trails of the
Sawtooth and White Cloud Mountains
by Margaret Fuller

Revised Edition

Cover photo: Middle Cramer Lake

Finger of Fate (Sawtooth Mountains)

trails of the

Sawtooth and White Cloud Mountains

by Margaret Fuller

Revised Edition

Signpost Books

Photo Credits

Stuart Fuller—xvi
B. W. Muir—Page 11
Lorry Roberts—Pages vi, 3
All other photos by Margaret Fuller

Library of Congress Cataloging-in-Publication Data
Fuller, Margaret.
   Trails of the Sawtooth and White Cloud Mountains / by
Margaret Fuller, — Rev. ed.
      p.   cm.
   Bibliography: p. 220
   Includes index.
   ISBN 0-913140-47-3
      1. Hiking—Idaho—Sawtooth National Recreation Area—
Guide-books. 2.. Sawtooth National Recreation Area (Idaho)—
Guide-books. 3. Trails—Idaho—Sawtooth National Recreation
Area—Guide-books.
I. Title.
GV199.42.I22S294 1988
917.96'04'3   88-31851
                                                              CIP

Trails of the Sawtooth and White Cloud Mountains, Revised Edition

Published by

Signpost Books
8912 192nd St. SW
Edmonds, WA 98020
   *Signpost Books welcomes inquiries from authors about
   prospective books.*

Foreword

By Cecil Andrus

Governor of Idaho

The Sawtooth National Recreation Area in the center of Idaho is one of those rare spots which remain little traveled and serenely remote, even though it is adjacent to popular vacation destinations. I know it well, for I have spent many hours in its soul-satisfying confines.

Only a few miles from the popular Sun Valley area, the Sawtooth National Recreation Area provides access to wild backcountry for thousands of visitors every year.

My efforts to preserve this region when I was first governor of Idaho are some of my most memorable and enjoyable accomplishments. Therefore it was with the greatest pleasure that I saw Margaret Fuller produce the Area's first comprehensive guide in 1979. In writing it Margaret compiled descriptions of all the trails she had hiked with her family in the Sawtooth, White Cloud and Boulder Mountains — the Sawtooth NRA's three rugged ranges.

Now she has revised and expanded *"Trails of the Sawtooth and White Cloud Mountains."* Those who travel only by motorized vehicle won't benefit as much from the new edition as those who travel by foot or on horseback. But this is the perfect reference and trail companion for those who explore this section of the Idaho backcountry.

On the following pages Margaret details some one hundred Idaho trails in the Sawtooth — White Cloud — Boulder Mountain area, an addition of two dozen hikes to the original book. They are grouped according to the lake, stream or other starting point from which they fan out into the wilderness.

For each trail she lists mileages from the starting point and also mileages to that starting point from the access. She notes elevation gains and the highest point and estimates the time required to complete the hike.

Pettit Lake

Her book includes also a general discussion about the area, a listing of campgrounds, and a history of the region, going back to early mining days.

It describes vegetation that will be found and lists wild animals that may be sighted. It tells how to obtain services of packers and guides. It offers advice on equipment, supplies and methods of guarding against over exertion. The would-be hiker is provided with safety precautions and first-aid suggestions.

If you've never tried an Idaho mountain trail, this book provides valuable information. If you've tried many trails but would like to experience some new ones, this book is likely to give you some ideas of where you could go.

It is my hope that this guide will continue to encourage visitors to the Sawtooth NRA to try the less-used trails and campsites and to disperse the public enjoyment throughout the Area.

This region is special to me. I hope this revision of Margaret's guide will help you share the very special Idaho experience in store for visitors to the Sawtooth National Recreation Area. It's a worthwhile addition to literature on how to really enjoy Idaho's unique quality of life.

Cecil D. Andrus

Acknowledgments

I would like to thank all those who helped me with the revision of this book, including Mose Shrum, supervisory forestry technician for the Sawtooth National Recreation Area; Mary Ann Cameron for editing; members of my family who went on hikes for the revision (my husband Wayne, and my children, Doug, Leslie, Neal, Hilary and Stuart); and several friends who hiked with me. I would especially like to thank Governor Cecil Andrus for writing a new forword for this edition.

The first edition of this book would not have been possible without the help and encouragement of Donna Parsons, director of the Snake River Regional Studies Center at the College of Idaho; Louise Marshall, publisher of Signpost Magazine and founder of Signpost Books, and Dave Lee, the first chief wilderness ranger for the SNRA. I would also like to thank those who helped with publicity for the first edition: *The Idaho Statesman, The Idaho Press — Tribune*, Lou Florence, the Idaho Lung Association, the College of Idaho, and the many organizations who have invited me to give slide shows for their members.

— Margaret Fuller

Sawtooth Wilderness and

National Recreation Area

WHITE CLOUD - BOULDER MOUNTAIN AREA

S. N. R. A.

● Moscow

● Lewiston

SAWTOOTH WILDERNESS

● McCall

Stanley

● Sun Valley

● Boise

Idaho Falls ●

Pocatello ●

Twin Falls ●

Table of Contents

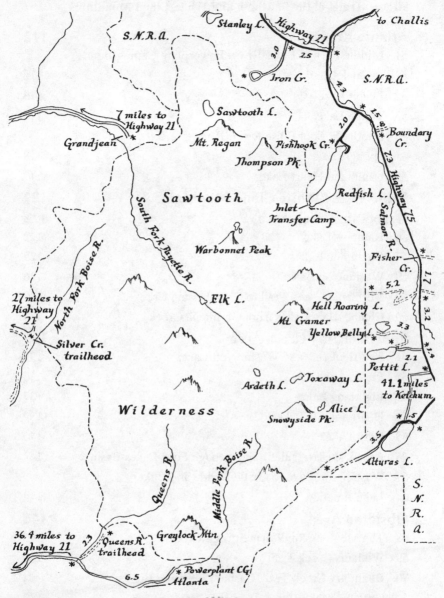

Sawtooth Wilderness

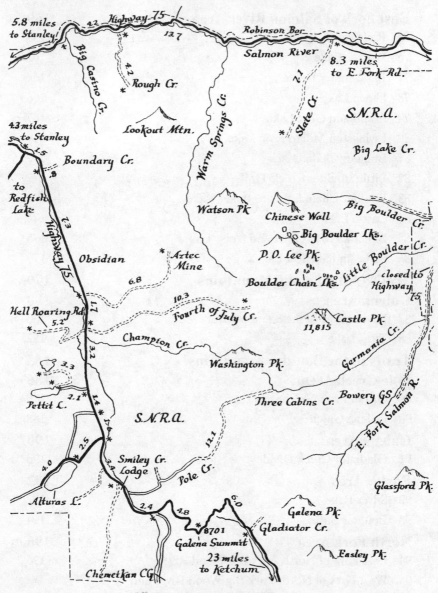

White Cloud Mountains

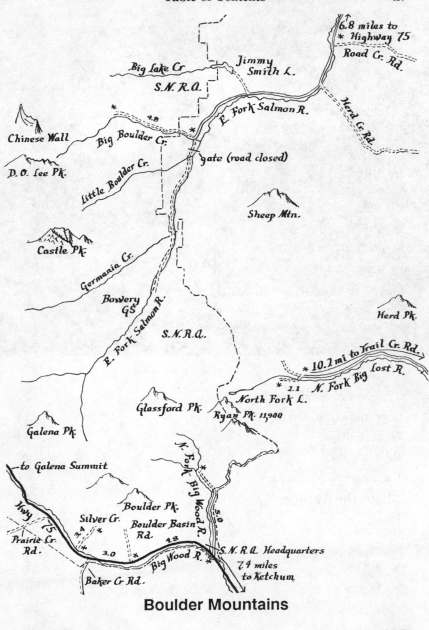

Boulder Mountains

Grand Mogul

List of maps with related hikes

Photographs

ABOUT THE AREA

A few miles north of Sun Valley, Idaho, the Sawtooth Mountains, like rows of saws set on edge, rise thousands of feet above the headwaters of the Salmon River. Across the silver curves of the river, behind wrinkled foothills, summits of the White Cloud Mountains resemble chunks of vanilla ice cream. Closer to Sun Valley, along the Big Wood River, the pink and gray striped Boulder Mountains overlook Idaho Highway 75. The three ranges have a unique beauty but are not as crowded as most ranges in the West. They are all part of the Sawtooth National Recreation Area. The highest summit is Castle Peak (11,815 feet) in the White Clouds.

The Salmon River, which separates the Sawtooths from the White Clouds, runs north down the Sawtooth Valley from its headwaters to the town of Stanley, where it turns east. The valley continues northwest of Stanley as a series of meadows called Stanley Basin. This basin separates the northern Sawtooths from the Salmon River Mountains of the Frank Church—River of No Return Wilderness. In June, camas flowers flood the meadows with blue.

The gray-green of big sagebrush covers the dry parts of these valleys above the green meadows and willows which follow the coils of the Salmon River. An occasional sheepherder's wagon with curved white top demonstrates that formation of the Sawtooth National Recreation Area preserved the traditional ranching of the valley. Place names such as Hell Roaring Lake remind us frontier days lasted into the twentieth century.

Forested moraines embrace large glacial lakes like Alturas, Pettit, Yellow Belly, Redfish and Stanley. Five-mile long Redfish is the best known and most popular. From the head of this lake granite needles march up both sides of Redfish Canyon. On the south the pinnacles of the Grand Mogul guard the entrance to this canyon. On the opposite wall, Mt. Heyburn's row of towers stands watch. At the head of Stanley Lake, McGown Peak in twin granite triangles, one higher than the other, looks down on the wooded moraines surrounding the lake.

PURPOSE OF THIS GUIDE

One purpose of this trail guide is to give enough information about the trails to encourage travel on the little-used ones. Another is to make known the beauty of the Sawtooth National Recreation

Area, so people will be inspired to help preserve it. A third purpose is to give directions to newcomers for some interesting hikes which are off-trail or are on unsigned trails.

The author is a hiker, so the guide gives information and times for foot travel, but horses can use most of these trails and mountain bikers can manage some of them, even though mountain bikes are not allowed in the Sawtooth Wilderness. The attractions of the scenery, the characteristics of the trails, and the need to protect the wilderness quality remain the same for all trail travelers.

This guidebook was first published in 1979 and has sold 10,000 copies. It is the guidebook hikers here carry in their backpacks. The revised edition you are reading contains 26 new hikes. In writing it, the author hiked again all but seven of the original hikes and consulted with Mose Shrum, supervisory forest technician for the Sawtooth National Recreation Area. The author has also written *Trails of Western Idaho* (Signpost Books, 1982) and *Trails of the Frank Church—River of No Return Wilderness* (Signpost Books, 1987) and the forthcoming "Mountains: A Natural History and Hiking Guide," John Wiley & Sons, New York.

VISITOR SERVICES

The main business district of Stanley, the largest settlement, consists of log buildings and dirt streets, three blocks long by two blocks wide. Behind it the snow-streaked Sawtooths look down on the town. Food, gasoline, lodging, gift shops and guide services are available here as well as at Smiley Creek, Galena, Obsidian, Redfish Lake, Clayton, Sunbeam, Grandjean and Atlanta.

Large developed campgrounds are at Alturas, Redfish and Stanley Lakes and on the Wood River. Smaller ones are at Iron Creek, Pettit Lake, Atlanta, Grandjean and along Highway 21 and the Salmon River Canyon. You can also camp at undeveloped sites along several dirt access roads which penetrate the backcountry. More than one million visitors use the Sawtooth National Recreation Area each year.

HISTORY

Mountain Shoshoni Indians, also called Sheepeaters, lived along the Salmon River and its tributaries for centuries before Alexander Ross visited the area with his fur trappers in 1824. He crossed the divide between the Big Wood River and the headwaters of the Sal-

Town of Stanley

mon, discovering and naming a small pond, Governors Punchbowl, on the way. Other trappers soon arrived: Warren Ferris of the American Fur Company in 1831, John Work of the Hudson Bay Company in 1832 and Captain Bonneville's men in 1833.

But it was 30 years before gold was discovered and people began to settle here. In 1863, Boise Basin miners found gold and silver quartz lodes on the nearby South Fork of the Boise River and established Rocky Bar. Prospectors from this and other mining towns soon found gold in the Sawtooths. In 1864, placer gold was discovered in the Stanley Basin and placer and lode gold at Atlanta. The basin is named for John Stanley, one of those prospectors.

In 1865, a road of sorts was built from Rocky Bar to Yuba City near Atlanta. It was called the Boiler Grade because once a boiler being packed along it fell off the road. Because of the area's remoteness, the first stamp mill wasn't brought to Atlanta until 1867, and the first three mills made little profit. In the mid-1870's, the Monarch and Buffalo mines smelted and shipped ore at Atlanta. By 1884, mining had declined here, but there have been new booms from 1902-11, in 1916, from 1932-36 and at the present time. From 1932-36 Atlanta produced more gold than any other Idaho area, reaching $6 million by 1938.

Silver was found on Silver Mountain on the North Fork of the Boise River in the 1860's. Matthew Graham, a miner at Atlanta and Rocky Bar, had Silver Mountain ore assayed in 1885. He built a mine and had a road constructed to it from Trappers Flat in 1887. A 20-stamp mill and mile-long tram were installed in 1888, when the population was 350. The largest settlement was called Graham. When the venture failed in 1889, the mine, tram and buildings were sold at sheriffs' sales for a total of $500 and the mill was sold for $9,500. On nearby Black Warrior Creek, mining occurred between 1900 and 1910 at the Double Standard, Rice Mammoth and Overlook Mines.

By 1869, placering was occurring in Stanley Basin and some hydraulic mining was taking place at Robinson Bar down the Salmon River from Stanley. By this time, Stanley had a store. In 1864, a road was built from Idaho City to Banner, near Lowman, and a pack trail ran from there to Cape Horn in the Stanley Basin. When mining on the Yankee Fork began in 1876 miners from that area spread into the Sawtooth Valley.

Levi Smiley found a quartz lode at the head of Smiley Creek in 1878, and in 1879 E.M. Wilson discovered the lode of the Vienna Mine. By 1880, the Pilgrim, Columbia and Beaver prospects were developed at Sawtooth City on nearby Beaver Creek, and a toll road was completed from Ketchum. Eastern developers brought in a 20-stamp mill for the Vienna Mine. At its height, Vienna had 200 buildings and 800 residents.

There were mines in the Alturas Creek drainage also, such as the ones in Eureka Gulch. By the winter of 1883-84, the boom was so great that the road to Ketchum was kept open all winter. In 1886 mail was carried between Sawtooth City and Atlanta on a sketchy road over Mattingly Creek Divide. By 1892 when the last mine operating, the Silver King, burned, the boom at Sawtooth City and Vienna was over. However, a 75-ton flotation plant was constructed and the Vienna Mine operated again for a few years in the 1930's.

Mining also occurred in the White Cloud and Boulder Mountains, but was much later and less extensive. The Livingston Mine, the most successful, at $2.3 million, was located by A.S. and W.S. Livingston in 1882, and shipped lead-silver ore by pack train. In 1922 a road, 200-ton mill and three-mile tramway were built and the mine operated until 1930. Some activity still persists.

Jess Baker located claims at Baker Lake in 1922. Molybdenum was discovered here in 1939, and the American Mining, Smelting and Refining Company (ASARCO) obtained these claims and located another 50 in 1967. Their application to build a road in 1970 was opposed by environmental groups and led to the formation of the Sawtooth National Recreation Area in 1972.

The first claims in Washington Basin were located in 1882. There were two mills, but only $50,000 in lead and silver was produced.

The settlement of Galena, founded in 1879 around lead and silver mining claims, grew until it had a 20-ton smelter, 800 people, four general stores and a stage line to Hailey.

David Clark started the first year-round ranch in Sawtooth Valley in 1899 at a hot spring on the east side of the valley. He was named postmaster of the first post office, called Pierson, in 1902. The name of it was later changed to Obsidian. Nearby on Fisher Creek in 1901, Frank Shaw was the second settler in the valley. Sheep were grazing Stanley Basin by 1879, but large bands weren't introduced until Frank Gooding (later governor) arrived with some in 1887. By 1907 the area was being overgrazed, as there were 364,000 sheep in the Sawtooth National Forest.

The first supervisor of the Sawtooth Forest Reserve was F. A. Fenn. The second was Emil Grandjean, a professional forester from Denmark. In 1908, when the Forest Reserves were changed to National Forests, the Sawtooth Forest was split, with the western part becoming the Boise National Forest. Grandjean became its first Supervisor, remaining in the position until 1923. The Sawtooth Forest was divided into three main ranger districts: Wood River, Salmon River and Boise River. Each of these was subdivided into several guard districts. William Horton was ranger for the Pole Creek District in Sawtooth Valley for 20 years. His log ranger station, built in 1909, still stands. In 1913, it had the first telephone in the area. Many of the roads, trails, buildings and campgrounds were constructed by the Civilian Conservation Corps from 1933 to 1941. CCC camps were located at Redfish, Ketchum and Big Smoky. In 1933, the 1424-acre Germania Creek fire, one of the first fought here, cost only $1,054 to extinguish.

In 1935, American mountaineers Robert and Miriam Underhill, accompanied by rancher Dave Williams on some trips, climbed at least 20 of the major Sawtooth Peaks, including Mt. Heyburn. Bob

Merriam, Paul Petzoldt, founder of the National Outdoor Leadership School, and four others from the Iowa Mountaineers, made the first ascent of Warbonnet in 1947. A northwest mountaineer, Fred Beckey, also made first ascents, such as South Raker and The Saddleback (Elephant's Perch). Louis Stur made the first ascent of the Finger of Fate with Jerry Fuller in 1958. Stur is best known for the route he pioneered on Mt. Heyburn, called the Stur Chimney.

In 1911, women's organizations in Idaho first proposed a national park in the Sawtooths, but a series of bills to establish a park have failed in Congress. In 1937 the Forest Service formed the 200,042 acre Sawtooth Primitive Area. In 1972, after studies and public hearings, Congress created the Sawtooth National Recreation Area, to be administered by the U.S. Forest Service, and designated the Sawtooth Primitive Area, a wilderness area of 216,383 acres in the National Wilderness System. The purpose of the Sawtooth National Recreation Area is to protect the salmon and other fish and conserve and develop the values in the area for public recreation and enjoyment.

The Sawtooth National Recreation Area Act directed the Secretary of the Interior to study the area and the adjacent Pioneer Mountains for a national park. In 1976, the Department of the Interior recommended a pair of national parks and a national recreation area for some of the surrounding land. Under the study, 686,080 acres qualified for a park, but one has never been established because most Idahoans feel park status would bring too many problems.

GEOLOGY

The Sawtooth Range is an uplifted fault block bounded by faults, and the Stanley Basin is a depressed fault block called a graben. The granite rock of the Sawtooths is closely jointed, or fractured, which has made the ridges sawtoothed because the jointing caused the rock to be easily eroded by glaciers. Half of the rock in the Sawtooths is the 88-million-year-old Idaho batholith, which is gray here, and most of the rest is the 44-million-year-old Sawtooth batholith, which is pink or apricot.

The 20-mile-long band of white rock giving the White Clouds their name is Paleozoic limestone and related rock. This rock has been changed by contact with molten granite to a type of rock called calc-silicate, similar to marble, but containing silicate minerals as well as calcite. Other types and colors of Paleozoic metamorphic and

Rock layers near Ocalkens

sedimentary rocks, such as argillite, quartzite, limestone and conglomerate, surround the band of white in a highly mineralized belt, which is 8 miles wide by 38 miles long and runs north-south through the center of the area. There are major deposits of zinc, fluorite, and low grade gold and molybdenum.

At the lower elevations in the eastern and southern part of the White Clouds, the vast volcanism of the Challis volcanics has left rhyolite and basalt lava and volcanic ash tuffs. The Challis volcanics are about the same age, 44 million years old, as the Sawtooth batholith and once covered half of Idaho. Mudflows in these volcanics formed Sullivan and Jimmy Smith Lakes.

PLANTS AND ANIMALS

Vegetation in the Sawtooth National Recreation Area changes with elevation, rock, soil and exposure to the sun. The lower slopes and valleys contain big sagebrush, Idaho fescue and bluebunch wheatgrass, as well as patches of lodgepole pine, Douglas fir and subalpine fir. Huckleberries often grow under the Douglas fir. Sagebrush and grass also can be found higher on south-facing slopes.

Along the streams, aspens and willows grow. Snowberry and elk sedge are found in aspen groves. The large wet meadows are awash with sapphire blue camas in late June and early July. Other common wildflowers in wet areas are elephant's head and white wyethia.

Where it is drier, patches of suphur plant, scarlet gilia, paintbrush, sego lily and whorled penstemon grow. On the western side of the Sawtooths near Atlanta, along the Queens River and near Grandjean, it is low enough for ponderosa pine. Associated shrubs here are snowberry, ninebark, serviceberry and chokecherry.

Most glacial moraines in the Sawtooths, such as those around Redfish Lake, are covered with lodgepole pine. Higher up, especially where it has been glaciated, subalpine fir, Douglas fir, snowberry, mountain alder, elk sedge and grouse whortleberry grow, and there are groves of aspen and lodgepole where fires have occurred.

The most varied vegetation is found around lakes in the cirque basins. There are subalpine fir, Englemann spruce, elk sedge, alpine bentgrass, alpine willow, grouse whortleberry, western *Ledum* (Labrador or trapper's tea), and red mountain heath. Other flowers are *Kalmia*, shooting star, mountain or explorer's gentian, and mountain bluebell.

Near timberline, at around 10,000 feet, whitebark pine replaces the other trees. Here also are found subalpine sagebrush, elk sedge, and Idaho and sheep fescue. Wildflowers include mountain sorrel, white mountain heath, and alpine buttercup.

Hikers sometimes see mountain goats. A few bighorn sheep are found only in the White Clouds. Other wildlife includes antelope, elk, black bear, cougar, lynx, bobcat, mule deer, coyote, beaver and muskrat. There are a few wolverine. Smaller animals include squirrels, mice, shrews, pikas, chipmunks, gophers, badgers, porcupines, rabbits, raccoons, otters, foxes, martens, weasels and skunks. Rainbow, eastern brook, cutthroat, Dolly Varden and California golden trout and steelhead swim in the lakes and streams. There were two runs of chinook salmon and one of sockeye, but almost none are left. Kokanee (landlocked) salmon occur in the larger lakes, such as Redfish.

There are ducks, Canada geese, owls, and three forest grouse: ruffed, blue and Franklin. Other birds include robins, woodpeckers, sparrows, chickadees, warblers, juncos, bluebirds, magpies, hawks, thrushes, ospreys, snipe, killdeer, siskins, golden eagle, dipper, and water pipit. The dipper is unusual as it runs underwater all year to look for insects.

The sandhill crane and the peregrine falcon are two endangered species living here. Another native, which probably has permanently disappeared, is the Rocky Mountain wolf. The grizzly bear vanished many years ago; the last one was seen in the 1940's.

ACTIVITIES

Cattle and sheep are driven and trucked to summer ranges to graze Recreation Area land. Hunting is permitted in accordance with Idaho fish and game laws. Logging is mostly limited to firewood cutting. It is difficult for the Idaho Fish and Game Department to maintain stocked lakes and streams in the Sawtooths because many lakes are infertile and streams are steep. Fishing is usually better in the White Clouds because water dissolves more nutrients from the types of rock found there. This provides nourishment for the small animals eaten by fish.

Some trails are open to motorized bike use. All trails in the area not within wilderness are open to mountain bicycles. Sailing, motor-boating and water skiing are popular, although the lakes are very cold.

Snowmobiling and cross-country skiing are the main winter activities. There are two nationally known cross-country resorts in the area, Galena Lodge and Busterback Ranch.

Because of their unique beauty, the Sawtooths, the White Clouds and the Boulders are especially attractive for hiking, backpacking and horseback riding. This guidebook describes some trails suitable for each of these activities, as well as some cross-country routes only for hikers. Travel plan maps are available from Forest Service offices. These maps show which trails are open to two-wheeled vehicles and which roads are open to all vehicles.

HORSE TRAVEL

In an average season, the high passes are not safe for horse travel until after the first week of August. Trying to cross with stock before the trails are bare of snow is hazardous and causes erosion of the fragile soils. When traveling by horse, use gentle horses trained to hobble or picket and stand quietly. The training should be done before they are taken into the mountains. The horses should also be conditioned by regular exercise before the trip, and should be accustomed to being with each other.

Picketing a horse to a log is safer and better for the grass than using a picket pin. Usually it is best not to picket more than one or two horses. The rest should be hobbled.

When trail conditions are unsafe, lead horses across the problem spot. Don't leave stock alone for more than a few hours. Use caution in passing hikers. Be aware that horses often spook when they see llamas, which are sometimes used on trails here.

The horse traveler should tie stock near campsites only when loading. Otherwise, tie them away from campsites and use the designated tie area if there is one. The location of stock tie areas can be obtained at Forest Service offices. Tying stock within 100 feet of streams, springs or lakes is prohibited. When attaching ropes to trees, protect the bark by either encircling the touching portion of the rope with burlap or a length of slit garden hose, or by placing small sticks against the tree and tying the rope over them. Horses can also be tied to rope hitchlines strung between two trees, provided the hitchlines are higher than the horses' heads and the halter-lines are long enough to let the animal's heads reach the ground.

Grazing within 200 yards of lakes is not allowed. Grazing damages fragile alpine meadows. It takes many years for this damage to be erased as plants at high altitudes have a very short growing season. Stock will have much less impact on soils and vegetation if you camp at lower elevations along the rivers and creeks. Then you can take day trips to the high lakes.

It is a good practice to carry as much feed as will be needed, but bringing hay or straw into the wilderness is not allowed. Some outfitters have found alfalfa cubes are the most satisfactory feed to carry. The cubes are cheaper than pellets and keep the horses from chewing poles and trees as they tend to do when fed pellets.

A permit (free) for all overnight pack stock use, or day use with more than nine head, is required, and parties of more than 30 head of stock are not allowed. The number of stock needed can be reduced by the use of backpacking foods and lightweight gear.

Some outfitters offer llama trips, and a few rent llamas, but llama renting hasn't yet become widespread in Idaho. Information on sources of llamas is available from the Idaho Outfitters and Guides Association. Learning to use llamas requires some orientation and practice, and the llamas used for packing should have already been trained by their owner to halter, lead and walk on trails carrying packs. Llamas are very smart and require you to make them think you are smarter. If you can do this, they will give you little trouble. They don't like going uphill very well, but will go readily if you keep insisting. They are fun animals to use for packing, and are easier for

Fishing in Toxaway Lake

the inexperienced to manage than are mules or horses. When using llamas, it is important to remember horses are afraid of them. Someone should walk ahead so if you meet horses you can be warned to get the llamas off the trail and out of sight.

OBTAINING PACKERS

When planning and preparing for a backpacking trip, you may find it impossible for your family to carry everything needed to be safe, comfortable and well fed. Consider using horses, mules or llamas, and trailbikes or mountain bikes in the non-wilderness areas. Families, especially those with young children, will need to have their gear spot-packed in by a commercial outfitter for some of the longer trips. A packer can carry packs and equipment to your destination while you hike or ride. To obtain a list of packers and outfitters contact the Idaho Outfitters and Guides Association, P.O. Box 95, Boise, Idaho 83701.

MOUNTAIN BICYCLING

When using a mountain bike, certain precautions are needed for your own safety and that of other trail users. Be a good citizen when riding your mountain bike. Always ride in control. Sound your bell or horn or call out at corners to warn of your presence. Yield to hikers and horseback riders. Be sure horses, mules or llamas hear you coming and hear you talk so they know you are a person. Move your bike off trail on the downhill side if possible to let horses pass. Stay on designated roads and trails and avoid riding during and after rain and on naturally boggy sections. Mountain bikes are not permitted within wilderness areas.

For your own safety, remember most bicycle injuries are from failure to control your bicycle, not from collisions.

Wear a bicycle helmet with a hard outside shell and foam-padded interior. Wear gloves, long pants and a long-sleeved shirt. Tuck pant legs into your socks or wear gaiters. Look ahead to anticipate hazards. Practice riding on gentle, smooth surfaces, to develop the skill needed on steep, uneven slopes. It is especially important to practice skidding on gentle, even slopes so you can control a skid on loose rocks on rough ground. It is also important to brake before a curve, not within it. To prevent problems in an emergency, carry the same 12 essentials you would if hiking. Put your gear in plastic bags inside bicycle bags to be sure it stays dry. Use rear-mounted bags; handlebar bags affect control of the bicycle. Also, carry bicycle tools, pump and a tire patch kit.

HIKING

The strenuous exercise of hiking will be difficult for your body to manage unless you are in good physical condition. Conditioning is essential before backpacking or day hiking more than five miles. A physical examination should precede a first-time trip. Exercise vigorously for several weeks before any trip. The exercise should be something which strengthens the heart and lungs, such as bicycling, running or swimming. Poor condition leads to fatigue, which can cause accidents.

Hikers who live at sea level shouldn't start a strenuous trip without allowing time to adjust to the altitude. Besides the unpleasant headache and nausea of altitude sickness, life-threatening conditions such as pulmonary or cerebral edema can develop, although they are rare at the elevations found here. Spending one to three days at the elevation of the trailhead before starting to hike will help prevent altitude sickness. Precautions needed vary with different people and the altitude at which they live.

On the trail, take your pulse occasionally so it doesn't stay above your target heart rate (70% of your maximum rate) for more than 20 to 30 minutes at a time. If it does, stop and rest for 10 minutes every half hour. If the rate is over your maximum rate (200 less your age), stop and rest immediately. Taking the pulse for five seconds and multiplying by 12 is accurate enough for this purpose.

In planning, try to find some others to go with you. Hiking is much safer when done with others. Hiking alone can be dangerous; in case of injury, no one may be around to go for help or treat you for shock or bleeding. Hiking alone on a cross-country hike could be fatal. On a cross-country route, a lone injured hiker might never be found as rescuers might not travel the same route. The cross-country hikes described here are only for experienced hikers and are not recommended for horses. If you won't listen to warnings and want to hike alone, take a survival kit and signal flare. Consider carrying a sleeping bag even on a day hike, to help prevent hypothermia at night if you are hurt.

Also in planning, consider the creek crossings. In this guide where trails are described as crossing creeks, they ford them or cross on stones or temporary fallen logs, unless a bridge is mentioned. Early in the season, some of the crossings without bridges are dangerous or impassable. Usually only experienced hikers or riders should attempt them before July 15. After July 15, young children on foot may still find them a problem. The spring runoff often washes away footlogs and even bridges.

Use caution in crossing streams. Unfasten the waist belt of your pack so it won't hold you underwater if you fall. It is safest to wade across (with boots on to protect your feet) in a wide, gravelly place. Wet logs and rocks are very slippery. Face upstream, move diagonally, use a stick for balance and move only one of your three "legs" at a time. Change to dry socks on the other side to prevent blisters.

SAFETY FOR ALL WILDERNESS TRAVELERS

Most trails have register boxes at or near the beginning. All hikers and riders should register for their own protection. Always let someone know where you are going and when you'll be back. A use permit must be obtained for parties of ten or more (20 is the maximum per party), for overnight stock use, or day use with more than nine head of stock. The maximum number of stock is 30 head.

These free permits are available at the Sawtooth National Recreation Area Headquarters, Star Route, Ketchum, Idaho 83340; at the Stanley Ranger Station, Star Route, HC64, Box 9900, Stanley, Idaho 83278; at the Lowman Ranger Station, Lowman, Idaho 83637, and at the Boise Ranger Station, 5493 Warm Springs Ave., Boise, Idaho, 83712. At these offices, current wilderness and backcountry regulations, Forest Service maps, and further information are available as well.

Because trail and access road conditions change with weather and season, it is wise to check with one of these offices before your trip. Snow or high water can block some trails before July 15, and the weather is uncertain, even snowy, after September 15. September and October weather can be beautiful even though cold (20 to 30 degrees) at night. Most of these trails can be traveled from about July 10 through October 15, but the times they open and close change from year to year because the weather here varies greatly. Trails usually open earlier or later than the others are listed in the Guide to Trips in the Appendix.

Because the weather can change to wintry in a few hours even in midsummer, when planning trips every hiker must be aware of the danger of hypothermia, which is probably the greatest danger in these mountains. Hypothermia, or the dangerous loss of body heat in cold and wet conditions, can occur in temperatures as high as 50 degrees F. It can cause death in only minutes. To prevent hypothermia, keep dry and warm by wearing raingear when needed and clothes which stay warm when wet, such as fleece, pile or wool. Wear tightly-woven fabric for the outside layer of clothing to protect from the wind, because wind chill can lower temperatures dramatically. Be sure to wear a hat because the head loses a large amount of body heat. Frequent snacks help maintain this heat.

If it is impossible to stay dry and warm, make camp and build a fire. Even on a day hike, it is wise to take a tarp, tube tent or aluminized plastic space blanket for an emergency tent. (For backpacking, a nylon tent with waterproof floor and separate rain fly is best.)

Persistent shivering is the first warning of hypothermia. Immediately help a shivering person who acts confused and uncoordinated get out of the wind and rain, change into dry clothes, obtain a hot drink and get into a warm sleeping bag. If the person is only semi-conscious, very gently remove clothing and place him or her into a sleeping bag with another person who is also nude. Skin to skin

The Temple

contact transfers body heat most effectively. In severe hypothermia, exertion, rough handling and attempts at rapid rewarming can cause fatalities. Horses can also get hypothermia, so keep them sheltered from wind and protected from cold.

Another danger, especially in the White Clouds, is old mines with dangerous shafts and tunnels. Plan your trip to avoid them. If you must pass some, keep away and watch children carefully.

In planning, be aware that even the clearest mountain water may be polluted. The only way to be sure water is safe is to boil it for five minutes or filter it with a special water filter. Therefore take a water filter or kettle with you. In recent years a protozoa, *Giardia lamblia,* has been brought into the area. This bug can cause severe diarrhea and painful stomach cramps from six days to three weeks after exposure, so don't risk the enjoyment of your vacation by failing to filter or boil your water — even once.

There are a few animal hazards. Ticks inhabit the brush all over the SNRA from May until about mid-July. Early season hikers should inspect themselves for ticks at least twice a day. To get a tick to back out, put insect repellant or white gas on the tick, or cover it with any kind of oil or grease. Or pull the tick out with tweezers

VERY slowly so it will relax its grip. If part of it remains under the skin it can cause serious infection. If bitten by a tick, see a doctor after your hike. Only a few ticks carry tularemia and Rocky Mountain Spotted Fever.

Larger animals can be a hazard too. Wild animals should not be fed, bothered or approached. Deer can kick with razor-sharp hooves. Chipmunks and ground squirrels sometimes carry bubonic plague. All animals can bite if fed by hand. When given handouts, animals tend to become dependent on humans and may die over the winter when that food source is removed. Black bears are not generally a problem in the Sawtooth National Recreation Area, but there are between 150 and 200 of them around. Especially in the brushy canyons on the west side of the Sawtooths, it is wise to hang food at night on a tree limb ten feet from the ground and six feet out from the tree trunk. Food should be protected at all times because chipmunks and ground squirrels can be pests. In some places they will even try to crawl into your pack during lunch.

THE TWELVE ESSENTIALS

For safety even on a day trip every backcountry traveler needs to carry some essential equipment.

1. Extra clothes — wear or carry long pants, sweater, insulated parka, rain poncho or jacket, rain pants or chaps, wool hat, wool gloves or mittens.

2. Extra food beyond needs of trip.

3. Pocket knife.

4. Waterproof matches or full butane lighter (take both, or two packets of matches stored in different places in case you lose one).

5. Firestarter — purchase stick or jelly type or make at home from paraffin and corrugated cardboard, or gather pitch in the forest.

6. First aid kit, including prescription pain medication in case of accident.

7. Flashlight — be sure it works and has extra bulbs and batteries.

8. Topographic map — know how to interpret it.

9. Sunglasses — if it snows, and it can any day in the summer here, you can suffer severe headache and even snowblindness without dark glasses.

10. Compass — know how to use it to find where you are.

11. Full water bottles and water filter, or pan for boiling water.

12. Emergency shelter — space blanket, tube tent or tarp.

One essential item on this list is a topographic map. This book contains sketch maps to help you plan trips, but they are an inadequate substitute for topographic maps. Most of the trails are shown on the United States Geological Survey maps (topographic maps) which have been made of the entire area. These maps can be ordered from the Distribution Branch, U.S. Geological Survey, Box 25286, Federal Center, Building 41, Denver, Colorado 80225, or bought in Boise or Ketchum at some outdoor and stationery stores. The Forest Service maps of the Sawtooth Wilderness and the White Cloud — Boulder Mountains are less detailed, but give good information on access roads. Topographic maps are essential for safety.

They will last longer if they are covered with plastic film. To cover them, place a piece of clear adhesive-backed vinyl shelf paper on a table, sticky side up. Peel off the paper backing. Then slowly unroll the topographic map on top of it, printed side down. When all of the map is stuck to the plastic, trim off unwanted edges, and fold the map so the plastic side is out and the name of the quadrangle is visible.

EMERGENCIES

Before setting out, be sure someone in your party has had a course in first aid or take a copy of an up-to-date first aid book with you (read it first). After administering first aid, the leader should decide what to do. A person who knows first aid will know the correct order of administering it (breathing, bleeding, and shock). Don't forget to treat for shock, especially in a mild injury, as shock can kill even when the injury itself is not fatal.

If the injured is unable to walk but not seriously hurt, and the party is large, the least expensive alternative is to carry him or her out. (A person with a suspected neck or back injury should not be moved by amateurs.) A heliocopter is available for emergencies, but is extremely expensive and its use must be approved by the Forest Supervisor. When going for help, leave one person with the victim and send two people out if possible. Write down the instructions for the authorities. Contact the county sheriff, who is responsible for all search and rescue. The western part of the Sawtooth Wilderness is in Boise County with Idaho City as the county seat. The northern part of the rest of the SNRA is in Custer County (Challis), and the southern part of the rest of the SNRA is in Blaine County (Hailey).

A makeshift litter for carrying someone out can be made from two poles and a sleeping bag. Rip the stitching out at the foot of the bag, insert the poles, and tie the person on top of the bag securely. For warmth, jackets or another sleeping bag can be wrapped and tied around the victim. Because of recent budget cutting, there are few trail crew members and wilderness rangers, so it is uncommon to meet a Forest Service employee with a radio.

An emergency clinic is located at Stanley; this clinic has its own ambulance. The nearest hospital is at Sun Valley.

There is no reason to get lost even on a cross-country hike if you know how to use a topographic map and compass. These mountains are not densely wooded and have many recognizable landmarks. Sometimes your objective may be impossible to find, but it is usually possible to find the way back to the trail or road.

If confused, sit down and orient the map and compass. First, make the compass needle point to N. Then set it on the map, turning the map so the needle is exactly parallel with the side edges of the map and points to the top of the map. Now turn the map with the compass on it so the needle points to 19 degrees east of north. (This 19 degrees, called the angle of magnetic declination, is the difference between the direction of the north magnetic pole and the true north pole at this location.) North on the compass dial is now north in your surroundings and matches north on the map.

On the topographic map of this area, the dark brown lines show 200-foot differences in elevation, and the light brown lines indicate 40-foot differences. (Topographic maps in other areas may have different scales and contour intervals.) When these lines, called contours, are very close together, they designate cliffs. Look for some landmarks which match peaks, cliffs, or notches on the map.

If still lost, build a fire and make camp. Keep the fire going as a signal, using great caution not to start a forest fire. In the morning, make another attempt to determine your location. Avoid actions, such as rushing about madly, which lead to panic; panic can kill.

WILDERNESS MANNERS

Chipmunks and squirrels may not know any better, but humans have no excuse for lack of manners. There is a code of proper be-

Sawtooth Lake

havior in the wilderness which shows your respect for our beautiful land.

One item in this code concerns shortcuts. On long switchbacks, it is tempting to take shortcuts, but don't do it. They cause erosion and washouts, and taking shortcuts is illegal. No one wants to have their taxes used to repair this kind of erosion when it is preventable:

Another is respect for other travelers. If you are hiking or biking and meet horses, stand still quietly on the downhill side of the trail while they pass. Then if a horse stumbles, it can recover itself by stepping uphill without stepping on you. If you have llamas with you and meet horses, get the llamas off the trail and out of sight before the horses spook from seeing them.

Another is to be sure to BURN or CARRY OUT all trash. Remember aluminum foil packaging envelopes will not burn! Attempting to burn them releases toxins into the soil. Mose Shrum says: "Put them in your litter bag and make the rangers smile." Try to leave the land the way you found it, or, if possible, in better condition. It is illegal to remove or collect any natural objects except berries and mushrooms and, with an Idaho license, fish and game animals in season. Burying any trash or garbage also is prohibited. Animals will dig it up and scatter it. The Sawtooths belong to everyone in the United States, so this wilderness is your home too. You need to keep your house clean even if someone else gets it dirty.

Respect for the land also means respect for prehistoric and historical items. Travelers should leave undisturbed the artifacts they see. Rangers may be able to answer your questions about them. These objects are part of the heritage of our country and should be left for future generations to see. Heavy fines and jail sentences await those who remove prehistoric and historical objects. Also, most historical sites here are on private property.

Use backpacking or other portable stoves as much as possible. Wood fires make black scars on the earth and rocks and require chopping up picturesque dead trees which are the homes of animals. If, however, you need a warming fire in cold, wet weather, be sure to use existing fire rings. If there is no fire ring, dig a hole for the fire and cover it after the fire is out. It is illegal to cut any *green* trees or branches. They won't burn anyway! In addition, within the Sawtooth Wilderness, cutting *dead* trees and their branches is not allowed. Remember to put the fire out before leaving camp. Remove any foil and other trash from the ashes (even if you didn't put it there) and take it with you.

Some lakeshore areas are posted with signs saying "over-used campsite. Please do not camp here". Please obey these signs, so the trampled vegetation will grow back and the trees will not die from having their roots damaged. If the bark on a root is worn through to the bare wood, that root will die. If enough of the roots die, the tree is lost.

Be sure your dog doesn't add to the problem. Keep it out of lakes and streams and bury its waste. If you're not willing to do this, leave it home. Your dog can also be a nuisance to wildlife and to other campers. If you bring your dog, make it mind so it won't bother other people or wildlife. In many other areas, inconsiderate dog owners led to dogs being prohibited except when on a leash.

Respect for the land also means choosing your campsite to avoid damaging the vegetation. In meadows, camping harms the grass and trenching tents kills it. Since the growing season in mountains is very short, the grass won't grow back for many years. At high elevations, such as high lake basins, the vegetation is the most fragile. Therefore, camp in the canyons below the lake basins, and take day hikes to the lakes. If you do this, you won't have to carry your backpack as far! Lake basins also have more mosquitoes and are often more crowded than the canyons.

On bare ground, trenching tents can cause erosion and unsightly scars. One set of trenches never fits another camper's tent, anyway. In the rain, use rocks to divert water from the tent if needed, and use a tarp or poncho on the tent floor inside the tent to help keep your gear dry. Be sure to replace the rocks after use.

Another provision in the wilderness code of ethics is to keep the water in all wilderness lakes clear and beautiful. To accomplish this, first be sure to wash dishes, bathe, and do laundry away from lakes and streams. It is illegal to use ordinary soap or detergent here. No one wants detergent foam in drinking water or old noodles at the edge of the lake. Use biodegradable soap and a lightweight container for washing. The container can be a cook pot, a folding plastic wash pan or even a large ziploc bag. Dump the used water at least 50 feet away from lakes, streams and campsites. Use a pan for cleaning and rinsing fish, and be sure to burn or carry out the fish entrails.

A second way to keep the water clean and the surroundings pleasant is to be sure to practice proper backcountry sanitation. For toilet purposes, dig a hole about six to eight inches deep at least 100 feet from lakes, streams, springs, or campsites. When there is no danger of fire spreading into dry tree litter or grass, burn toilet paper to keep animals from digging it up. Cover the hole completely with earth after use. Latrines can be dug for large groups, but should be long, shallow trenches at least 300 feet from water and be partly covered after each use. Cover a latrine completely before leaving camp and restore the ground to its original appearance.

If you have planned your trip well, taken precautions for your safety and are prepared to leave the land the way you found it, you are ready now to read about the trails of these mountains.

ORGANIZATION OF ROUTE DESCRIPTIONS

At the beginning of each hike description, you will find the round trip mileage from the nearest trailhead, highest point reached, elevation gained, elevation lost (return climb) if any, time to allow on foot, topographic maps and the location and quality of the access road. For the descriptions which begin at a trail junction some distance from a trailhead, an additional line says: "This section one way: x miles, y feet gain." All other mileages are round trip. In each trip description and in the Guide to Trips in the Appendix, the routes are rated according to difficulty for hikers.

All official trails are marked with **blazes** cut in the bark of trees and shaped like upside-down exclamation marks. Because some trails may be hard to follow in places, the blazes do help. The word **talus** means loose boulders and rocks with no dirt between. A **rock**

bench is a large rounded or flat place of solid rock. **Switchback** means the trail doubles back on itself. The term **cairn** refers to a small pile of rocks marking the route. **Transfer camp** means a trailhead with a campground located beside it.

Mileages may not agree with Forest Service signs, but all mileages have been checked against Forest Service trail logs and the author's experience. Mileages for trails never logged have been calculated with a map-measuring instrument, taking into account switchbacks not shown on the topographic maps. Landmarks described here may change or disappear due to natural causes or trail rerouting.

In planning, consider the access road as well as the trail. Mileages may change in the future from those given here as trails and roads are rerouted. The access roads are described as paved, dirt and primitive. Unpaved roads may become impassable after rain or snow. Primitive roads usually require a vehicle with a high clearance (but some small foreign cars may be able to travel them) and may be open only part of the summer due to mud or washouts. The average driving speed possible on most primitive roads is less than 10 miles an hour. In planning your trip, remember that mountain bikes, trail bikes and carts are not allowed in the Sawtooth Wilderness.

You may want to plan your trip to avoid crowds. Some of the main trails on the eastern side of the Sawtooths are becoming crowded. Only one third as many people go in from the west side. On this side, trails to lakes are longer, but the canyons are more beautiful than those on the east. The White Cloud and Boulder ranges are also less crowded than the east side of the Sawtooths. A list of little-used trails is in the Guide to Trips and most trails in the Appendix get little use. Also, trails are used less during the week than on weekends and during September than in midsummer.

HOW TO REACH THE SAWTOOTH N. R. A.

To reach the area, take Idaho Highway 75 north from Ketchum and Sun Valley over Galena Summit to the Sawtooth Valley. Stanley is 60 miles northwest of Sun Valley by road. You can also reach the area by driving northeast from Boise on State Highway 21 and taking gravel roads to Atlanta and Grandjean, or continuing on Highway 21 to Stanley. From the east, you can get to Stanley by driving south and west on Idaho Highway 75 up the Salmon River from Salmon.

trails in the
SAWTOOTH
MOUNTAINS

Mt. Regan and Sawtooth Lake from trail to McGown Lakes

ALTURAS LAKE AREA

1 ALPINE CREEK LAKES
Map 1

round trip: 7.6 miles (1.4 miles cross-country) to west lake, 10.4 miles to north lakes (4.2 miles cross-country)
elevation gain: 1,442 feet to west lake, 2,087 feet to north lakes
highest point: 9,167 feet at north lakes
map: Snowyside Peak
time: 7 hours for west lake, 8 hours for north lakes
ability: expert
access: From Ketchum, drive north 39.5 miles on Highway 75 to the Alturas Lake Road. Turn left (west) on paved road and drive past lake and off pavement to a ford of Alpine Creek at 6.5 miles.

Several wild and lonely lakes in rugged country are scattered beyond the end of the maintained trail in Alpine Creek Canyon above Alturas Lake. The largest lake is the closest but reaching it requires a careful climb beside a rushing waterfall. At the lower end of the lake, a cracked gray monolith stands guard over this waterfall and two tree-masted islands. At the head of the lake, a jumble of granite peaks forms a wrinkled backdrop for the cliffs and ledges surrounding the clear blue water. Among the jumble hide clusters of satellite lakes. From the waterfall, the zigzag wall dividing the north branch of Alpine Creek from Alice Lake is visible. Under this wall are strung four more lakes, one of them right under the dragon's back of Snowyside Peak.

To reach the trailhead, follow access directions above. Park in the parking area (7,080 feet) on the near (east) side of the ford. Walk north 50 yards to find the level trail in woods. At .5 mile the trail begins to climb. At 1.0 mile, it passes a rock knoll on the right into a sagebrush basin. From here, there is a fine view of the jagged north wall of the canyon and the peaks at the head of it. This mile makes a fine walk in itself.

The trail continues through the sagebrush and strips of trees. At 1.7 miles, the path crowds the aqua-green creek. At a campsite, the route enters forest and the official trail ends, but the path continues for another 1.4 miles.

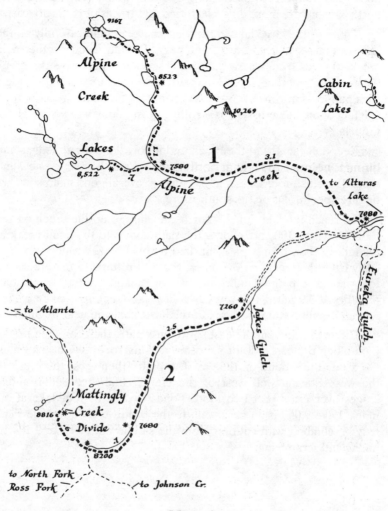

Map 1

The route ascends the canyon through forest and over granite benches. At 1.5 miles, the path turns up to the right (north) through willows. The trail stays out of the canyon bottom, then drops to edge a flat meadow. At 2.5 miles, the way crosses above another meadow on a sagebrush hillside, then re-enters woods and fords a side creek. The trail reaches the main creek (7,580 feet) 3.1 miles and 500 feet above the trailhead. Beyond here, the routes up both the west and north canyons are more difficult to find, but traces of paths do exist.

To reach the large lake in the west canyon, climb carefully up the left side of a waterfall on a faint path. To find it, go up the main creek 20 yards from where the trail reaches it. Then cross the creek on logs. On the other side, find a path zigzagging up a wooded ridge. This path cuts northwest towards the outlet of the lake. At 3.2 miles, 200 feet above the crossing, is a rolling grassy area with a view of the waterfall.

Keep left (south) of the creek and follow the path up ledges and through willows beside the falls. A handhold may be needed now and then. The 8,522-foot lake is at 3.8 miles. Several good campsites are on three peninsulas on the south shore.

To reach the lakes in the north canyon, go up the creek on the right (east) for 100 yards when the path comes to the main creek at 3.1 miles. Then take a path marked by oval blazes which turns up away from the creek. At 3.5 miles, the trail returns to the creek and follows it. The path dwindles in a rolling meadow dotted with subalpine firs at 3.9 miles, but you can follow the creek to a lake at 8,523 feet at 4.2 miles. Campsites are at the lower end and near the inlet.

Circle this lake on the east shore on a path, then continue up the path along the east side of a stream to a narrow pond at 4.4 miles. Go around this pond on the east (no path), then cross the creek to the west. Staying well west of the creek, climb between rounded ledges over grass past two more ponds to a 9,167-foot lake at 5.2 miles. Lake 9,050 is an easy walk to the southwest. Snowyside Peak may be climbed with caution from the saddle above Lake 9,167 by hiking and scrambling.

2 MATTINGLY CREEK DIVIDE
Map 1

round trip: 12 miles
elevation gain: 1,736 feet
highest point: 8,816 feet
time: 6 1/2 to 8 1/2 hours
maps: Snowyside Peak, Marshall Peak
difficulty: strenuous
access: Turn west from Highway 75 at Alturas Lake, 39.5 miles north of Ketchum. Drive 4.5 miles on a paved road, then 2 miles on a dirt road to a ford.

Across Mattingly Creek from the red and white mountain heaths of Mattingly Creek Divide, jagged peaks crowd the canyon wall. Four rock towers, one brick red and the others gray, peer over a gap like giant chessmen. Hikers seldom climb the divide, even though trail bikers often ride to the Johnson Creek Junction, .6 mile below it.

To reach the trailhead, follow access directions above. This hike begins at the ford of Alpine Creek on the Alturas Lake Road at 7,080 feet unless you have a four-wheel drive vehicle with a high wheelbase. Beyond the ford, the road is level through the forest, but is washed out in more than one place between the ford and a junction with the Eureka Gulch Jeep Trail at .3 mile. This trail goes 3 miles with a 1580-foot elevation gain to the old mines of Eureka. The rocky road then winds along through forest beside the creek to the register box at Jakes Gulch (7,260 feet) at 2.2 miles.

The first part of the trail is a road through trees. It reaches an open sagebrush area at 2.7 miles below striped outcrops. This route was a rough wagon road to Atlanta in the days of Sawtooth City. From 2.7 miles to a ford of Alturas Lake Creek at 4.7 miles (7,680 feet) the trail threads through a succession of large sagebrush-grass meadows, crossing six intermittent streams on the way.

At 4.7 miles, ford the creek or cross on an upstream footlog. Beyond the ford is a campsite. The route climbs 1,200 feet through thick forest in the next 1.2 miles. At 5.0 miles, cross a stream. The first side trail shown on the map does not exist. The creek now runs below the trail in a 40-foot ravine. At 5.4 miles (8,200 feet), is a .5 mile side trail which leads to a junction with the Johnson Creek and

North Fork of the Ross Fork trails 240 feet above. This Johnson Creek Trail (another is near Graham) goes 7.6 miles with a 2,055-foot descent to the Ross Fork of the Boise River Jeep Trail. The North Fork of Ross Fork Trail descends 1,835 feet in 5 miles to a point 3.5 miles farther up the same jeep trail.

The trail to the divide returns to the right of the creek at the head of the canyon at 5.7 miles, then climbs a hilltop to the summit (8,816 feet) at 6.0 miles.

The divide and the trail down Mattingly Creek give cross-country access to a lake at the head of the south fork of Alpine Creek and two small lakes on the side of Mattingly Peak. The trail down Mattingly Creek drops 2,866 feet in 6.4 miles from the divide to the Middle Fork of the Boise River Trail, 4.5 miles above Powerplant Campground near Atlanta.

3 CABIN LAKES

Map 2

round trip: 7.2 miles
elevation gain: 1,998 feet
highest point: 9,078 feet
maps: Alturas Lake, Snowyside Peak
time: 7 to 8 hours
difficulty: strenuous
access: From Ketchum, drive north on Highway 75 for 39.5 miles to the Alturas Lake Road. Turn left (west) and drive 3 miles to a junction with the Cabin Creek Road. Turn right (north) and drive .7 mile. Turn left onto a dirt road and drive .4 mile to a parking area.

The sandy crest of McDonald Peak, freckled with pines, bars the canyon above Cabin Lakes. A trail not on maps reaches one of the five small lakes. At this first and deepest lake, cracked gray cliffs plunge into aquamarine water, and a rippling waterfall cascades into it. On granite shelves above, the highest lake sprawls among granite peninsulas, flowered turf, and golden sand. The lower two lakes are really only one, divided by a ten-foot wide channel.

To reach the trailhead, follow access directions above. From the parking area (7,080 feet), walk northwest through trees and up a sagebrush hillside for .1 mile to the register box. The trailhead was

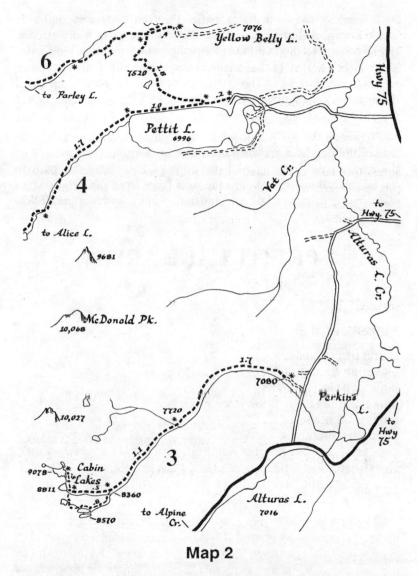

Map 2

relocated to its original site at the end of 1987. This is at the end of the side road showing three buildings on the map. The route then goes west along the edge of the forest below the sagebrush ridge.

At .8 mile, the trail begins alternating between woods and open grassy areas. At 1.7 miles, it ascends a side creek for 200 yards before fording it. The trail continues to climb, occasionally crossing streams.

At 2.7 miles, beyond a grassy basin, the trail hops a second side creek, approaches the main creek and disappears in a dry stream. (Here a route to the twin lakes turns off, which allows a loop trip.) Keep right (north) of the main creek where the path reappears beyond granite ledges. The path climbs between rock ledges and through trees above the ravine of the creek to the first lake (8,811 feet) at 3.3 miles and ends.

To reach the 9,078-foot upper lake, go .2 mile around the east side of the first lake and turn northeast up a gully, which is right of the one containing the creek between the lakes. Climb this gully to the lake at 3.6 miles. To reach the twin lakes from the first lake, go south over a ridge to a lake which dries up in midsummer and follow a creek down to them.

PETTIT LAKE AREA

4 ALICE LAKE

Maps 2 and 3

round trip: 12 miles
elevation gain: 1,600 feet
highest point: 8,596 feet
maps: Alturas Lake, Snowyside Peak
time: 8 1/2 hours
difficulty: strenuous
access: 42.5 miles north of Ketchum, turn left (west) on the Pettit Lake Road. Go 1.6 miles on a gravel road to a four-way junction. Turn right (north) and go .5 mile to Tin Cup hikers' transfer camp.

The arrangement of the gnarled lodgepoles and subalpine firs on the granite peninsulas around Alice Lake seems designed by a super-natural landscape gardener. Two ponds just below it take shelter under the pale orange skyscraper wall of El Capitan. Across the upper end of the blue green lake parades a row of dragon peaks, one with two heads looking in opposite directions.

To reach the trailhead, follow access directions above. The trail starts out through trees and across a sagebrush flat to a view of 6,996-foot Pettit Lake, then goes 20 feet above the shore. At .2 mile, a side

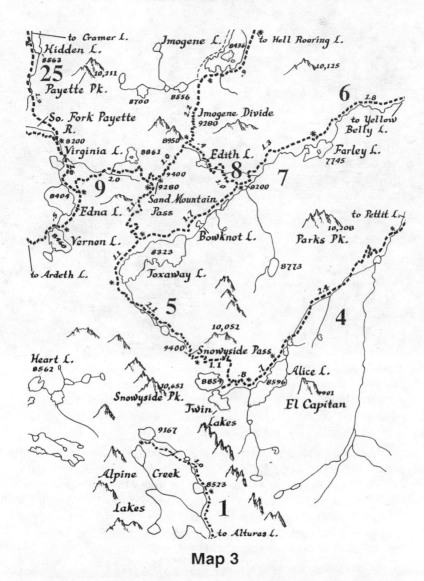

Map 3

trail leads 1.8 miles and 524 feet over a ridge to the Toxaway Lake Trail. This cutoff trail allows loop trips from Pettit Lake.

At 1.2 miles, the Alice Lake Trail leaves the lake and continues level through Douglas and subalpine firs, blueberry and grouse whortleberry for .6 mile before beginning to climb. At 2.1 miles, it edges the base of cliffs. The trail crosses the creek to the east side on

Pond below Alice Lake

a narrow footlog at 2.9 miles. Then at 3.5 miles it fords back to the right (west) of the creek. Here the canyon opens to show granite walls and a split in the canyon ahead.

The path switchbacks through talus and brush above a log-strewn pond, then goes along the base of a 600-foot cliff into the right branch of the canyon at 4.0 miles. At 4.1 miles, the path crosses to the left (east) of the creek on a logjam, then returns to the west on logs at 4.3 miles. Ahead the route climbs a knoll in the center of the canyon in switchbacks not on the map. Above a waterfall at 4.8 miles, the trail returns to the east on a bridge, then levels.

At 5.0 miles, the way returns to the west (right) on logs, then reaches the first of two shallow blue-green ponds. Alice Lake is a few more yards along the trail at 5.3 miles. The path runs along the shore to a peninsula at 6.0 miles before climbing to Twin Lakes. Campsites on this peninsula are over-used, so camp elsewhere. Three ponds above the upper end of the lake make a good cross-country side trip.

5 FROM ALICE LAKE OVER SNOWYSIDE PASS TO TOXAWAY LAKE

Map 3

loop trip from Pettit Lake: 18 miles
elevation gain: 2,404 feet
this section one way: 5.1 miles, 804 feet gain, 1,000 feet loss
highest point: 9,400 feet
map: Snowyside Peak
difficulty: strenuous
access: using directions in Hike 4 (Alice Lake) hike to Alice Lake.

The trail up Snowyside Pass from Alice Lake first passes Twin Lakes, which are divided by a strip of granite outcrops. In season, reflected snowbanks whiten the dark blue water. The two-headed dragon peak is closer now and a peninsula in the lower lake stabs at it. From the upper lake, talus and flower-filled grass sweep to the slabs and cliffs of the curving summit of Snowyside Peak. From the trail up Snowyside Pass, Twin Lakes are sapphires inlaid in a gray granite brooch. Above them a whole row of dragon peaks marches toward the pass from Alice Lake. On the other side of the pass, the trail zigzags down beside wildflower gardens to two turquoise ponds, but Toxaway Lake is hidden.

This hike description begins at 8,596-foot Alice Lake where the trail leaves the lake for Twin Lakes. For directions for hiking there see Hike 4 (Alice Lake). From this point, 6.0 miles and a 1,600-foot climb from the trailhead, the trail ascends west up the creek between Alice and Twin Lakes. At a marshy meadow and pond, the trail turns right into woods, then left across boulders to a sign (at .8 mile) for a .2 mile path to Twin Lakes.

From this sign to the ponds above Toxaway, the trail has been rerouted since the topo map was printed. Half way around Upper Twin Lake and well above it, the route heads north into a grassy area with a pond, then switchbacks left, right, and then .6 mile to the left (west). It jogs again before the 9,400-foot pass at 1.9 miles. The trail crosses the pass at the notch northeast of the one on the map. This pass may not be open to stock until after the first week in August. Hikers can travel it sooner, but crossing the snow on the north side is hazardous.

Twin Lakes from Snowyside Pass

On the far side, the path follows a stream as it descends 14 zig-zags over rocks, turf and mountain heaths to run above the first pond at 3.2 miles. At the second pond, the trail descends to the shore, across from an inlet which gurgles through the white flowers of parrot's beak in season.

Below this pond, the trail runs beside the thin sheet of the stream as it slides over granite to a third tiny pond. Then the route angles down through boulders and subalpine firs, making more switchbacks than shown. At 3.8 miles, the trail crosses the creek on logs below another waterslide. At 4.0 miles, Toxaway Lake is below as the trail passes to the right of a campsite.

The route edges the lake on granite benches and in forest, cross-ing two or three side streams. Beyond the end of the lake, the White Clouds and the scalloped gray wall of Parks Peak are visible. At 5.1 miles (8,400 feet) in the open above a peninsula of rock benches and tiny trees is a junction with the trail to Sand Mountain Pass.

6 FARLEY LAKE

Map 4

round trip: 6.6 miles
elevation gain: 724 feet
highest point: 7,800 feet
map: Snowyside Peak
time: 5 hours
difficulty: easy
access: 42.5 miles north of Ketchum on Highway 75, turn left (west) on the gravel Pettit Lake Road. Go 1.6 miles to a four-way intersection. Turn right (north) and cross a bridge over the outlet. Turn right (north) again on a road to Tin Cup horse transfer camp. At .5 mile, keep straight ahead (east) where a road turns off to the horse camp. Drive on a primitive, rocky road to a signed trailhead at the west end of Yellow Belly Lake, 3.3 miles from the Pettit Lake Road.

Three granite islands, one with a crew of trees, sail the teal blue water of Farley Lake below the furrowed cliffs of Parks Peak. From these cliffs, white ribbon waterfalls plunge into the clear depths. Across from the cliffs and falls, avalanche chutes clogged with tiny firs gouge the sides of an unnamed orange mountain. Just below the lake, the creek thunders between jaws of rock into a meadow.

To reach the trailhead, follow access directions above, but don't attempt the Yellow Belly Lake Road in a passenger car. In early season and when it rains, four-wheel drive is needed. If unable to reach the trailhead by car, begin on the Alice Lake Trail at Pettit Lake. At .2 mile turn onto a cutoff trail over a 524-foot forested ridge. This 1.8 mile trail meets the Yellow Belly Lake Trail .4 mile from Yellow Belly Lake.

From the west end of Yellow Belly Lake (7,076 feet) the trail runs through sagebrush flats and forest to the Mays Creek Junction. Here the cutoff trail comes in from Pettit Lake and a .2 mile side trip north reaches 7,097-foot McDonald Lake, a shallow green lake in marsh grass and partially burned woods.

From this junction, the trail continues through woods to a log crossing of Farley Lake Creek at 1.5 miles. Then the trail begins to climb in forest, passing a waterfall on the creek in woods at 2.4 miles.

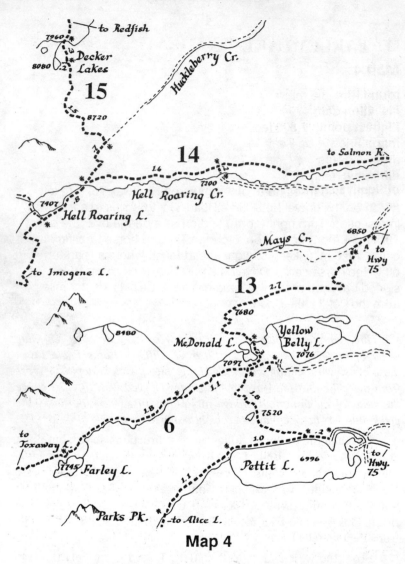

Map 4

A rocky meadow with small trees is at 2.5 miles. From switchbacks above it, you can see the White Clouds and Castle Peak to the east and a large waterfall below.

At 3.0 miles (7,800 feet) is an overlook of the lower end of the 7,745-foot lake. Here a path turns down to campsites. There are also sites on a peninsula at 3.3 miles, as well as off-trail sites at the upper end of the lake.

7 FARLEY LAKE TO TOXAWAY LAKE

Map 3

round trip: 12.6 miles
elevation gain: 1,247 feet
this section one way: 3 miles, 600 feet gain
highest point: 8,400 feet
map: Snowyside Peak
time: 8 hours
difficulty: strenuous
access: Hike to Farley Lake by following directions in Hike 6.

Above the west end of Toxaway Lake, the shoulder of Snowyside Peak resembles a dinosaur with a triangular, jagged back and a massive head which looks right down at the blue-green water. To the left of the dinosaur, the fissured gray and orange face of Parks Peak borders the lake on the south. Granite peninsulas scallop the flower-embroidered shores of the mile-long lake, the longest backcountry lake in the Sawtooths. Drowned peninsulas, decked with lodgepoles and subalpine firs, create islands.

To reach 7,745-foot Farley Lake where this hike description begins, start at Yellow Belly or Pettit Lakes. To reach either lake, follow directions listed above. It is 3.3 miles and a 724-foot climb to the peninsula half way along Farley Lake. That's where this hike description begins.

From here the trail runs above Farley Lake across rocks and among aspens, sagebrush and subalpine firs. Beyond the lake, the trail climbs above a horseshoe-shaped lagoon on the creek, then re-enters forest. At .6 mile, talus slides into meadows and ponds. Next the path goes over a lodgepole ridge to more talus, and the White Clouds are visible. The trail bridges the outlet of Edith Lake and climbs through forest to a junction with the Edith Lake Trail at 1.3 miles.

Next the main trail reaches a narrow pond with a good view of Snowyside Peak. Above the pond, the creek slides over glacier-polished granite. The path edges another marshy pond before arriving at green Bowknot Lake at 2.0 miles. Two peninsulas almost cut this marshy lake in two below a miter-shaped shoulder of Parks Peak. The trail winds through lodgepoles, subalpine firs and granite benches to Toxaway Lake at 2.4 miles. The route is 50 feet above the north shore as it goes to a junction at 3.0 miles with the Sand Mountain Pass Trail. There are many campsites on the peninsulas.

8 EDITH LAKE

Map 3 or 5

round trip: 11.2 miles to lake, 12 miles to junction with Imogene Divide Trail
elevation gain: 1,874 feet
this section one way: 1.4 miles to junction, 750 feet gain
highest point: 8,950 feet at junction with Imogene Divide Trail
map: Snowyside Peak
difficulty: strenuous
access: Following directions in Hike 6 (Farley Lake) and Hike 7 (Farley to Toxaway Lake), hike to the Edith Lake Junction.

Little Edith Lake huddles under corrugated peaks below Imogene Divide and Sand Mountain Pass. It is a pleasant spot to rest or camp before tackling one of these passes. From the granite knolls northwest of the lake, fluted cliffs stairstep down to Imogene Divide from a sharp-pointed orange peak. On the south side of the lake, high white granite peninsulas slide into blue-green water.

To reach the Edith Lake Junction (8,200 feet) where this hike description begins, follow directions listed above. This junction is 4.6 miles and an 1,124-foot climb from the trailhead at Yellow Belly Lake. From the junction, the trail switchbacks up granite on the south side of Edith Lake's outlet. A ford where the creek slides over granite slabs is at .5 mile. The trail returns to the south side of the creek at .8 mile, then hops back to the north again just below the 8,650-foot lake at 1.0 mile. The way edges the east and north sides of the lake, then passes a miniature pond at 1.2 miles. The path wanders up a slope of grass and rocks to a tinier pond and a junction (8,950 feet) at 1.4 miles with the trail from Sand Mountain Pass to Imogene Divide.

9 TOXAWAY LAKE TO EDNA LAKE

Map 3 or 5

round trip: 20.8 miles
elevation gain: 2,204 feet
elevation loss (return climb): 876 feet
this section one way: 4.1 miles, 880 feet gain, 876 feet loss
highest point: 9,280 feet
map: Snowyside Peak
time: 2 to 3 days
difficulty: strenuous
access: using directions in Hike 6 (Farley Lake) and Hike 7 (Farley to Toxaway Lake), hike to Toxaway Lake.

Mountains with delicate points and smooth sides ring Edna Lake. Between them to the north, the canyon of the South Fork of the Payette drops away, giving an end-of-the-world effect. The wide expanse of blue water and needle-carpeted groves of firs and pines are relaxing. From the trail, the prongs of the Rakers are visible in the distance. On the way to the lake from the pass, a pond, sometimes called Rendezvous Lake, gleams in a meadow of tiny firs below a gabled orange mountain.

This hike description begins at the junction (8,400 feet), on the north side of Toxaway Lake, which is 6.3 miles and a 1,324-foot climb from Yellow Belly Lake. To get there follow directions in the hikes listed above. The route begins by climbing a sandy ridge in switchbacks as long as .2 mile. Only a few of these are on the map. From this section, sandy slopes drop hundreds of feet to the lake. The trail gradually circles left of a rocky hill. At 2.1 miles, the trail drops to the sandy notch of the divide (9,280 feet). Here the trail to Imogene Divide goes to the north. The high point (9,400 feet) is .3 mile towards Imogene Divide on that trail.

The trail on to Edna Lake zigzags down through whitebark pines to the edge of the meadow surrounding Rendezvous Lake (8,861 feet) at 2.8 miles. From here the trail descends grassy slopes, follows a creek on the north and crosses the outlet of Rendezvous Lake. A junction with the trails to Ardeth Lake and Grandjean is at 4.1 miles in tiny firs above Edna Lake. Campsites may be reached from either trail.

10 EDNA LAKE TO ARDETH AND SPANGLE LAKES

Maps 5 and 14

round trip: 29 miles via Edith Lake
elevation gain: 3,390 feet
elevation loss (return climb): 1,881 feet
this section one way: 5.2 miles, 1,186 feet gain, 1,005 feet loss
maps: Snowyside Peak, Mt. Everly
time: 3 to 4 days
difficulty: strenuous
access: The shortest way to reach Edna Lake, where this hike description begins, is to hike in 9.3 miles from Yellow Belly Lake by way of Edith Lake. See hikes 6, 7 and 8.

Spangle Lake contrasts with Little Spangle Lake: Spangle Lake is round, deep, and dark blue, while Little Spangle is sprawling, shallow, and olive green. Here at dawn, white granite slabs and islands spangle the water with reflections below a ridge of short gray cliffs. From the trail near the divide between Edna and Ardeth Lakes, gray granite boulders and benches climb Glens Peak from the grass and granite shore of tiny Summit Lake.

To reach Edna Lake, the shortest route is from Yellow Belly Lake by way of Edith Lake. It is 9.3 miles and a 2,324-foot climb by that route. For directions, see hikes listed above. From the junction (8,480 feet) with trails from Grandjean and Ardeth Lake above the east shore of Edna Lake, take the trail towards Ardeth Lake. It goes south above the shore, then climbs to Vernon Lake at .5 mile. Here carved granite slopes rise to crumbled cliffs of a wide-triangle peak. There are campsites on the east shore of the lake and near the inlet. A side trail goes south around the lake to a pond above it.

Take the main trail around the north side of the lake. Cross the outlet on logs and then, at .8 mile, the creek from Summit Lake. The path zigzags through woods, returns to the north side of the creek, and arrives at Summit Lake at 1.5 miles. At the west end of the lake, a rise forms the 8,866-foot summit of the divide between Edna and Ardeth, a 464-foot climb from Edna Lake.

Now the trail drops 638 feet in switchbacks over loose rocks and through trees to 8,228-foot Ardeth Lake at 2.4 miles. At 2.7 miles, the

Map 5

trail fords the outlet of Ardeth Lake to a junction at 2.8 miles with the Tenlake Creek Trail. A good campsite is west of this junction and others are off trail to the southwest.

The trail on to Spangle Lakes climbs the side of a ridge to a meadow and pond at 3.1 miles. Then it switchbacks in rocks to the 8,952-foot divide at 4.3 miles, 724 feet above Ardeth Lake. From the divide, a cross-country side trip up Glens Peak balances on large boulders just below the summit. The view from this peak is worth the effort.

The trail drops only 367 feet through whitebark pine and subalpine fir to a meadow on the east side of 8,585-foot Spangle Lake. It goes along the shore to a junction with the Middle Fork of the Boise River and Benedict Creek trails at 5.2 miles. There are plenty of campsites around both Spangle Lakes. Mosquitoes can be bad at Little Spangle in wet years.

11 INGEBORG, ROCK SLIDE AND BENEDICT LAKES

Map 14 or 20

round trip: 36 miles
elevation gain: 3,700 feet
elevation loss (return climb): 2,536 feet
this section one way: 3.5 miles, 310 feet gain, 655 feet loss
highest point: 8,920 feet
map: Mt. Everly
difficulty: strenuous
access: Hike to Spangle Lakes from Yellow Belly Lake (14.5 miles, 3,390 feet gain) or from Atlanta (14.5 miles, 3,145 feet gain). See hikes 6,7,9 and 10.

A scalloped ridge of crumbling granite lines the west side of Lake Ingeborg. Down the canyon of Benedict Creek, a single scallop drops talus into Rock Slide Lake. Farther down, Benedict Lake and its meadows are trapped between invisible summits which hide behind granite benches. From the trail between Ingeborg and Rock Slide Lakes, the orange and black fangs of the Raker Peaks are visible. One of these resembles the end of a deformed foot, with a big toe, but only three little toes.

This hike description begins at the junction of the Middle Fork of the Boise River Trail with the trail from Ardeth Lake at Spangle Lake. This spot can be reached in 14.5 miles (3,390 foot climb), from Yellow Belly Lake or in 14.5 miles of trail in a 3,145-foot climb from Atlanta.

The trail to Lake Ingeborg first fords the outlet, then edges the south shore of Spangle Lake. Next it switchbacks the side of the canyon to a pond under a row of cliffs at .6 mile. Here the trail turns north and climbs to 8,890-foot Lake Ingeborg at 1.1 miles. The trail edges the right shore of the lake near campsites, then goes up a few feet to a 8,895-foot divide.

The way drops past a marsh to Rock Slide Lake (8,668 feet) at 2.1 miles. This lake is so small it has few campsites. The trail descends to a pond and junction with a trail to Three Island Lake at 3.0 miles. This side trail climbs 200 feet in .6 mile to that lake.

Below this junction, the trail keeps dropping, crosses the creek and zigzags down to the shore of 8,240-foot Benedict Lake at 3.5 miles, where there are several campsites. The trail continues down Benedict Creek 4.6 miles to the South Fork of the Payette River with an 1,060-foot descent.

12 SAND MOUNTAIN PASS AND THE IMOGENE DIVIDE

Map 5

round trip: 25.0 miles from Yellow Belly Lake
elevation gain: 2,654 feet
elevation loss (return climb): 1,294 feet
this section one way: 4.1 miles, 450 feet gain, 1,294 feet loss (starting at Sand Mountain Pass)
highest point: 9,400 feet
map: Snowyside Peak
difficulty: strenuous
access: Use directions from Hikes 6, 7 and 9 to hike to Toxaway Lake and then to the junction of the Edna Lake and Imogene Divide trails on Sand Mountain Pass.

Next to a pleated orange ridge, Imogene Divide overlooks a dozen 100-yard switchbacks, set in gray talus. In the distance below them, white granite peninsulas notch the edges of sapphire blue Imogene Lake. The high point on the trail is .2 mile towards the Imogene Divide from the junction with the trail down to Edna Lake on Sand Mountain Pass. From this point, the curved gap of Imogene Divide is ahead to the north, and the dinosaur back of Snowyside Peak and dark, craggy wall of Parks Peak to the south.

To reach the junction on Sand Mountain Pass where this hike description begins, follow directions in the hikes listed above. It is 8.4 miles and a 2,204-foot climb to this junction from Yellow Belly Lake. From the junction (9,280 feet) the trail towards Imogene Lake zigzags to 9,400 feet at .2 mile. Then it switchbacks down through talus, scree and a few whitebark pines. Above a tiny pond in the grass at 1.0 mile is a junction (8,950 feet) with the Edith Lake Trail.

Next the way climbs 330 feet up a sandy slope, dotted with whitebark pines, to 9,280-foot Imogene Divide at 1.9 miles. Then the trail switchbacks the north side of the pass, dropping   into timber and reaching a stream at 2.8 miles. Beside a marsh at the inlet of the 8,336-foot lake at 3.2 miles, it meets a path around the west side of the lake. There are several campsites along both trails.

Take the main trail east of the lake past three peninsulas with campsites. From this trail, ribbed, jagged mountains near Mt. Cramer are seen below the lake. The trail joins the path west of the lake just below the lower end of the lake at 4.1 miles.

HELL ROARING AREA

13 MAYS CREEK TRAIL TO McDONALD LAKE

Map 4

round trip: 6.8 miles
elevation gain: 830 feet
elevation loss (return climb): 583 feet
highest point: 7,680 feet
maps: Mt. Cramer, Obsidian, Snowyside Peak
time: 5 1/2 hours
difficulty: moderate
access: On Highway 75, turn left (west) 45.7 miles north of Ketchum onto Hell Roaring — Decker Flat Road. Cross a bridge over Salmon River and turn left (south) to a junction at 1.6 miles. Take the left branch and park beside Mays Creek at 1.7 miles.

The Mays Creek Trail is a pleasant, shady walk with veiled glimpses of Sevy and Parks Peaks. Not shown on the topographic map, this trail leads over a ridge to McDonald Lake, a two-lobed lake entirely in marsh grass. Willows, blueberries and shrubby cinquefoil edge the marsh. Behind them, peaks in Farley Lake Canyon and a sphinx-like shoulder of Mt. McDonald peer through lodgepole pines. The trail links the Yellow Belly and Hell Roaring Creek Trails, making loop trips possible.

To reach the trailhead, follow access directions above. Park before the ford of Mays Creek at 6,850 feet to avoid mud and rocks. When the Mays Creek Road beyond the ford climbs a hill, turn left (south) at blazes onto an old logging road. Walk 200 yards to a "no motorized vehicles" sign, where the trail begins .4 mile from the ford.

The path winds up the side of a wooded ridge to its crest at 1.2 miles. Here it turns west along the top of the ridge. At 2.3 miles (7,680 feet) the route drops south from the ridge, at first straight down, then in long switchbacks on grassy shelves. Just above the 7,097-foot lake the trail heads for the shore. The path then follows the shore, fording the outlet at 3.1 miles, into an area of burned trees. The trail then goes south to a junction with the Yellow Belly Trail at 3.4 miles. Yellow Belly Lake is .4 mile east of this junction.

14 HELL ROARING LAKE

Map 4

round trip: 8.8 miles
elevation gain: 207 feet
highest point: 7,407 feet
map: Mt. Cramer
time: 3 1/2 hours plus driving time
difficulty: easy
access: From Highway 75, turn left (west) 45.7 miles north of Ketchum and cross the Salmon River in .3 mile. Turn left and go 1 mile on a gravel road and .5 mile on a dirt road to a junction with the Mays Creek Road. Turn right and drive 3.4 miles up this primitive ROUGH road to the trailhead. (Trailhead is scheduled for change in the near future.)

This shady trail ambles through woods carpeted with red-berried grouse whortleberry to the silvered logs and lime green marsh grass of the lower end of blue-green Hell Roaring Lake. The slanting 800-foot tower of the Finger of Fate points from granite ridges behind the lake. On either side of it, granite gnomes bear the fanciful names of The Ar-

Hell Roaring Lake

rowhead and *The Birthday Cake*. Next to these, a dark gray accordion of cliffs zigzags towards the boulders and slabs of Mt. Cramer.

To reach the trailhead, follow access directions above. At the road junction at .2 mile, a longer trail to Hell Roaring Lake begins. This trail is used when the rough upper part of the road is too muddy for travel. Beginning here makes the hike five miles one way. The trailhead for the shorter trail is under reconstruction. The primitive rough part of the road will be closed and replaced with a new trail. The new trail will begin 100 feet before the road bridge over Hell Roaring Creek and roughly follow the creek for 1 mile up to meet the old trail 3 miles from the lake, making a total round trip distance of 8 miles.

From the current upper trailhead (7,200 feet) at the end of the rough road, the trail first crosses Hell Roaring Creek on a complex of logs. Children or the elderly may need help. At .2 mile, the trail intersects the one from the Salmon River, and at .3 mile, comes to the register box.

There is little water on this trail and often lots of dust. The trail winds through a lodgepole forest, past a a couple of meadows, and crosses an intermittent stream at 1.5 miles. At 1.8 miles is a junction with a trail to Redfish Lake just above 7,407-foot Hell Roaring Lake.

Turn left (southwest) and cross the creek on a bridge to get the best view of the Finger of Fate and surrounding mountains. There are several campsites on both sides of the lake.

From the upper end, a side trip reaches an unnamed lake right under the Finger of Fate. To do this, leave the main trail at 2.6 miles on a path around the west end of the lake. Follow it to the inlet at the west corner of the lake. Go up the right (north) side of this inlet to the 8,200-foot lake, 3.6 miles from the trailhead and 800 feet above Hell Roaring Lake.

15 HELL ROARING TO DECKER LAKES
Map 4

round trip: 8.4 miles
elevation gain: 1,560 feet
elevation loss (return climb): 680 ft.
this section one way: 2.4 miles, 1,360 feet gain, 680 feet loss
highest point: 8,720 feet
time: 8 hours
map: Mt. Cramer
difficulty: moderate, with .1 mile cross-country
access: Follow directions in Hike 14 to hike to Hell Roaring Lake.

Sheets of white granite embrace blue tarns and then soar to the crinkled walls and sloping snowfields of Decker Peak. The true summit is the 10,704-foot peak 1.3 miles southwest of the Decker Peak marked on the topo map. The lowest tarns, the two Decker Lakes, shimmer on branches of Decker Creek west of the trail from Hell Roaring to Redfish Lake.

To reach the beginning of this hike description, follow directions in the hikes listed above to reach Hell Roaring Lake (7,407 feet), a 1.8 mile walk and 200-foot climb from the present Hell Roaring trailhead. From the junction at the lower end of the lake, the trail towards Decker Creek and Redfish Lake switchbacks northeast in woods to meet the Huckleberry Creek Trail at .7 mile. This trail goes 3.8 miles with a 1,430-foot elevation loss to Decker Flat.

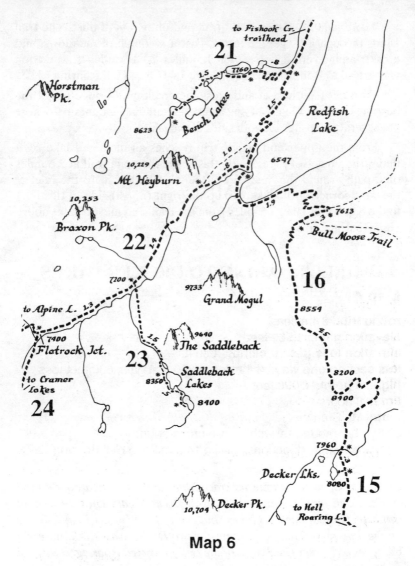

Map 6

The main trail climbs to the 8,720-foot crest of the ridge at 1.0 mile, 1,360 feet above Hell Roaring Lake. From the north side of the ridge, you glimpse the snowy face of Decker Peak through the trees. At 1.5 miles the trail turns north and drops in a ravine along a stream which is often dry.

Where the ground flattens at 2.2 miles, turn west and climb 100 feet cross-country to the largest lake (8,080 feet) at 2.4 miles. There is no path. Approaching from Decker Creek (2.6 miles from Hell Roaring Lake), there are downed timber and steep slopes along the way to the lakes. Reach the smaller, upper lake by circling the larger lake and cutting northwest .1 mile.

Do this hike in early summer, as later the water line is lowered. The best campsites are located near the trail, not at the lakes. The only water on this hike is at Hell Roaring or Decker Lakes.

16 DECKER LAKES TO REDFISH INLET TRANSFER CAMP

Map 6

through trip from Hell Roaring Creek Road: 11 miles
elevation gain: 2,354 feet
elevation loss: 2,967 feet
this section one way: 7 miles, 794 feet gain, 2,287 feet loss
highest point: 8,554 feet
map: Mt. Cramer
time: 9 hours, plus time for car shuttle and boat ride from the inlet back to Redfish Lake Lodge by prearrangement with the lodge
difficulty: strenuous
access: Following directions in Hikes 14 and 15, hike to the turnoff to Decker Lakes 4 miles from Hell Roaring Creek.

On this trail, lodgepole pines screen views of the pale shapes of the White Clouds and the immense turquoise of Redfish Lake. From the descent to the lake, Mt. Heyburn is seen as only the first of a string of peaks along the Redfish Canyon wall. Avalanche chutes claw great scratches on this wall.

To reach the beginning of this hike description at the turnoff for Decker Lakes, .3 mile above Decker Creek (7,960 feet), follow directions in hikes listed above. After descending to the creek, the trail climbs north, drops northeast and then begins to climb seriously. At a 90-degree bend at 1.1 miles, an old trail to Decker Flat goes to the right. The trail turns west up the center of a ridge at 1.4 miles with a view of the White Clouds near the top.

At 2.2 miles, the path switches north with glimpses of Redfish and Little Redfish. Then the trail drops 200 feet to the head of an all-year stream. The route climbs the side of another ridge at 2.6 miles. The trail runs north along the center of this ridge to its 8,554-foot high point at 3.0 miles. From here, Mt. Heyburn is ahead and the Grand Mogul is on the left. From the brow of the ridge at 4.0 miles, Redfish Lake is below and Cabin Creek Peak in the Salmon River Mountains is in the distance.

At 4.8 miles, the Bull Moose Trail goes 4.5 miles to Decker Flat with a 1,020-foot elevation loss. Then at 5.1 miles in a low point in the ridge, the trail to Sockeye Campground heads northeast. It is 4.2 miles with a 1,060-foot elevation loss to that campground. At this junction, take the trail towards Redfish Inlet. This trail zigzags down the side of the ridge to run 30 feet above the lake at 6.0 miles.

At 6.4 miles the trail drops to the beach for 50 yards and then returns to forest. At high water, wade or take a rough path through brush. Next the trail bridges a creek, then climbs 160 feet to meet a path to the Lily Pond at 6.7 miles. The way drops to a ford of Redfish Creek next to the transfer camp at 7.0 miles. Be sure to arrange in advance for the boat from the lodge to meet you or allow for the five-mile hike and 973-foot climb around the lake to the road.

17 IMOGENE LAKE

Map 5

round trip: 11 miles
elevation gain: 1,236 feet
this section one way: 3.7 miles, 1,029 feet gain
highest point: 8,436 feet
maps: Mt. Cramer, Snowyside Peak
time: 8 hours
difficulty: strenuous
access: From Highway 75, turn left (west) 45.7 miles north of Ketchum at a sign for Hell Roaring Creek and cross the Salmon River on a bridge. Follow directions in Hike 14 to reach the trailhead and hike to Hell Roaring Lake.

The arms of Imogene Lake flood one of its high granite peninsulas and make it an island in early season. Above the upper end of the lake, a wide shoulder of Payette Peak holds fluted cliffs. From the lake, a chain of little lakes set in grass and wildflowers skips up a hanging valley towards the peak. Along the trailside of the lake, orange rock need-

les climb a wall of unnamed mountains. The chain of little lakes, Imogene Divide, the unnamed lake sometimes called Lucille, and Profile Lake all make beautiful side trips from Imogene.

To reach the lower end of Hell Roaring Lake (7,407 feet) where this hike description begins, follow access directions above. From here the trail goes along the left (southeast) shore of Hell Roaring Lake. At the head of the lake at .8 mile, the path switchbacks up ledges and through forest across the canyon from crinkled cliffs. Between 1.6 and 2.0, miles the trail goes along an open hillside amid tiny trees.

At 2.1 miles, the trail circles the left side of a small snow pond, not shown on the topo map. The path edges a tiny pond full of water lilies at 2.6 miles and it runs along the east side of a larger, sprawling pond at 2.7 miles where the pleated dark cliffs of the canyon of Profile Lake are visible. At 3.5 miles, the trail crosses to the west side of the outlet of Imogene on logs, then goes along the right side of another tiny water lily pond. At 3.6 miles, the trail crosses the outlet again to the east before arriving at the 8,436-foot lake at 3.7 miles. The trail has been rerouted from what is shown on the topo map.

To make a side trip to the chain of tiny lakes at the head of the lake, follow the trail along the east side of Imogene Lake to the junction in a meadow with the west trail at 4.6 miles. Turn right (north) onto this trail, which fords the inlet. Just before a corduroy bridge over a stream a faint path turns left (southwest). Take this path up granite ledges near a waterfall. Once beyond the ledges, the path is obvious to the first lake. A sign here says the name of the lake is "Esther."

At this shallow lakelet, bays and coves sprawl between granite benches and grass. Here, you look up the canyon to the roof-like side of Payette Peak. Go cross-country around the right (north) side of the first lake to reach the next small, grassy pond. Continue up the inlet, through ledges and between benches to the third lake which has boulders, scree and tiny trees, and turquoise water. Here huge sawteeth rise from the ridge. Follow the stream to the highest lake at 8,950 feet, 1.3 miles and a 520-foot climb from Imogene. For directions for reaching the large unnamed lake (8,733 feet), sometimes called Lucille, northwest of the lower end of Imogene, see the following hike description.

18 PROFILE LAKE

Map 5

round trip: 15 miles
elevation gain: 2,333 feet
elevation loss (return climb): 240 feet
this section one way: 2 miles, 1,224 feet gain, 160 feet loss
side trip to Lucille Lake: additional .2 mile one way
highest point: 9,500 feet
maps: Mt. Cramer, Snowyside Peak
time: 12 hours or 2 days
ability: expert
access: For access directions, see Hike 14 (Hell Roaring Lake) and Hike 17 (Imogene Lake).

Northwest of Imogene Lake, great granite triangles overshadow an unnamed lake, sometimes called Lucille, at 8,733 feet. Lichens color these giant sawteeth dark green. Near the lower end of the lake, a white granite peninsula thrusts into the turquoise water. Orange ledges stairstepping to the summit talus of Mt. Cramer to the right (west) of this wall complete the backdrop. Seven hundred feet up these ledges in a bowl of rocks blue Profile Lake takes the shape of a bust of George Washington. The creek connecting the two lakes tumbles in a series of waterfalls. From Mt. Cramer, rock soldiers lead north to the summit of Sevy Peak. Hikers can use these lakes as a route up Mt. Cramer.

To reach the lower end of Imogene Lake (8,436 feet) 5.5 miles from the trailhead, where this hike description begins, see hikes listed above. Take the unofficial trail around the west side of Imogene. Go around the lower end of the lake on this trail to the narrow bay at the northwest corner of the lake.

Turn off the trail and climb west to the small pond shown on the map. Then go north to a slot between rock benches at 8,560 feet and descend to a small pond (8,400 feet) at .5 mile. From the pond, walk west along the base of ledges (not following a creek) to a second pond at .8 mile. Detour to ford the outlet 100 to 150 yards below the pond where it spreads out over flat granite. Go around the pond on the north, then climb rock benches on the right of the inlet. When the inlet splits, continue up the right of the one draining Profile Lake, not the outlet of Lucille. At 1.3 miles, cross the creek on logs below a narrow pond. From here, it is a .2 mile side trip to Lucille Lake

(8,733 feet) at 1.5 miles. The wooded side of the lake has several campsites.

To continue to Profile Lake, return to the lower end of the narrow pond and follow a faint path up a series of grass-filled gaps in the granite ledges to the left (west) of the outlet of Profile Lake. At 1.8 miles (.5 mile from the narrow pond) is a tiny rocky pond. Above it, the gaps run into steep talus above the gorge of the outlet. So turn west away from the creek and climb gentler ledges to the top of a rounded granite ridge. From here, it is possible to descend carefully to the 9,500-foot lake at 2.0 miles. The ground is too rocky for camping.

To climb Mt. Cramer, return to the granite ridge and follow it west over slabs and boulders. When it steepens, cut to the right of a rectangular snowbank which is prominent much of the summer. Follow the southeast ridge of the peak to the summit. It is .8 mile and a 1,216-foot hike from Profile Lake to the summit of Mt. Cramer.

REDFISH LAKE AREA

19 FISHHOOK CREEK MEADOW
Map 7

round trip to meadow: 4.4 miles
elevation gain: 242 feet
highest point: 6,800 feet
map: Stanley
time: 3 hours
difficulty: easy
access: On Highway 75, turn left (south) 56.2 miles north of Ketchum on the paved Redfish Lake Road and drive 2 miles to the backpackers' parking lot.

Pale aqua and crystal Fishhook Creek meanders in the meadow which is the destination of this hike, alternately hiding under high grassy banks and winding over golden sand. At the head of the meadow, a 200-yard beaver dam holds a quiet pond. The pointed towers of Mt. Heyburn jut above the left side of the meadow. To the right of Mt. Heyburn, the double black hump of Horstmann Peak crouches like a black cat. Right of the meadow, a ridge of square teeth leads toward

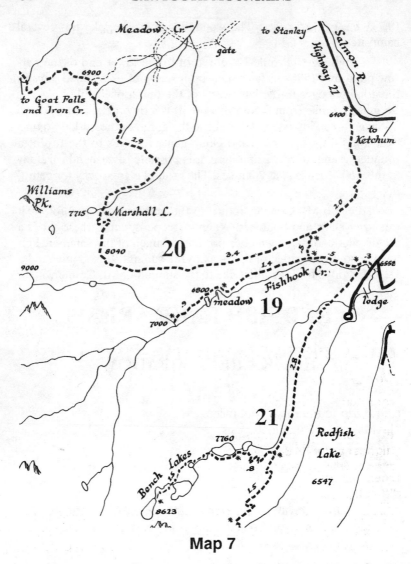

Map 7

shoulders of Thompson Peak. Between these mountains at the head of the canyon, the umbrella-tent of Mt. Ebert is pitched.

To reach the backpackers' parking lot (6,558 feet) where the hike begins, follow directions above. On the Redfish Lake Road, keep straight ahead at a junction 2 miles from the highway. The parking lot is on the right. From it, walk northwest across the lodge road and find a hiker sign and old road leading west up the right side of Fishhook Creek. Most of the hike is along this old road, which is now closed to motor vehicles. The track climbs 120 vertical feet up the creek. Near the top, a trail to the Redfish Corrals turns right. At the top at .3 mile, a trail goes 3.6 miles with a 1,522 foot climb to Bench Lakes, and a branch of this trail goes on up Redfish Canyon..

Continue on the old road, avoiding side tracks, through Douglas fir and lodgepole forest. At .8 mile is a junction with a trail climbing 480 feet in .5 mile to the Alpine Way Trail. By this shortcut, Marshall Lake is only 5 miles instead of 6 miles via the Alpine Way Trail. At 1.5 miles, the old road ends at a washout of the creek bank. Take a blazed trail to the right (northwest) through the trees. At the edge of a steep ridge, the path curves left to follow the base of it. At 2.2 miles (6,800 feet) the trail reaches the edge of the meadow. The beaver pond is .1 mile beyond.

The trail continues past the pond through forest to a creek crossing at 3.1 miles. Experts can continue cross-country an additional 4 miles to the Stephens Lakes. This is a difficult route due to a long stretch of talus blocks in the bottom of the canyon.

20 ALPINE WAY AND MARSHALL LAKE
Map 7

round trip: 20 miles
elevation gain: 2,382 feet
elevation loss (return climb): 1,180 feet
highest point: 8,040 feet
maps: Stanley, Stanley Lake
time: 2 days
difficulty: strenuous
access: 57.4 miles north of Ketchum between the Redfish Lake Road and the Stanley Ranger Station, turn left (west) on a paved spur road and drive 100 yards to two dirt roads leading left which begin at the same point..

Near the beginning of the Alpine Way Trail, across Fishhook Creek is a backdrop of the towers of Mt. Heyburn and the black face and nose of Horstmann Peak. Just off the trail, at 5 miles, tiny Marshall Lake nestles close to cliffs laced with waterfalls. Lodgepoles and subalpine firs blur the stripes of Williams Peak above the shallow green lake. Far-

ther along the trail Goat Falls tumbles in steps, each one split into white ribbons by black boulders.

To reach the trailhead (6,400 feet), follow access directions above. Drive 100 yards along the right (west) road and park in the trees. Then walk south along the old road which continues .5 mile. The topographic map is confusing because it shows only the spur road to the ranger station, and the left (east) of the two dirt roads is shown as a trail. At .6 mile, the road becomes a trail and climbs the end of a wooded ridge. At 1.0 and 1.3 miles, it passes trails to the left (east) to Redfish Corrals. Just before the register box at 2.0 miles is a junction with the cutoff Marshall Lake Trail from Fishhook Creek which has climbed 480 feet in .5 mile. A few feet off trail south of the register box is a fine view of Mt. Heyburn and Horstmann Peak which is a good destination for an evening walk on the Alpine Way Trail or the cutoff. At 2.1 miles, a spur trail turns left to a viewpoint of these mountains and others above Fishhook Creek.

For the next mile plus, the trail is within a few steps of this view and in the open. At 3.2 miles, the route returns to forest. The way steepens at 4.0 miles and at 4.5 miles, it turns a corner to the north, where the immense crown of Thompson Peak is visible.

At this point, expert hikers may turn south to begin a side trip to the round lake under Thompson Peak. Use caution and avoid steep slopes in descending to a pond southwest of the trail. The route is easier if you keep just east of the pond as you descend. From the pond, the climb is steep to the round lake, but not as abrupt as it is cutting directly to the lake from the trail. A gully northwest of the pond is the best route up to the lake.

Beyond the corner, the Marshall Lake Trail reaches its high point (8,040 feet) on an open, grassy slope, then descends through woods. At 5.0 miles, the route drops in switchbacks to a .1 mile spur trail to 7,715-foot Marshall Lake at 5.3 miles. At 5.4 miles, the Alpine Way Trail crosses the outlet of Marshall Lake on logs.

Beyond here, the trail goes northeast down the canyon of Marshall Lake's outlet, then downhill northwest through lodgepoles resembling a pole forest. At 8.3 miles (6,900 feet), is a jeep track from Meadow Creek from the west. This track climbs 450 feet in 1.2 miles from a pasture 3 miles southwest of Stanley. Access to it is blocked by posted private property, so don't use it. Skirting the property is so much trouble it is not worth the miles saved.

From here, the main trail turns west along the side of a ridge. At 9.2 miles, the path drops to a ford of Goat Creek which can be difficult in early summer. Next the route switchbacks a wooded hillside to an unsigned junction (7,400 feet) at 10.0 miles. Here, a well-worn path goes to Goat Falls. From this point, the Alpine Way Trail continues north to the Iron Creek Trail and to Stanley Lake. For a description of this see Hike 30 (Goat Lake).

Water on this hike is available only at the two creek crossings and Marshall Lake. The only good campsites are at the lake.

21 BENCH LAKES

Map 7

round trip to Lake 2: 7.8 miles, add 1 mile cross-country one way and 863 feet gain to see higher lakes
elevation gain: 1,202 feet
highest point: 7,760 feet at second lake, 8,623 feet at fifth lake
maps: Stanley, Mt. Cramer
time: 6 hours; add 3 hours to see higher lakes
difficulty: moderate; expert for upper lakes
access: On Highway 75, turn left (west) 56.2 miles north of Ketchum, and drive 2 miles on a paved road to the backpackers' parking lot.

This hike goes close to the pleats and notches of the 1,000-foot face of Mt. Heyburn. In early summer, snow fills the chimneys between the orange and gray towers of this wall. Each of the blue-green lakes comes closer to this face, until at the fifth lake, the chockstones caught in the chimneys are visible. Below the trail, the clear blue of Redfish Lake reaches out to Redfish Canyon and its rows of spiked peaks, which march toward the lake like a vast rocky army led by Mt. Heyburn.

To reach the trailhead, follow access directions above. From the parking lot (6,558 feet), walk west across the paved lodge road and find the trail at a hiker sign. The trail begins as an old dirt road up Fishhook Creek. At .3 mile is a junction with the Redfish to Baron Lakes Trail. Turn left (south) here. The trail zigzags through forest and sagebrush up the moraine above the lake. Beyond an intermittent stream at 1.2 miles, the trail overlooks the lake as it begins to follow this moraine. Much of the trail is in the open and there is no water. On the ridge at 3.1 miles, a trail turns right (north) to Bench Lakes.

Beyond this turnoff, the Redfish-Baron Trail continues well above the lake past its upper end and into Redfish Canyon. 1.5 miles from the Bench Lakes Junction, a branch trail drops .5 mile to the Inlet Transfer Camp at the upper end of the lake. Taking the boat to the end of the lake cuts 1 mile off the Bench Lakes hike.

From the Bench Lakes Junction, the trail to the lakes makes switchbacks in brush and woods not shown on the topo map. At 3.7 miles is the grassy edge of the first lake, which has few large trees because of an old forest fire. The second lake, at 3.9 miles (7,760 feet), nestles below a wooded ridge guarded by Mt. Heyburn. The official trail ends here, but a path goes much of the way to the upper lakes.

This path circles the left (south) shore of the second lake, then crosses the inlet and climbs on the right (north) of it to the tiny third lake at 4.5 miles. To get to the fourth lake, circle the third on the right (north) and follow a faint path up a steep slope to the lake at 4.8 miles. Go around this lake on the north and cross its inlet. Climb a wrinkle left (south) of this inlet to the fifth lake (8,623 feet) at 5.3 miles.

Campsites are few, but there are two or three at each lake. Avoid camping at the over-used lower lakes.

22 REDFISH INLET TO FLATROCK JUNCTION

Map 6

round trip: 7 miles
elevation gain: 853 feet
highest point: 7,400 feet
maps: Mt. Cramer, Warbonnet Peak
time: 5 1/2 hours
difficulty: easy
access: Go by boat from Redfish Lake Lodge to the Inlet Transfer Camp or around the lake on foot. To reach the lodge, turn left (west) on the paved Redfish Lake Road 56.2 miles north of Ketchum and drive 2.3 miles.

Jagged peaks fringed with delicate spires line both sides of Redfish Canyon. This glacial trough cuts off hanging valleys containing lakes like Saddleback Lakes. Deep blue Redfish Lake, enclosed by glacial moraines, meets this canyon below the jumbled points of the Grand Mogul and the fluted cliffs of Mt. Heyburn. Every bend of the canyon brings more crags into view. The orange Saddleback on the southeast wall of the canyon at 2 miles is one of the most dramatic. It looks like an oversized saddle, complete with horn. At Flatrock Junction, the trails to Alpine and Cramer Lakes diverge. Near it Redfish Creek slides in shining sheets over white granite. This hike gives the essence of the Sawtooths with little effort. Even a boat ride to the trailhead at the upper end of the lake is worthwhile.

To reach the Inlet Transfer Camp where the hike begins, take the lodge boat or walk 5 miles around the lake. If taking the boat, leave your car in the backpackers' parking lot to avoid congesting the lodge parking area.

The trail to Flatrock starts in the campground and goes northwest 200 yards to a register box. Avoid a trail leading northeast from the boat landing as it backtracks to connect at .5 mile with the lodge trail at a point 1 mile closer to the lodge than the other trail. The trail through the campground joins the lodge trail at .8 mile.

The joined trails continue up the canyon alternating open areas with trees and giving views of the lake beginning at 1.2 miles. At 1.4 miles, the path crosses a side creek. Statue-like towers on the canyon wall and enormous boulders along the trail at 1.6 miles create an area called "Garden of the Giants". At 2.0 miles, the trail crosses another creek, then passes an unmarked junction for Saddleback Lakes at 2.2 miles.

The route continues in trees and over rock benches beside cascades to Flatrock Junction (7,400 feet) at 3.5 miles. There are campsites and picnic spots a few yards away near the ford of the creek on the Cramer Lakes Trail.

23 SADDLEBACK LAKES
Map 6

round trip: 7.4 miles, from Redfish Inlet, 3 miles cross-country
elevation gain: 1,803 feet
this section: 1.5 miles, 1,150 feet gain; additional .5 mile
one-way for upper lake, 50 feet gain
highest point: 8,400 feet at upper lake
map: Mt. Cramer
time: 8 hours
ability: expert
access: On Highway 75, turn left (west) 56.2 miles north of
Ketchum, and drive 2.3 miles west to Redfish Lake Lodge. Take
the boat from the lodge to the upper end of lake or hike 5 miles
to the Inlet Transfer Camp.

*The top of the Saddleback resembles a saddle for giants complete
with saddlehorn. From the summit, an orange granite wall plunges
1,300 feet into the lowest turquoise lake. Climbers call the face "The
Elephant's Perch". Across the lakes, the dark gray needles of Goat and
Eagle Perches face this wall. Above the highest lake, teeth on Decker
Peak peer over a striped jagged ridge. Some people call the lakes
"Shangri-La", a name describing the feeling this basin inspires.*

To begin this hike, take the trail up Redfish Canyon from the
Inlet Transfer Camp. At 2.0 miles the trail fords a stream coming
from the northwest. Once across, watch for an unsigned path turning
left (southeast) at 2.2 miles to Redfish Creek, where logs serve as a
crossing 100 yards upstream (treacherous in early season).

Across the creek, a path pushes up through brush away from the
creek for 30 yards and then turns right. It goes up the creek 100 yards
from it for 150 yards. Next the route turns up to the left (south) over
rock benches. There are several paths in the same general direction.
Stay on the benches to keep out of the gorge of the outlet.

In grass and small trees at .7 mile, descend from the benches so
they are on the left (east), but stay between them and the creek. At
1.0 mile, climb 500 feet up steep gravel beside the cascading outlet.
In a tiny meadow above the cascade at 1.2 miles, cross the creek to
the west. At 1.3 miles, skirt the right (west) side of a narrow sliver of
a lake to reach the flat granite benches at the lower end of the

second lake (8,350 feet) 1.5 miles from the trail and 3.7 miles from
Redfish Inlet. Campfires are not allowed within 200 yards of Saddleback Lakes.

To reach the highest lake, take a path around the west side of the
second lake. The higher lake (8,400 feet), is 2.0 miles from the trail
and enclosed by sentinels of Decker Peak. Best campsites are along
the west side of the second lake.

24 FLATROCK JUNCTION TO CRAMER LAKES

Maps 5 and 8

round trip: 14.4 miles
elevation gain: 1,834 feet
this section one way: 3.7 miles, 981 feet gain
maps: Mt. Cramer, Warbonnet Peak
time: 10 1/2 hours from Redfish Inlet Transfer Camp
difficulty: strenuous
access: Using directions in Hike 22 (Redfish Inlet to Flatrock
Junction), hike to that junction.

*A meadow sprinkled with wildflowers and a giant arrowhead on top
of the mountain wall make Upper Cramer Lake inviting. The outlet of
this lake thunders into the water of the middle lake in a short, wide
waterfall. Above the lakes, the flat 800-foot face of Mt. Cramer and the
needled ridge of The Temple edge the cirque leading to Cramer Divide.
In the distance to the north, a rock feather caps a peak on Baron
Divide.*

This hike description begins at Flatrock Junction (7,400 feet),
which is 3.5 miles and 853 feet above Redfish Inlet Transfer Camp.
For directions for reaching this point, see hikes listed above. The
trail to Cramer Lakes begins with a 25-foot ford of Redfish Creek. A
log jam is about 100 yards downstream, but it can be dangerous at
high water.

The path is level through woods for .8 mile. It then curves
southeast and climbs along the side of the canyon with the outlet of
Cramer Lakes. From 1.5 to 2.0 miles the trail switchbacks, then
levels in forest which veils Elk and Reward Peaks to the southwest.
At 2.5 miles, the path climbs gently along the canyon wall, crossing

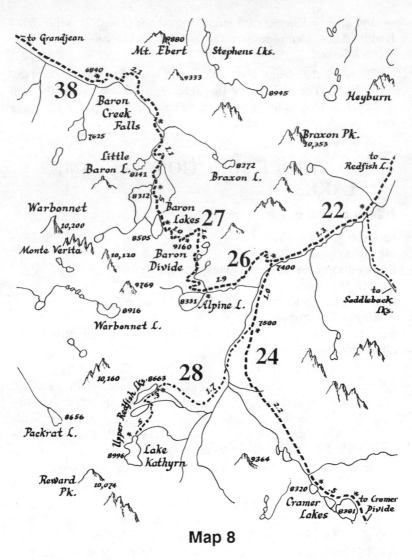

Map 8

small side streams, and at 2.7 miles, it runs above an unnamed grassy lake. The route crosses another side stream at 3.0 miles to reach Lower Cramer Lake (8,320 feet) at 3.2 miles. The path continues on the northeast side of the lakes to the middle lake at 3.5 miles and the upper lake (8,381 feet) at 3.7 miles. The trail then heads through a wildflower meadow towards Cramer Divide. There are several campsites at all three lakes.

The Arrowhead from Upper Cramer Lake

25 CRAMER LAKES TO EDNA LAKE
Map 5

round trip: 29.4 miles
elevation gain: 3,137 feet
elevation loss (return climb): 1,280 feet
this section one way: 7.5 miles, 1,303 feet gain, 1,280 feet loss
highest point: 9,480 feet·
maps: Mt. Cramer, Warbonnet Peak, Snowyside Peak
time: 4 days

access: Using directions in Hike 22 (Redfish Inlet to Flatrock Junction) and Hike 24 (Flatrock Junction to Cramer Lakes), hike to Upper Cramer Lake.

From Cramer Divide, rows of peaks march in every direction, beginning with the splinters of The Temple which run east to the sliced-off summit of Mt. Cramer. This ridge continues east to jumbled Sevy Peak and The Arrowhead, a rock resembling the tip of an arrow sticking out of the mountain. South of the divide, rocks and wildflowers edge the crystal water of Hidden Lake, which filters into a marsh at the south end. East of the lake, granite benches and ledges soar to the wide tri-angle of Payette Peak.

From Upper Cramer Lake (8,321 feet) the trail climbs granite benches, crosses a creek at .7 mile and the outlet of a pond at 1.3 miles. Next it switchbacks past a smaller pond in rocks and zigzags up talus below a wall of cliffs to the divide (9,480 feet) at 2.3 miles. The trail over the divide is often snow-covered and impassable for saddle and pack stock until August 10 or so. Hikers will be able to travel it sooner, but it will be a challenge.

On the other side, the trail drops south along a ridge through whitebark pines, overlooking a narrow blue pond. Then the path zigzags to a crossing of the inlet in a meadow at 3.3 miles. The trail continues down grassy slopes to the shore of Hidden Lake (8,563 feet) at 4.0 miles. The path edges the west shore of the lake and a narrow pond below it. At 4.9 miles the way crosses the outlet of the lake, then descends through forest and angles over to join the South Fork of the Payette River Trail (8,200 feet) 5.9 miles from Upper Cramer Lake.

From here, take the South Fork Trail to reach Edna Lake. It is .5 mile to the end of Virginia Lake, a shallow lake in marsh grass and woods. On the way, the trail fords the river and a creek coming from Sand Mountain Pass. The route then climbs 200 feet to the lower end of Edna Lake at 6.9 miles. The trail edges the north side of the lake to a junction at 7.5 miles with trails to Sand Mountain Pass and Ardeth Lake.

26 FLATROCK JUNCTION TO ALPINE LAKE

Map 8

round trip: 10.8 miles
elevation gain: 1,784 feet
this section one way: 1.9 miles, 931 feet gain
highest point: 8,331 feet
map: Warbonnet Peak
time: 8 1/2 hours
difficulty: strenuous
access: On Highway 75, turn left (south) 56.2 miles north of Ketchum and go 2.3 miles to Redfish Lodge. Take the boat from Redfish Lodge or hike 5 miles around the lake to Redfish Inlet Transfer Camp. Use the directions in Hike 22 and hike up Redfish Creek to Flatrock Junction.

On the west, the furrowed cliffs of a pointed granite mountain hang above Alpine Lake. Lodgepole pines, subalpine firs and granite benches hold in the other three sides of the lake. Spires near Baron Divide peek over a ridge to the northeast. From Flatrock Junction the trail to the lake zigzags 931 feet up cliffs stairstepping out of Redfish Canyon.

Follow access directions above to hike to Flatrock Junction (7,400 feet). The left branch of the trail goes to Cramer Lakes. Turn right (west) towards Alpine Lake. This trail switchbacks through grass and brush, crossing back and forth over a side stream. At .7 mile, it comes to the cliffs and the groves of trees growing on them. It levels out at 1.6 miles and fords an inlet. At 1.9 miles, the trail reaches the lake (8,331 feet). Campsites on the trail side of the lake are over-used, so try the upper end or across the outlet. Campfires are not allowed within 200 yards of Alpine Lake.

27 ALPINE LAKE TO BARON LAKES
Map 8

round trip: 17.0 miles
elevation gain: 2,613 feet
elevation loss (return climb): 848 feet
this section one way: 3.1 miles, 829 feet gain, 848 feet loss
highest point: 9,160 feet
map: Warbonnet Peak
time: 2 - 3 days
difficulty: strenuous
access: Using directions in Hike 22 (Redfish Inlet to Flatrock Junction) and Hike 26 (Flatrock Junction to Alpine Lake), hike to Alpine Lake.

From Baron Divide peaks and crags and serrated ridges stretch in every direction into blue haze. Below, Baron Lakes perch in a hanging valley at the head of the canyon of the South Fork of the Payette River. On the south side, the cylindrical folds of Monte Verita overhang the lakes. On a ridge northwest of that mountain, granite pinnacles form the feathers on a warbonnet, but the peak with the name Warbonnet is hidden. On the north end of this ridge Big Baron Spire is topped with a pinnacle resembling the tip of a bent thumb.

This hike description begins at Alpine Lake (8,331 feet). For directions for reaching that lake, see the hikes listed above. The trail to the divide makes four 300-yard switchbacks in woods and then climbs along the outlet of a series of ponds, crossing this creek twice. At .7 mile, the path edges the west side of the first pond.

Next, the trail goes towards the head of the canyon on partly open slopes. It turns south sharply at 1.3 miles. The path zigzags up in rocks to the 9,160-foot divide at 1.6 miles. On the other side the trail hairpins down through ledges, talus and whitebark pines to the rocky edge of Upper Baron Lake, (8,505 feet) at 2.6 miles. It continues along the edge of the lake and, at 2.8 miles, a path turns off to some campsites. The route descends in woods to the lower lake (8,312 feet) at 3.1 miles. The best campsites are northeast of Upper Baron Lake and at the lower end of Baron Lake.

28 UPPER REDFISH LAKES
Map 8

round trip: 14 miles, 5 miles cross-country
elevation gain: 2,449 feet
this section one way: 2.5 miles, 1,496 feet gain
highest point: 8,996 feet
maps: Mt. Cramer, Warbonnet Peak
time: 10 1/2 hours or 2 days
ability: expert
access: Using directions in Hike 22 (Redfish Lake to Flatrock Junction) and Hike 24 (Flatrock Junction to Cramer Lakes), hike to Flatrock Junction and go 1 mile above it on the Cramer Lakes Trail.

Snowfields splash the 800-foot charcoal gray sawteeth of Elk Peak above the three Upper Redfish Lakes. Needles also guard the ridge between this peak and the talus cap of Reward Peak. Elk Peak and this ridge, white granite knolls, turquoise water, and whitebark pines swollen with burls make the upper lake, Lake Kathryn, beautiful. The two lower lakes, set between trees, granite outcrops and flower-splashed meadows, have a different view. On the northeast, pickets of an orange mountain fence in the aqua water of the twin lakes. This is a rugged hike with no path, so it is for experts only.

Use the access directions above to hike to a point 1 mile (at 7,500 feet) towards Cramer Lakes from Flatrock Junction. This point is 4.5 miles from the Inlet Transfer Camp. At the turn off, the trail jogs uphill to the left and begins to climb. Leave the trail here and descend to Redfish Creek, following a faint path for .5 mile through dense forest, downed timber and boggy areas. Cross the creek at about .6 mile on logs while the ground is still level.

Go along the right (west) side of the canyon above the creek. Just before reaching the outlet of Cramer Lakes at .8 mile the banks of the creek steepen. Climb away from the creek 100 yards onto a little ridge and follow it. At 1.0 mile the creek divides again into three sections. Climb on the right (north) of the right branch through shrubs. At 1.2 miles, the canyon gets even steeper and the branch of the creek you are following splits again at the outlet of the lower lake (not shown on the map).

Keep to the right of both streams and work up ramps between granite ledges, but AVOID cliffs on the right. This route is easier than the brush between and to the left of the streams. Each time the creek splits, keep to the right of all branches of it. The stream runs through a series of cascades and waterfalls before the granite flattens into pavement at 1.5 miles. At 1.7 miles is the lower lake (8,663 feet). Go left (south) around the lower lake and cut across a strip of land to the middle lake at 2.0 miles.

The upper lake, Lake Kathryn, can be reached from the lower end of the middle lake after a .5 mile scramble up a 300-foot ridge to the south. To find this route, cross the outlet of the lake and circle the ridge to the left of it until you can climb between granite benches to the crest. Then follow the flattened summit of the ridge and climb down over the benches to the lake (8,996 feet) near its outlet.

IRON CREEK AREA

29 ALPINE, SAWTOOTH AND McGOWN LAKES

Map 9

round trip: 9.6 miles
elevation gain: 1,720 feet
side trip to McGown Lakes: add 1.5 miles one way and 330 feet gain, 255 feet loss
highest point: 8,430 feet
map: Stanley Lake
time: 8 hours
difficulty: strenuous
access: 2.5 miles north of Stanley on State Highway 21, turn left (west) on the gravel Iron Creek Road and drive 3 miles to the transfer camp.

Above the lower end of Sawtooth Lake, the largest lake in the Sawtooth Wilderness, sculptured granite curves from the shore to the cap-like summit of the dominant peak, Mt. Regan. From the trail to Mc-Gown Lakes the twisted rust and silver trunks of dead whitebark pines frame this peak and the immense sapphire platter of the lake. A mile below the lake, the cracked cliffs of Alpine Peak fall to two orange

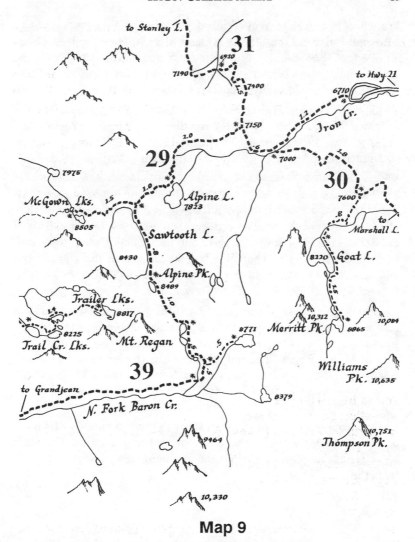

Map 9

*peninsulas which pierce the lime and blue-green water of Alpine Lake.
From the trail above this lake, two hills to the east resemble potatoes,
one with its jacket on and the other opened and topped with sour cream
and chives.*

To reach the trailhead (6,710 feet) follow access directions
above. The trail, which begins at a wooden map, is heavily used. It
begins in a flat lodgepole forest, comes close to Iron Creek at .5 mile,
then climbs a knoll and winds to a trail junction with the southern

branch of the Alpine Way Trail at 1.2 miles. This branch goes to Marshall Lake and the Stanley Ranger Station. Now the Iron Creek Trail edges the right side of a round meadow and climbs gently. At 1.8 miles, the north branch of the Alpine Way Trail turns off to Stanley Lake. Here a side canyon contains a sliced-off dome.

The Iron Creek Trail angles up the side of the ridge and makes four switchbacks. The way fords cascading Iron Creek on rocks at 2.9 miles to a wildflower meadow. The trail zigzags up a forested ridge to a junction at 3.8 miles with a 200-yard path to Alpine Lake (7,823 feet).

The main trail switchbacks through granite benches above Alpine Lake. At 4.5 miles, the path flattens as it bridges a stream, then climbs the rest of the headwall to a grassy pond at 4.7 miles. The trail crosses the outlet of Sawtooth Lake and back again on logs to the left (east) side. It reaches a junction a few yards from the edge of the lake at 4.8 miles. The right (west) branch goes 1.5 miles with a 330-foot gain and 255-foot loss to McGown Lakes.

For a good view of the lake (8,430 feet) take the south branch past a snow pond to a grassy area at 5.2 miles. From here it is .8 mile to the south end of the lake, where a pond sits in flowers under the wall of Mount Regan. The only good places to camp near Sawtooth Lake are at the two ponds below it, one towards Alpine Lake and the other at the head of the North Fork of Baron Creek. Campfires are not allowed within 200 yards of Alpine and Sawtooth Lakes.

You may want to retrace your steps to the junction and take the other fork to McGown Lakes, which are set in gray talus. The main reason for taking this side trip is the excellent view of Sawtooth Lake from the trail.

30 GOAT LAKE

Map 9

round trip: 7.6 miles
elevation gain: 1,590 feet
elevation loss (return climb): 80 feet
highest point: 8,220 feet
map: Stanley Lake
time: 5 to 6 hours
ability: expert
access: 2.5 miles north of Stanley on Highway 75, turn left (west) onto the Iron Creek Road and drive 3 miles on a gravel road to the transfer camp and parking area.

Two small permanent snowbanks with aquamarine edges spit large chunks of ice into Goat lake. These snowbanks hang at the base of an 1,800-foot wall above navy blue water. On the wall, rock towers thrust out of the cliffs like gigantic divers ready to plunge. On the other three sides of the lake, shorter cliffs enclose shallower blue-green water. Above the upper end, strands of a braided waterfall weave through lime green grass from a cluster of higher lakes. Behind the falls, the tip of Thompson Peak resembles feathers on an arrow. To reach this lake, you must climb a slippery path beside Goat Falls.

To begin this hike follow directions above to the Iron Creek trailhead at 6,710 feet (see Sawtooth Lake). Take the Iron Creek Trail to the junction at 1.2 miles (7,000 feet) with the Alpine Way Trail going south.

Turn left on that trail and cross Iron Creek on a footlog. The trail goes east through woods, then turns south in a ravine full of alders and grass at 1.6 miles. The trail follows a tiny stream up the ravine and crosses it in mud at 2.0 miles. Now the path turns northeast up the side of a ridge and rounds the end of the ridge still climbing.

At 3.0 miles, at a junction marked only with blazes, peaks behind Goat Lake are visible. Here the main Alpine Way Trail turns east downhill. Take the more worn path towards the mountain wall through two open areas. The second open area contains a dry stream bed and cliffs above it resembling a flatiron on top. At 3.2 miles at the far side of this open area and 100 yards from Goat Falls, turn

Goat Lake

right at a sharp angle on a path towards ledges above. Take time to find the right path; it is well-worn.

The path ascends left (north) of the ledges on the right of the falls. The first 300 feet are the steepest. The track gradually goes closer to the falls through tiny firs. Be careful at the top of the falls where the route crosses a big slab covered with sand. Now the way follows the creek and then goes away from it in boulders. At 3.6

miles, cross the creek to the left on logs or rocks to avoid enormous blocks of talus. Early in the season, you may need to cross farther up or not at all. The path climbs through forest and over granite outcrops to the 8,220-foot lake at 3.8 miles. The only campsites are between granite benches above the east side of the lake. This hike is not recommended for children under 12 because of the dropoffs and slippery climb. Campfires are not allowed within 200 yards of Goat Lake.

Experts may wish to continue cross-country 1.5 miles to the upper lakes. To do this, take a path around the east side of the lake to the upper end. The path begins by climbing between the benches and then drops to the shore near the upper end. From the left (east) lobe of the upper end of the lake, aim for a rock ramp leading to the 150-foot high bench on the near (east) side of the two inlets. Get onto the ramp by scrambling up a ten-foot cliff. Climb the ramp to the top of the bench and then along it until you can descend onto the elongated snowfield shown on the map. Walk up the snowfield past the first tiny lake in talus to the largest of the upper lakes (8,865 feet), 645 feet above Goat Lake. A dark knoll separates this lake from a teardrop lake west of it.

31 NORTH ALPINE WAY AND LAKES
Maps 9, 10

through trip: 8.8 miles
elevation gain: 1,530 feet
elevation loss (return climb): 1,720 feet
this section one way: 5.8 miles, 1,090 feet gain, 1,200 feet loss; additional 1.5 miles one way and 849 feet gain to see off-trail lakes
highest point: 7,760 feet at saddle, 8,609 feet at highest lake
map: Stanley Lake
difficulty: strenuous; expert for lakes
access: 2.5 miles north of Stanley turn west on the Iron Creek Road and drive 3 miles to the Iron Creek trailhead. Then hike 1.8 miles to the Alpine Way Trail.

This trail passes under cliffs and crosses side canyons lined with delicate spires, notched crags, and chuckling waterfalls. In the northern section, the towers seen are those on McGown Peak, the double-

pointed mountain of Stanley Lake. From the high point of the trail, a side trip reaches two tiny lakes in a sawtoothed canyon. West of the lower lake, the gray granite of McGown Peak is indented by crescent-shaped hollows and etched by wandering veins of white rock. On the east, the lake is guarded by a granite gargoyle. A narrow flower-strewn moraine holds in the upper lake. North of this lake, a sandy slope climbs the side of McGown Peak. To the west, the ridge holds even triangular teeth similar to those on a saw.

To reach the beginning of this hike description, follow access directions above to hike the Iron Creek Trail to the junction with the North Alpine Way Trail at 1.8 miles. The turnoff to the off-trail lakes is .8 mile closer to Stanley Lake than to Iron Creek.

The trail begins by angling up the side of a grassy ridge to a flat summit at .5 mile. Then the path switchbacks down in trees, crosses a small creek and then Crooked Creek (6,920 feet) on logs at 1.5 miles. The trail skirts the base of the mountain wall in woods and in sandy areas. At 2.5 miles, it fords a small creek in a gorge, then climbs straight to a saddle (7,760 feet), the high point of the trail, at 3.0 miles.

To reach the lakes, turn southwest and go up the end of a ridge. Follow a sandy deer path along the east side of the towers of the ridge spine to a notch at .3 mile where the ridge smooths out so you can follow the top of it. At .5 mile, the ridge ends in a cirque of grass and rocks. Climb the headwall of the cirque along the creek on the left side past a waterfall. At the top, go around a shallow pond, shown as a marsh on the topo map, and turn right (north). Climb through a gap between two hills to the lower lake at 1.0 mile. To reach the upper lake 1.5 miles from the trail, return to the marsh and walk up to the head of the valley.

From the high point at the turnoff to the lakes, the trail to Stanley Lake descends a ridge in trees with a view of towers of McGown Peak. Beginning 3.8 miles from the Iron Creek Trail, it descends in .2 mile switchbacks. At 4.5 miles, the path crosses a creek on logs or rocks, but the rocks are very slippery. The path descends the left side of the creek in lodgepole and grouse whortleberry. At 5.0 miles as it flattens, the trail turns north toward Stanley Lake Creek, which it fords at 5.5 miles. At 5.7 miles, the trail passes a register box for this trail and at 5.8 miles intersects the Stanley Lake Creek Trail, 1.2 miles from the trailhead at Stanley Lake.

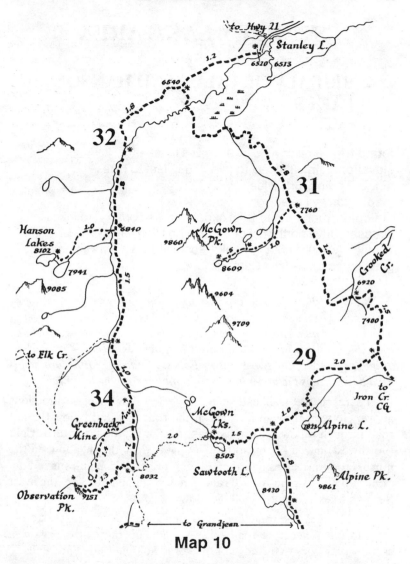

Map 10

STANLEY LAKE AREA

32 BRIDALVEIL FALLS AND HANSON LAKES

Map 10

round trip: 8 miles to falls, 9.6 miles to lakes
elevation gain: 320 feet to falls, 1,582 feet to lakes
highest point: 8,102 feet
map: Stanley Lake
difficulty: moderate to falls, expert (cross-country) to lakes
access: Drive northwest of Stanley on Highway 21 for 5 miles. Turn left (west) on Stanley Lake Road and go 3.8 miles on a gravel road to the Inlet Campground.

Bridalveil Falls puffs out at the top, then plunges in a cascade of lacy water, just like a veil. Clumps of turf hold red paintbrush, magenta mimulus and pale blue bluebells in the bride's bouquet. Above the falls, a double-humped monolith, textured by fractures, overlooks the deep turquoise water of the two Hanson Lakes. A natural earth dam stabilized by firs keeps the upper lake from tumbling into the lower lake.

To reach the trailhead at 6,520 feet, follow access directions above. Go west through the gate at the trail sign and follow the old road through willows near the creek. At .5 mile, the track turns right (northwest) into a big meadow. The path edges the meadow on the north, crosses streams and then enters forest. At 1.2 miles is a junction with the Alpine Way Trail. Keep straight ahead to the west through trees and more small meadows.

At 2.3 miles, the route begins to climb southwest across a step in the canyon. Where the road turns straight up the canyon again, a sketchy path goes to the edge of the gorge holding Lady Face Falls.

The main trail at 3.0 miles fords Stanley Lake Creek. Footlogs here are underwater in early season. At 3.8 miles, in sand, turn onto a path to the creek. Ford the creek (6,840 feet) and take a path southwest to view the falls at 4.0 miles. In doing this, keep to the lowest and most level branch. DO NOT climb the dangerous sandy paths on the right of the falls, even to get to Hanson Lakes.

To reach the lakes safely, go look at the waterfall and return to the ford. At the ford, notice three vertical sandy ridges leading up the canyon wall to the right (north) of the waterfall. To the right of them, a strip of brush parallels the ribs. Climb the right (north) side of this brushy area on a zigzag path, skirting the edge of the forest. When the steepness lessens, the path cuts left 25 feet to a small creek and disappears.

Cross this creek and contour across the hillside to a small flat meadow where paths reappear. Follow the one which crosses a flat, rocky slope and plunges through mossy springs to intersect the distinct but dangerous path that has come up beside the falls. (A few feet down this path, a big X on a tree marks the point where the path plunges 600 feet in .2 mile.)

After intersecting this path, turn right (southwest) on it and go along the right side of the creek to the lower lake (7,941 feet) .7 mile from the ford. A path to the right (north) of this lake and up the right (northeast) side of the inlet reaches the upper lake (8,102 feet) 1.0 mile from the ford.

33 ELK MEADOW AND LAKE
Map 11

round trip: 3.4 miles for meadow, additional 1.2 miles one way for lake, 40 feet gain
elevation gain: 120 feet
elevation loss (return climb): 40 feet
highest point: 6,805 feet at lake
map: Elk Meadow
time: 4 1/2 hours for both meadow and lake
difficulty: easy for meadow (except for ford), expert for lake
access: 5 miles northwest of Stanley on Highway 21 turn left (west) on gravel road and drive 3.4 miles to a junction. Turn left onto a primitive road and drive as far as the second sharp curve of the creek at 2 miles.

From the vast green bogs of Elk Meadow, views of McGown Peak and the canyon wall of upper Elk Creek entice hikers. This route to Elizabeth Lake is easier than the one from Stanley Lake as it avoids a 560-foot return climb. In addition, near the beginning you can use a compass to take a short cross-country side trip through thick woods to a marshy green lake twice as large as Elizabeth Lake, but with a similar view.

A register box for a direct route through the meadow which no longer exists misleads hikers. (The box will be relocated in the future.) Few know of the drier route on a stock driveway to the Elizabeth Lake Trail. Hikers must still cross the wet meadow on the Elizabeth Lake Trail to reach that lake, but this route avoids the endless bog of the old trail. The meadow alone is a fine destination, especially in late June when the wildflowers are at their best. To reach the trailhead (6,680 feet) follow access directions above. In early season, park before the road goes into a muddy meadow, 2.3 miles from the highway at the first sharp bend in the creek.

There are two routes to the stock driveway from the road. One is on a path down to the creek at the far end of the muddy meadow. The path fords the creek in sand in two shallow sections, so is not difficult if you can find it. Across the ford, the path climbs southwest up a tongue of land into a lodgepole forest where it becomes a good trail.

The other way to find this trail is to continue walking on the road past the register box to a pole fence .2 mile beyond the meadow. Walk through the gate in the fence and then down the fence to the creek and ford it. Here it is deeper and swifter than at the other crossing. On the other side, walk up a path to the trail.

The blazed stock trail wanders through level forest and sagebrush flats above the meadow. To stay on the right path, look for blazes. At 1.5 miles, the trail crosses a tongue of meadow, then returns to forest. At 1.7 miles, the route joins the Elizabeth Lake Trail at the edge of Elk Meadow at 6,760 feet. This trail is faint or nonexistent within the meadow.

To reach the unnamed lake, once through the pole fence mentioned earlier, stay on the old road as it goes uphill through forest. Where the road turns up to the right and ends .5 mile from the fence, take out your compass and topo map and plot a course to the lake. There is no trace of the trail shown on the map. The route climbs over a small hill, down to the upper end of a swampy meadow, then up to the lake (6,805 feet), 1.2 miles from the first path to the ford.

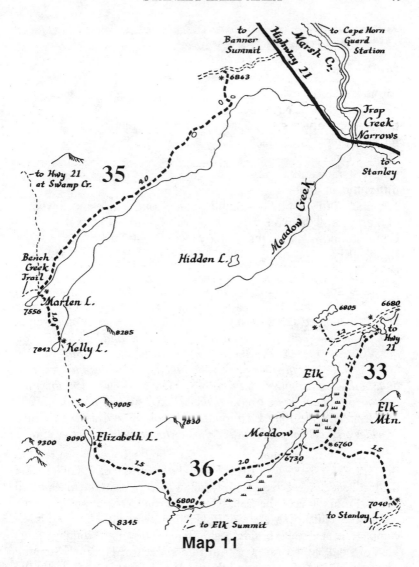

Map 11

34 OBSERVATION PEAK

Map 10

round trip: 16.6 miles
elevation gain: 2,631 feet
this section one way: 4.5 miles, 2,311 feet gain
highest point: 9,151 feet
time: 2 days
map: Stanley Lake
difficulty: strenuous
access: Turn west on the Stanley Lake Road 5 miles northwest
of Stanley and drive 3.8 miles on a gravel road to the Inlet
Campground. Walk up the Stanley Lake Creek Trail to the
Bridalveil Falls turnoff. See Hike 32 (Bridalveil Falls and Hanson
Lakes).

*From this sandy hill above the Trail Creek—Stanley Lake Creek
Divide, the jagged spires of the Sawtooth Range stretch southeast, becoming bluer with distance, to the needles of North and South Raker on
the skyline. Across the canyon dark cliffs sweep to the rounded top of
Mt. Regan. One of the blue peaks, Warbonnet, resembles the crest of a
dark blue wave rushing east. From here, there are views back down the
canyon of Stanley Lake Creek to the serrated wall of McGown Peak
and west into the rounded mountains above Elk Creek. This hike
provides an excellent panorama of the Sawtooths with moderate effort.*

This hike description begins on the Stanley Lake Creek Trail at
the turnoff for the view of Bridalveil Falls at 6,840 feet, 3.8 miles from
the trailhead. To reach this point, follow directions in the hikes listed
above. From the falls, the trail, still an old road, crosses an open area
below the cliffs of McGown Peak, then continues in woods. A
campsite is at .7 mile beside a side stream flowing through a large
area of sand. At 1.5 miles, a trail turns west to Elk Creek Summit.
This trail climbs 1,520 feet and descends 1,780 feet in 9.5 miles to the
Elizabeth Lake Trail.

At 2.0 miles, the main trail threads a narrow meadow below a
wall of boulders and cliffs and passes a campsite. At 2.5 miles, the
old road to the Greenback Mine turns up the canyon wall. The trail
continues along the creek but well above it. At 3.2 miles is the flat of
the Trail Creek—Stanley Lake Creek Divide (8,032 feet).

View from Observation Peak

Here is a junction with trails to McGown and Sawtooth Lakes, Trail Creek and Observation Peak. You can camp here, but there is no water. The Trail Creek Trail descends 1 mile to the Trail Creek Lakes Junction with a 451-foot elevation loss and then goes to Grandjean (see Hike 37, Trail Creek Lakes). McGown Lakes are 2 miles toward Sawtooth Lake, with a 600-foot gain and 120-foot loss. The trail to Observation Peak climbs 1,119 feet in 1.3 miles up a sandy hillside sprinkled with whitebark pines to the gentle summit at 4.5 miles.

To see the site of the Greenback Mine on the return, descend north from Observation Peak .7 mile cross-country to a round pond. Follow its outlet .5 mile to a swampy meadow and the mine road. The mine is 200 yards up the road, but the only building remaining is a log crib over the shaft. To return to the trail, descend .7 mile on steep road switchbacks. This 1.4 mile route saves .6 mile over the trail, but the cross-country hiking along the pond's outlet is rough.

35 MARTEN AND KELLY LAKES
Map 11

round trip: 10 miles
elevation gain: 979 feet
elevation loss (return climb): 40 feet
highest point: 7,842 feet
maps: Elk Meadow, Banner Summit
time: 7 hours
difficulty: moderate
access: 8.5 miles north of Stanley on Highway 21, turn west on a dirt road at a sign for Marten Lake. Drive through a creek at .2 mile and continue to the register box at .7 mile.

Similar tree-dotted cliffs and peaks of gentle triangles back Marten and Kelly Lakes. They differ only because marsh grass edges Marten Lake and red mountain heath and Labrador tea surround Kelly Lake. From the trail, east across Stanley Basin, stand the striped ramparts of Cabin Creek Peak. This route is a gentle climb through cool woods, but few take it because it is north of the main rocky mass of the Sawtooths. The stillness may be broken only by the cry of a jay or the sighing of the pines.

To reach the trailhead (6,863 feet), follow access directions above. The trail wanders through lodgepoles and, at .5 mile, crosses a basin of snow ponds. At 1.0 mile is a tiny marshy lake with a view of the peaks. At 2.5 miles, the path climbs along the base of an open hillside. In woods at 3.5 miles, the route crosses four sections of a branch of Trap Creek. Crossing the largest is on a log. The trail continues along the creek to Marten Lake (7,556 feet) at 4.0 miles, where there are several campsites.

Just before the lake is an unsigned junction with a trail to the north. This trail splits in a few yards into the Bench Creek and Swamp Creek trails. The Bench Creek Trail goes west 5.4 miles to Highway 21 near the Bull Trout Lake Road, with a 644-foot climb and 1,280-foot descent. The Swamp Creek Trail goes 6 miles north to Highway 21 just south of the Thatcher Creek Campground with a 910-foot elevation loss. The trail to Kelly Lake crosses the outlet of Marten Lake on a log, then wanders over a gentle ridge through subalpine firs to a stream crossing at .5 mile. The path rounds the east end of the ridge and turns south to the lake (7,842 feet) at 5.0 miles.

Camping here is limited. The trail continues beyond Kelly Lake 1.5 miles with a 491-foot gain and 243-foot loss to Elizabeth Lake.

36 ELIZABETH LAKE
Map 11

round trip: 10 miles
elevation gain: 1,410 feet
elevation loss (return climb): 360 feet
highest point: 8,090 feet
time: 8 1/2 hours
maps: Banner Summit, Elk Meadow
ability: expert
access: From Highway 21, turn west 5 miles northwest of Stanley onto the gravel Stanley Lake Road. Drive 3.4 miles to the second junction, marked Elk Mountain. Turn right (west) and drive to a trailhead at 5.2 miles.

This little lake of marshy edges and green water hides behind lodgepole pines and subalpine firs below ridges of crumbled granite cliffs. Beyond the lower end two small jagged peaks cling to the wall of Elk Creek Canyon. Just before the lake, McGown Peak and the White Clouds seem to float in the distance. On the way to the lake, huge Elk Meadow, threaded with creeks and sodden with bogs, makes route-finding difficult and damp. Therefore, this hike is best for late summer and dry years.

To reach the trailhead (6,960 feet), follow access directions above. From the register box, the trail leads north over a flat ridge and then turns west as it drops to the edge of the huge meadow at 1.5 miles. There is no sign for the 3.4-mile stock driveway trail from Elk Meadow Road which comes in here.

Take a cowpath going left into the meadows and disappearing at two metal stakes. Ignore the trail shown on the topo map until you are .7 mile from the west end of the meadow. Do not try to skirt the meadow on the near side because bogs extend into the forest. Cattle graze in the meadow but won't bother you. Walk to an electric fence in the center of the meadow and along it for .3 mile to a gap in the fence. Go through the gap and ford Elk Creek at 6,730 feet.

Beyond the ford, cut over toward the woods at the far side of the meadow, crossing two or three side creeks on the way. Aim for the willows where the far edge of the meadow jogs toward you. A path with blazes should appear along the edge of the forest. The correct route passes a tiny log cabin. Sixty yards beyond the cabin is a junction before a ford of Elk Creek at 3.5 miles. The Elk Creek Trail continues across the ford 6.0 miles to Elk Creek Summit with a 1,780-foot climb. It goes an additional 3.5 miles and 1,520 feet down to the Stanley Lake Creek Trail.

Turn right (west) on the Elizabeth Lake Trail along the edge of Elk Creek and a side creek. Avoid side paths before the climb; the trail is the least-used route crossing the other paths at right angles. At 3.8 miles, the trail climbs straight up the wooded hillside. The way turns away from the creek at 4.0 miles and then turns back to the left at 4.3 miles and crosses the creek. The route ascends a steep hill to the left away from the creek. Finally it tops a ridge and follows it. At 5.0 miles, an unsigned path drops left (west) 100 yards to the lake (8,090 feet). The trail continues 1.5 miles with a 243-foot climb and 491-foot loss to Kelly Lake.

GRANDJEAN AREA

37 TRAIL CREEK AND TRAILER LAKES
Map 12

round trip: 9.2 miles
elevation gain: 2,820 feet to first Trail Creek Lake
highest point: 8,000 feet at first Trail Creek Lake, 8,817 feet at highest Trailer Lake
side trip to Trailer Lakes: 1.4 miles one way and 880 feet additional gain
maps: Grandjean, Stanley Lake
time: 9 hours for Lower Trail Creek Lake, 4 additional hours for Trailer Lakes
difficulty: strenuous; expert for cross country route to upper lakes and Trailer Lakes
access: 37.2 miles northwest of Stanley on Highway 21, turn left (east) on the gravel Grandjean Road. Drive 7.1 miles to the trailhead in the campground.

The second Trail Creek Lake

The lowest Trail Creek Lake reflects a dark triangular peak with hunched shoulders. At the base of the peak, a tilted slab touches the blue-green water with one corner. Lodgepoles, subalpine firs and granite benches lead along the opposite shore to the inlet cascading in a flower-dusted notch. Notice the trail gains 2,800 feet in only 5.2 miles, so plan accordingly. Cliffs of the triangular peak also hang over the second lake, but a grassy peninsula and talus distinguish its shoreline. In front of granite knolls and whitebark pines, marsh grass and Labrador tea wreath the dark green water of the third lake. On the skyline above it, jagged teeth march up a ridge to the summit of a peak roofed with sloping slabs. Above the island dotting round green Regan Lake, peach talus climbs to a ridge of cliffs with scribbled stripes.

The highest of the two Trailer Lakes is only a turquoise pool in the rocks above the fish-shaped largest lake, which looks up with an eye made of a pile of talus. Above it, pale orange cliffs sweep to the lumpy summit of Mt. Regan.

To reach the trailhead (5,180 feet) on the east side of the campground, follow access directions above. The trail first goes through woods to a bridge over Trail Creek. At a junction on the

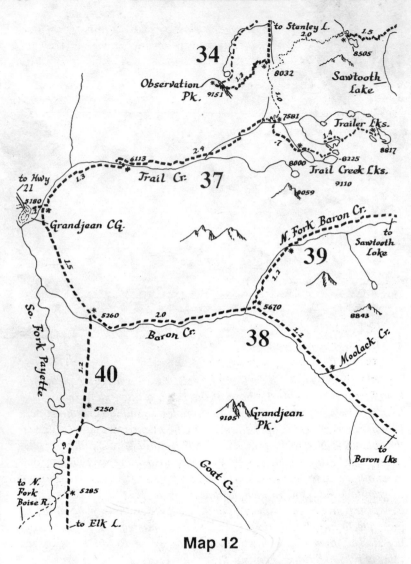

Map 12

other side at .2 mile, turn left (north) on the Trail Creek Trail. This trail twice switchbacks up a sagebrush hillside, then follows the creek on a steep, grassy slope across from rock towers.

At 1.0 mile, the trail hairpins away from the creek, then returns to it in brush at 1.2 miles. The route crosses to the north side of the creek at 1.5 miles on footlogs which will be underwater in early season.

From the ford, the route makes a big switchback up a talus slope, and at 2.0 miles returns to forest and brush. At 2.4 miles, the trail zig-zags up a brushy slope. The trail is washed out for a few yards at 3.1 miles just before it fords the creek again to the south.

In the next section, 16 switchbacks up to 200 yards long climb 320 feet up granite ledges in .3 mile. At 3.3 miles, the trail runs gently along the ravine of the creek and crosses it back to the left (north) on a log at 3.5 miles. At 3.7 miles, after the creek splits, the way crosses the north branch of the creek in alders. The next section has another 20 switchbacks, but they are in woods and climb only 300 feet in .7 mile.

At 3.9 miles (7,581 feet) is the sign for Trail Creek Lakes. The main trail climbs 451 feet in 1 mile to the Trail Creek—Stanley Lake Creek Divide. Take the Trail Creek Lakes Trail across Trail Creek in mud, and go up the right (west) side of the outlet of the lower lake. At 4.5 miles, the route skirts a talus slope occupied by pikas. The lower lake (8,000 feet) is at 4.6 miles. Campsites are at the lower end and half way around the left (north) side of the lake.

To reach the upper lakes, go around the north shore of the lake and find a path leading east up a ravine to the left of granite benches. Where the path disappears in a dry creek bed, turn right (south) cross-country to the lower end of the second lake (8,225 feet), which is .5 mile from the outlet of the lower lake.

To reach the third lake (8,245 feet), go half way along the north side of the second lake. Then turn left (north) and walk past a pond to the lake at .7 mile.

To get to the Trailer Lakes, go around the third lake on the north to its upper end. From here there are two possible routes, and both are more difficult than reaching the Trail Creek Lakes. The steeper route climbs the inlet shown on the map in a gully of tiny trees. From this gully, continue up a slot in the rocks to the flat sand and granite benches near the smallest, highest lake, which is .1 mile above the large, fish-shaped lake (8,817 feet).

The second route gives a view of Regan Lake on the way. To follow this route head north from the north side of the third lake near the upper end for 200 yards up a little canyon. Turn east and go between a series of granite knolls to a low saddle (8,600 feet), 1.4 miles from the lowest Trail Creek Lake. Regan Lake is .2 mile below to the north. Reaching the Trailer Lakes from here is difficult because you must go east above cliffs on the side of the ridge.

38 BARON CREEK TRAIL TO BARON LAKES

Maps 12 and 8

round trip: 22.4 miles to the upper lake
elevation gain: 3,325 feet
highest point: 8,505 feet
maps: Grandjean, Stanley Lake, Warbonnet Peak
time: 2 to 3 days
difficulty: strenuous
access: 37.2 miles north and west of Ketchum on Highway 21, turn right (east) and drive 7.1 miles on a gravel road to Grandjean Campground.

The trail from Grandjean to Baron Lakes ascends a canyon shadowed with spires and embroidered with waterfalls. Southwest of Baron Lakes, the face of Monte Verita resembles the pipes of an organ. The ridge connecting this peak with a shoulder of hidden Warbonnet Peak holds a row of tilting feathers. To the northwest, Big Baron Spire looks like the profile of an Indian squaw with one small crooked feather on her head. Below the lakes, the great pleated wall of Baron Peak forms a backdrop of sawteeth. This pinnacle-surrounded lake basin epitomizes the name "Sawtooth".

To reach the trailhead at 5,180 feet, follow access directions above. The trail begins at the end of the campground and goes over Trail Creek to a junction at .2 mile with the trail to Trail Creek Lakes. Stay on the level South Fork of the Payette River Trail, which rambles under lodgepole and ponderosa pines and through occasional grassy areas.

At 1.7 miles, turn left (east) on the Baron Creek Trail, which climbs along the north side of Baron Creek through forest and open brush below granite cliffs. At 3.6 miles, the trail fords the North Fork of Baron Creek, where a footlog is usually present. There is a campsite beyond the ford. At 3.7 miles, the North Fork of Baron Creek Trail turns off to Sawtooth Lake.

Up the canyon of Baron Creek, the folded face of Grandjean Peak is above the south wall. At 4.9 miles, the trail fords Moolack Creek to two small campsites. The trail comes close to Baron Creek at 5.5 miles at a campsite marked by a trailside boulder. Above in an open grassy area, the grade steepens. At 6.8 miles, a waterfall tumbles from Tohobit Peak.

Switchbacks begin opposite another falls at 7.3 miles. They climb 1,000 feet in 1 mile, through woods and shrubs, but mostly over rocks, where it can be hot. Close to these rocks rushes Baron Creek Falls. Above the falls at 9.0 miles is a campsite.

The trail bridges the creek at 9.4 miles. From here an unmaintained path goes up the creek to the site of an old trail crew camp below Braxon Lake. The main trail has three more creek crossings (at 9.8, 10.1 miles and 10.4 miles) but no more bridges. The last ford is just below the lower end of 8,312-foot Baron Lake which appears at 10.5 miles. The best campsites are near the outlet.

The trail to the upper lake zigzags through forest and then up the ridge to 8,505-foot Upper Baron Lake at 11.2 miles. The best campsites are off-trail northeast of the lower end of the lake.

Two interesting side trips from the lakes lead to Little Baron Lake and an unnamed lake on the side of Monte Verita. To reach Little Baron Lake, climb through a notch in the ridge at the lower end of Baron Lake and descend 200 feet in forest. For the unnamed lake, follow the trail around Baron Lake, cross the outlet of Upper Baron Lake (not shown on the map) and the inlet draining from Monte Verita. Climb the right side of this inlet over grassy slopes and granite benches to the lake at 1.2 miles, 708 feet above Baron Lake.

39 NORTH BARON TRAIL TO SAWTOOTH LAKE

Maps 12 and 9

round trip: 19.4 miles
elevation gain: 3,309 feet
elevation loss (return climb): 59 feet
this section one way: 6 miles, 2,819 feet gain, 59 feet loss
highest point: 8,489 feet
maps: Grandjean, Stanley Lake
time: 2 to 3 days
difficulty: strenuous
access: Follow directions for Hike 38 (Baron Lakes) to hike to the crossing of North Baron Creek, 3.7 miles from Grandjean.

This trail climbs the canyon of the North Fork of Baron Creek be-
tween pleated granite walls trimmed with pinnacles. Across the canyon
from the trail up the headwall, orange stripes etch the charcoal pleats of
a 1,500-foot face. From the top of this climb, it is a short side trip to a
round turquoise lake in a bowl of scalloped cliffs. Above, the trail pas-
ses three aquamarine ponds in talus and wildflowers right under the
orange cliffs of Mt. Regan. Around a corner, the high rounded point of
Mt. Regan hangs over the great sapphire sheet of Sawtooth Lake.

This hike description begins at the junction (5,670 feet) of the
Baron Creek Trail with the North Fork of Baron Creek Trail, which
is 3.7 miles from Grandjean. For directions for hiking to this junction, see above.

The North Baron Trail switchbacks a grassy area into brush and
Douglas firs. At 1.2 miles, the trail fords the North Fork. In late summer, cross on a downstream log and brush pile, but in early summer,
pick your way across the treacherous avalanche logs just above the
ford.

Once across, the trail continues to switchback through brush and
rock slabs, then runs through alders, willows and cottonwoods with
occasional washed-out sections. At 3.0 miles, the route crosses open
slopes of grass, tiny firs and sagebrush. Then it climbs scree and talus
to a ford at 4.0 miles. This crossing can be difficult in early summer.

Next the path hairpins up the wall of the hanging valley containing the lake, crossing back and forth over a white quartz outcropping.
As soon as the trail levels, at about 8,240 feet and 4.5 miles, but
before the first of two tiny ponds in the woods, a cross-country side
trip goes northeast to the 8,771-foot round lake on the canyon wall
under Merritt Peak.

To take this side trip, cut towards the outlet of that lake, but keep
high enough to stay out of its gorge. Follow a strip of dirt between
the talus on the west and the forested gorge below. Just below the
lake, a big snowbank lingers in a hollow. For the last 200 yards, walk
up the creek or scramble along ledges on the side of it. At the lake,
which is .5 mile and 600 feet above the trail, climb out of the stream
bed to the right to avoid cliffs.

Back on the main trail, both ponds in the woods have campsites,
the first since Baron Creek. The path then threads a wildflower garden and talus to two larger ponds in the talus at 4.7 and 5.0 miles.
There are campsites on the wooded knoll between these ponds.
Above the upper pond (8,271 feet), the trail zigzags through talus to

its high point opposite still another pond (8,489 feet) in the grass right under Mt. Regan. Then the way drops to the shore of Sawtooth Lake (8,430 feet) at 6.0 miles. From here, the trail goes .8 mile along the east shore to the Iron Creek Trail (see Hike 29, Alpine, Sawtooth and McGown Lakes).

40 SOUTH FORK OF PAYETTE RIVER: GRANDJEAN TO ELK LAKE

Maps 12 and 13

round trip: 23.2 miles
elevation gain: 1,470 feet
highest point: 6,650 feet
maps: Grandjean, Edaho Mountain, Warbonnet Peak
time: 2 to 3 days
difficulty: strenuous
access: 37.2 miles northwest of Stanley, turn left (east) onto the Grandjean Road. Drive 7.1 miles on the gravel road to Grandjean Campground.

Along the way to Elk Lake from Grandjean, Taylor Spring bubbles from emerald moss at the side of Big Meadows. These vast meadows stretch five miles of green velvet along the meandering South Fork of the Payette River. A fir forest crowds lime green marsh grass at the edges of Elk Lake. Across the clear water, the spired and fractured north wall of the canyon faces rock ridges bristling with trees.

To reach the trailhead, follow access directions above. The trail crosses Trail Creek on a bridge at .2 mile, then passes a turnoff for Trail Creek Lakes. The route is level for the first 6.5 miles through trees and grassy areas. At 1.7 miles, the Baron Creek Trail turns east. Continue south on the river trail, mostly through forest. At 2.9 miles, the trail bridges Goat Creek.

At 3.8 miles, a trail turns off to the North Fork of the Boise River. This trail crosses the South Fork of the Payette in a 120-foot ford, which is a problem most of the summer. It goes 11.8 miles up a ridge and down the North Fork of the Boise to meet the Bayhouse Trail 1 mile from the primitive Graham Road. There is a 2,271-foot climb and 1,656-foot elevation loss along the way.

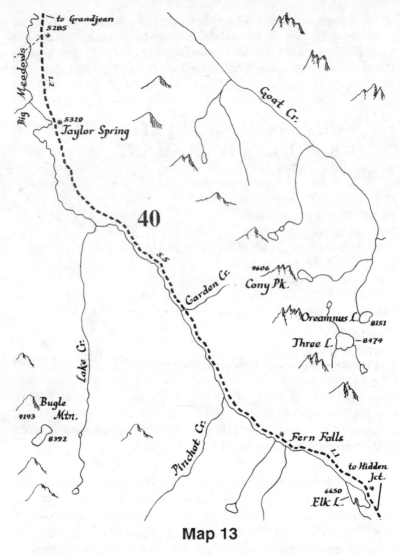

Map 13

On the South Fork Trail, an old jeep trail parallels the main trail on the east for 2.5 miles, giving access to the site and grave of Deadman's Cabin. This site is .3 mile south of Taylor Spring. The spring at 5.0 miles is only 140 feet higher than the trailhead at Grandjean. At the spring, the trail coincides with the jeep road for 300 feet. Previously hidden grassy meadows and several campsites are here.

At 6.5 miles, the trail begins to climb. Below Garden Creek at 8.0 miles are waterfalls on the South Fork and a campsite. Mud slides have caused washouts above here, but the trail has been repaired. There are many switchbacks in brush beyond, but none are shown on the topo map. A campsite .5 mile below Fern Falls sits off-trail in a grassy area toward the river. Fern Falls at 10.5 miles is actually two short waterfalls. At 11.6 miles, the trail comes close to Elk Lake, (6,650 feet) half way along it. There is one campsite earlier, down a path near the lake at 11.0 miles, but the more attractive sites lie at the upper end of the lake at 12.0 miles. In this canyon, water can be obtained from the river when the trail is near it or from stream crossings.

41 SOUTH FORK OF PAYETTE RIVER: ELK LAKE TO HIDDEN LAKE JUNCTION

Map 14

round trip: 35.2 miles
elevation gain: 3,020 feet
this section one way: 6 miles, 1,550 feet gain
time: 3 to 4 days
maps: Warbonnet Peak, Mt. Everly, Snowyside Peak
difficulty: strenuous
access: Using directions in Hike 40 (South Fork Payette River Trail: Grandjean to Elk Lake), hike to Elk Lake.

Along the South Fork of the Payette River above Elk Lake, glacier-polished rocks glide to spires and turrets on the canyon walls. Similar spires bar the head of each side canyon. Just below Benedict Creek, the river foams in a glistening cascade known as Smith Falls. In this trail section, the route fords Benedict Creek once and the river three times.

To reach Elk Lake (6,650 feet), follow access directions listed above. Above the lake, the trail climbs through woods to a 120-foot ford of the river at 1.9 miles. This ford is to the south, and is usually one to two feet deep, but it may be dangerous in June and early July. Beyond the ford, the trail climbs to a junction with the Benedict Creek Trail at 2.9 miles. This trail gains 960 feet in 3.5 miles to a junction with the Queens River Trail below Benedict Lake.

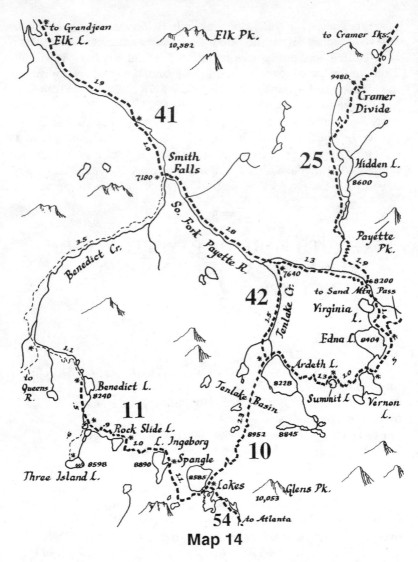

Map 14

Next the South Fork Trail crosses Benedict Creek on logs, then fords the river to the left (north) and climbs more steeply. At Tenlake Creek at 4.7 miles, the trail fords the South Fork again to the south side to a junction (7,640) with the Tenlake Creek Trail.

Between this junction and the Hidden Lake Junction, the trail switchbacks up 600 feet through lodgepoles and grouse whortleberry. At the junction at 6.0 miles (8,200 feet), trails turn off to Hidden

Lake and Edna Lake (described in Hike 25, Cramer Lake to Edna Lake). From Elk Lake to this junction, water can be obtained only at the river crossings and campsites are few.

42 TENLAKE CREEK TRAIL

Map 14

round trip: 35.6 miles
elevation gain: 3,048 feet
this section one way: 1.5 miles, 588 feet gain
highest point: 8,228 feet
map: Mt. Everly
time: 3 to 5 days
difficulty: strenuous
access: Using directions in Hikes 40 and 41, hike from Grandjean up the South Fork of the Payette River Trail to Tenlake Creek.

The destination of this trail is Ardeth Lake, a .5 mile-long blue lake set below the wide triangle of Glens Peak in a basin containing ten lakes. The topmost cliffs of this peak peer at the lake over a 600-foot shelf of solid granite. Two slanting chimneys, usually snow-filled, divide the sides of the shelf into three leaning granite grain elevators. The other nine lakes perch on this shelf, accompanied by dozens of tiny ponds.

This trail begins at 7,640 feet on the South Fork of the Payette River Trail, 16.3 miles and a 2,460-foot climb from Grandjean. The trail ascends Tenlake Creek through thick forest, and at .2 mile fords Tenlake Creek to the right (west). At 1.2 miles, just below Ardeth Lake, the route returns to the left side of the creek. These fords have deep, rushing water and could be a problem in early summer. The trail joins the Edna-Spangle Lakes Trail in woods near campsites at the lower end of Ardeth Lake (8,228 feet) at 1.5 miles.

GRAHAM AREA

43 BAYHOUSE AND JOHNSON CREEK TRAILS

Map 15

round trip: 15.2 miles
elevation gain: 1,780 feet
elevation loss (return climb): 720 feet
highest point: 7,040 feet
maps: Swanholm Peak, Nahneke Mountain
time: 11 hours or 2 days
difficulty: strenuous
access: From Highway 21 at Edna Creek Campground 18 miles northeast of Idaho City, drive to the Silver Creek trailhead on the primitive, ROUGH Graham Road.

From the summit of the Graham Road, the splintered panorama of the entire Sawtooth range outlines the horizon. This road is for the brave, since it is rocky, steep and hangs above deep canyons. It requires four-wheel drive as it is a primitive road receiving little maintenance in the last ten years. From the road, the Bayhouse Trail climbs through a cool fir forest over a ridge and down through sagebrush to the Johnson Creek Trail. The trail meanders with the creek in and out of meadows and lodgepole groves below the granite spurs of Big Buck Mountain. This is the shortest route to Pats Lake (10.1 miles).

The road to Graham turns northwest from the Atlanta Road at a point 4.3 miles from Edna Creek Campground, which is 18 miles northeast of Idaho City. The route follows the Pike's Fork of the Crooked River, gradually becoming steeper and rockier. At a summit 13.0 miles from the turnoff, the road looks down on 1,000-foot deep Jackson Creek Canyon. The track skirts the canyon wall to a junction with a side road to Jackson Peak Lookout at 14.6 miles.

From this point, the road is suitable only for four-wheel drive vehicles with high clearance. The track drops 300 feet into two-mile long Trapper Flat at 15.5 miles. The road next climbs the Crooked River to 8,080 feet with a view of the Sawtooths at 21.7 miles. After ups and downs, the road crests again at 25.0 miles. In the next five miles, the road descends 2,000 feet with some turns so sharp drivers

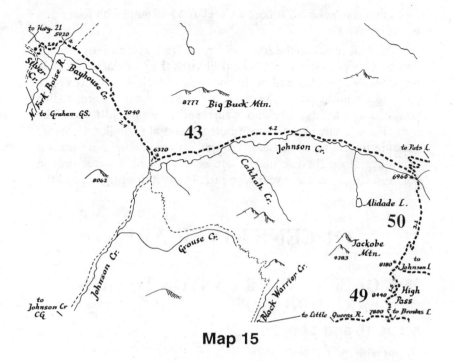

Map 15

must back up to make the curve. At 28.1 miles (32.4 miles from Highway 21), the road reaches the Silver Creek trailhead. The road continues another four miles, passing the Graham Bridge Campground and unused guard station, to the Johnson Creek Campground.

The level trail from the Silver Creek trailhead (5,904 feet) fords Cow Creek at .2 mile and the North Fork of the Boise River at .8 mile. There is a log, but the crossing may be difficult in early summer. A trail turns up the North Fork of the Boise at 1.0 mile. The trail up the North Fork climbs 1,656 feet and descends 2,271 feet in 11.8 miles to meet the South Fork of the Payette River Trail 3.8 miles from Grandjean.

Beyond this junction, the Bayhouse Creek Trail climbs southeast 1,140 feet through forest and meadows. At 1.9 miles, it crosses a branch of Bayhouse Creek. The path crests a summit, (7,040 feet) at 2.5 miles with a view of the lower end of Johnson Creek Canyon. The route drops 720 feet on an open sagebrush slope to a junction (6,320 feet) at 3.4 miles with the Johnson Creek Trail, which has come 5 miles and 700 feet from Johnson Creek Campground with four fords of the creek.

Turn left (east) up the Johnson Creek Trail, which winds through pines and brush. At 5.5 miles, the trail fords the creek in a sprawling meadow. At the other end of the meadow at 5.9 miles, it fords back again to the north side of the creek. Up the canyon, the horns of two peaks form a headwall behind Azure and Rock Island Lakes. The trail climbs gently in the canyon bottom, and at 6.7 miles angles up the side to join the Pats Lake Trail at 7.6 miles. There are several campsites along the canyon. In late season, there is water only in Johnson Creek, and in a year with little snow, it dries up beyond the first ford.

QUEENS RIVER AREA

44 QUEENS RIVER CANYON TO PATS LAKE JUNCTION
Maps 16 and 17

round trip: 24.8 miles
elevation gain: 3,080 feet
highest point: 8,280 feet
maps: Atlanta West, Atlanta East, Mt. Everly
time: 3 days
difficulty: strenuous
access: 18 miles north of Idaho City on Highway 21, turn east at Edna Creek Campground and drive 36.4 miles on a gravel road to the Queens River. Turn left (north) and drive 2.3 miles on dirt road to a transfer camp.

Cracked gray cliffs 1,000 feet high line the canyon of the Big Queens River from its mouth to the Pats Lake Junction. The first three miles of trail run through groves of ponderosa pines draped with yellow-green moss, but higher up, the route traverses open grass, brush or talus with views of fluted peaks ahead. Beyond Nanny Creek, streams pour down the side of the canyon and make bogs on the trail. Near the head of the canyon, a 1-mile side trip leads to an unnamed lake on an old trail incorrectly signed Bluejay Lake. A dagger-shaped tongue of grass along the inlet cuts into this oval, green lake below a ridge topped with short cliffs. Above this turnoff, vertical streaks of black and white stripe some of the walls. At the Pats Lake Junction, the infant river babbles through moss in a rocky meadow under the gray granite hat of Mt. Everly.

To reach the trailhead, turn right (east) at the Edna Creek Campground 18 miles north of Idaho City onto gravel Forest Road 384. At 13.7 miles, turn left (east) along the North Fork of the Boise River on Road 327. At 26.6 miles, turn left again at a four-way intersection onto the Middle Fork of the Boise River Road 268 and drive to the Queens River Road 206 at 36.4 miles. Turn left (north) to the transfer camp at 38.7 miles. There are signs for Atlanta at each turn on the approach, but on the way out, find your way by the road numbers. The Queens River Road continues beyond the parking area into an informal campground.

From the parking area, the trail begins as an old road, closed to motor vehicles, which drops left (north) to cross the Queens River on a bridge. At .2 mile, the trail splits into the Queens River and Little Queens River trails. A loop trip will take five to eight days.

Of the two, the Queens River Trail climbs more gradually, wandering through Douglas firs and ponderosa pines, crossing side creeks at 1.4 and 2.0 miles, and coming closer to the cliffs of the canyon wall. At 2.3 miles, the trail approaches the river and appears to cross it on a ponderosa log but doesn't. The Joe Daley Trail joins from the south at 2.6 miles at an unmarked junction. This trail goes 4.5 miles in a 1,320-foot climb over a ridge to primitive roads leading to Atlanta.

At 3.3 miles, the Queens River Trail crosses the river to the right (south) on a log jam 150 yards upstream. The first three crossings of the Queens River can be hazardous early in the season.

Once across the logs, go back down the creek ten yards, then up a dry side stream to find a path to the trail. Next, the trail ascends in trees away from the river into brush below the canyon wall.

At 3.8 miles, the trail hops a side creek, and at a campsite, returns to the river and crosses it to the left (north) on a log jam 25 feet west of the trail. On the other side, head upstream to find the trail, which soon reaches an open, brushy area extending upstream three miles. On the wall above, waterfalls hide in clefts in the cliffs. Just before Nanny Creek, the trail returns to forest, then crosses the river at 6,500 feet in several sections at 6.9 miles to a flat on the right (south) side of the river with campsites beside Nanny Creek.

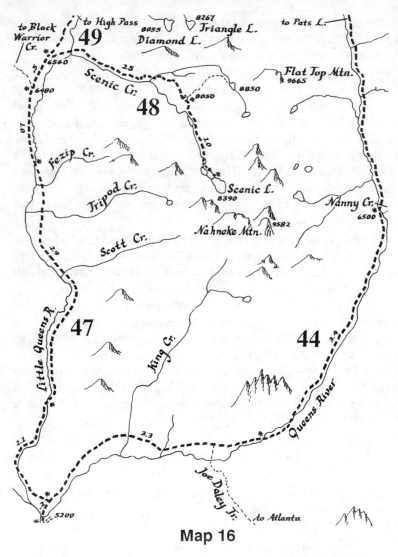

Map 16

Beyond here, the trail is in open grass and rocks with ledges above. At 7.9 miles, the trail is flooded for 60 yards at high water. Grassy and wooded flats at 8.0 miles have campsites.

Now the trail crosses open grass, with side streams and patches of woods. At 9.6 miles, the path jogs 90 degrees to the right (east) for 100 yards at a "trail" sign and cairns, then continues up the canyon.

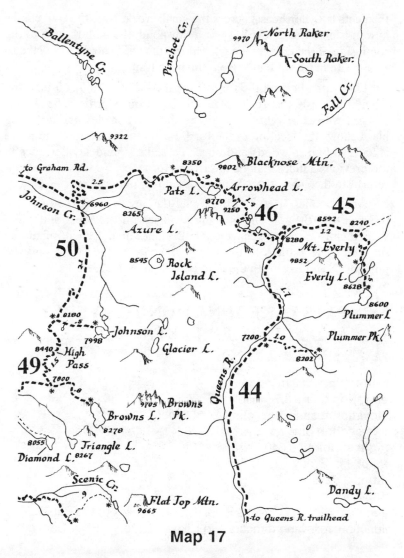

Map 17

At 10.7 miles at a sign for Bluejay Lake, a path goes off to the right, but the lake (8,200 feet) is unnamed.

To make a side trip to this lake, take this path angling steeply up the side of the ridge. The route goes through a patch of alders, switches back to the right, curves left again, and winds up the hillside. At .5 mile, the trail is above a 100-foot gorge which holds the lake's outlet. The ground flattens in a grassy area below talus at .7 mile, then cuts left (northeast) across the small creek. Now the trail climbs in woods near the creek. West of a tiny pond, the path returns to the south side of the creek, then goes above the west shore of the lake to a campsite in trees 1.0 mile from the main trail.

Fifty yards beyond the turnoff for the side trip at 7,360 feet, the main trail fords the river, then climbs through grass. The way is marked with cairns, but there is no path. When descending, a big blaze shows the location of the ford. Beyond the meadow, the route is hard to find in woods and bogs. These bogs, and smaller ones in the previous 3 miles, can be hazardous for stock. Gradually the path returns to the creek, then switchbacks mostly in the open.

At 11.6 miles, it crosses back over the now six-foot wide river to the right (north) and angles along a ridge with the black and white striped cliffs across the canyon. At 12.3 miles among small subalpine firs, the route returns to the left (west) side of the creek, and the junction (8,280 feet) with the Pats Lake Trail is at 12.4 miles.

45 PATS LAKE JUNCTION TO EVERLY AND PLUMMER LAKES

Map 17

round trip: 29.2 miles
elevation gain: 3,764 feet
elevation loss (return climb): 352 feet
this section one way: 2.2 miles, 684 feet gain, 352 feet loss
highest point: 8,640 feet
map: Mt. Everly
time: 3 days
difficulty: strenuous
access: Hike the Queens River Trail 12.4 miles to the Pats Lake Junction, following directions in Hike 44 (Queens River Canyon).

The trail to Everly and Plummer Lakes climbs under the towering cliffs of the dark gray northern face of Mt. Everly. From the white granite benches surrounding the turquoise water of Everly Lake, ledges and cliffs soar to the double-hump of this mountain. The lake is around a corner from the great dark face. Granite benches also enclose Plummer Lake, except on the east where cliffs rise 700 feet to two triangular peaks. A scalloped blob of black rock splashes the right one, Plummer Peak. Even though the lakes are only .2 mile apart, Everly

Lake drains into Benedict Creek, a tributary of the Payette River, and Plummer Lake empties into the Queens River, a tributary of the Boise River.

To reach the beginning of the hike, follow access directions above. From the junction with the Pats Lake Trail at 8,280 feet, take the Queens River Trail east up a grassy basin and through woods. The trail passes through two flat meadows to a 8,592-foot divide at .7 mile with a view of the face of Mt. Everly.

Then the way crosses a grassy flat and drops through trees to a triangle of trails at 1.2 miles (8,240 feet). This triangle is the only sign of the junction to the lakes. From here, the Queens River Trail drops to the Benedict Creek Trail in .9 mile with a 360-foot descent. Turn right (south) at the triangle and ford a small creek to a meadow. The trail then winds back and forth through trees and granite outcrops up the right side of the outlet. It crosses the outlet on built-up rocks just below Everly Lake (8,628 feet) at 1.7 miles.

The trail edges the left (east) side of the lake below granite benches to campsites. From these, a path leads east to a tiny pond, then south up between the benches and down to the north end of Plummer Lake (8,600 feet) at 2.2 miles.

46 PATS LAKE JUNCTION TO PATS LAKE
Map 17

round trip: 31.4 miles
elevation gain: 4,050 feet
this section one way: 3.3 miles, 970 feet gain, 840 feet loss
highest point: 9,250 feet
map: Mt. Everly
time: 3 to 4 days
difficulty: strenuous
access: Hike up the Queens River Trail 12.4 miles to Pats Lake Junction, following directions in Hike 44 (Queens River Canyon).

The trail to Pats Lake hairpins 400 feet up the canyon wall from the trail junction in less than a mile. Along the way, two ponds hug the grass, like blue mirrors on green velvet. At the larger pond, granite hills frame the fissured wall of Mt. Everly across the canyon. Gentians, buttercups and shooting stars carpet the grass in season. From the top of the divide, the view is back into the misty gulf of the Queens River

Canyon and ahead into cobalt blue Arrowhead Lake and teal blue Pats Lake below it. Above these lakes, cracks in the wall of cliffs make them resemble a row of buildings.

To reach the beginning of this hike at the Pats Lake Junction (8,280 feet) 12.4 miles and a 3,080-foot climb from the Queens River trailhead, follow access directions above. From the junction in the rolling meadow, the trail climbs through woods and rock benches to the first pond at .7 mile. A second, larger pond is in turf at 1.0 mile. At 1.2 miles, the path passes above a third tiny pond in granite benches. Camping at the ponds is poor because of the lumpy turf. Next, the trail passes left of a snow pond in a grassy basin, then switchbacks up granite ledges to 9,250 feet. It drops into a notch (9,200 feet) at 1.7 miles. The trail over this divide is often snow covered well into August. Crossing with stock before the trail is bare of snow is dangerous and promotes erosion.

On the other side, the trail hairpins down slabs and talus 200 feet in .3 mile to a tiny pond. At 2.4 miles is 8,770-foot Arrowhead Lake with only a few, small campsites.

The trail to Pats Lake (8,350 feet) zigzags down through ledges and trees, then circles the north side of the lake 60 feet above and 200 yards from it. At the lower end at 3.3 miles, a path goes 100 yards to campsites along the shore.

47 LITTLE QUEENS RIVER TO SCENIC LAKES JUNCTION

Map 16

round trip: 13.4 miles
elevation gain: 1,360 feet
highest point: 6,560 feet
maps: Atlanta West, Nahneke Mountain
time: 9 hours
difficulty: strenuous
access: See Hike 44 (Queens River Canyon).

This makes a beautiful early summer walk through a rainbow of wildflowers below vanilla-scented ponderosa pines. Douglas firs feather the canyon walls above. Along the trail, which is an old wagon road for the first three miles, ruins of silvered wood and remnants of rusted iron from old mines give a feeling of stepping back in time.

To reach the trailhead, follow directions for the hike listed above. At the junction at .2 mile, take the left (west) branch of the trail up the Little Queens River in an open, brushy forest of Douglas fir and ponderosa pine. The trail bridges the river to the west at 1.1 miles. Once across, the trail runs at the base of a steep hillside, crossing Browns Creek at 1.7 miles.

At 1.8 miles, the path is in a sagebrush flat beside ruins of cabins and across the river from an old mine tunnel. At 2.3 miles, the trail fords the river back to the east in two sections. A sign for "foot trail" directs hikers through willows to a large ponderosa log 300 yards upstream A steep path connects the log with the trail on the other side.

A log cabin is at 3.0 miles in a grassy flat across from mine diggings. Beyond here, the old road becomes a trail which climbs away from the creek in forest for two miles. In this section, the trail crosses Scott Creek at 3.9 miles, Tripod Creek at 4.7 miles and Fezip Creek at 5.0 miles. At 5.2 miles, the path fords back to the west side of the river. In late season, hikers cross on rocks, but in early summer, this crossing may be difficult.

Now the path threads sagebrush and grass slopes. At 6.2 miles is a junction with the Neinmeyer Creek Trail, which goes 7.6 miles with a 2,080-foot climb and 2,320-foot descent to the Johnson Creek Trail .6 mile south of the Bayhouse Trail Junction. The Little Queens River Trail edges a beaver pond, then joins the Scenic Lakes Trail at 6.7 miles.

48 SCENIC LAKES
Map 16

round trip: 20.4 miles
elevation gain: 3,190 feet
this section one way: 3.5 miles, 1,840 feet gain
highest point: 8,390 feet
map: Nahneke Mountain
difficulty: strenuous
access: Follow directions above under Hike 44 (Queens River Canyon) and Hike 47 (Little Queens River) to hike to the Scenic Lakes Junction, 6.7 miles from the Queens River Transfer Camp.

On a dark gray face overhanging the turquoise water of the tiny lake below Scenic Lake, two dark gray stripes point together in a V. The thinner of these ends in an arrowhead with melting tip. Above Scenic Lake, a curved line of dark brown splotches the cliffs and two more dikes, round and weathered, resemble gigantic brown candles imbedded in Nahneke Mountain. Along the way to the lake, the route becomes a foot trail climbing 500 feet in .5 mile.

To reach the Scenic Lakes Trail, follow the access directions listed above. At .2 mile from the Scenic Lakes Junction, the trail fords the 75-foot wide Little Queens River. Then the way winds above the canyon of Scenic Creek in alternate forest and open grass. At 1.0 mile, the route begins zigzagging through brush, with a view from one trail corner of a waterfall on the creek. At 1.7 miles, a sign warns "horse travel not recommended beyond this point".

A foot path climbs straight up in grass and brush with a view of towers to the left, then cuts to the right below cliffs. Next the route zigzags up to the right of the cliffs, then angles along the side of the canyon wall again at 2.1 miles.

The trail descends left of an orange and white outcrop, and circles to the right of a pond to a junction with a line of blazes (no path) to Flat Top Lakes at 2.5 miles. This route climbs 800 feet in .7 mile to the first Flat Top Lake.

The Scenic Lakes Trail winds across a boggy meadow, over a granite outcrop, and along the center of the first of three large meadows. Beyond the first of these, the path runs on the left of the creek between it and granite ledges. In the second, narrower meadow, the trail disappears, and reappears at a cairn on an outcrop half way along the meadow. Now the trail follows the creek next to ledges. After crossing the third, smaller meadow, ford the creek at 3.2 miles to the right (west). The smaller, unnamed lake, where the official trail ends, is at 3.4 miles. A few small campsites are nearby.

To reach the upper lake, ford both branches of the outlet to the left (east) and go along the edge of the lake below a granite knoll. At the far end, the path ascends a slope of grass and rocks into woods to reach the upper lake, 8,390 feet, at 3.5 miles. A rocky campsite is on a bench near the outlet, with another site below it.

49 SCENIC LAKES JUNCTION TO BROWNS LAKE, HIGH PASS AND JOHNSON LAKE JUNCTION

Maps 16 and 17

round trip: 21 miles
elevation gain: 3,240 feet
elevation loss (return climb): 260 feet
this section one way: 3.8 miles, 1,880 feet gain, 260 feet loss
side trip to Browns Lake: add .8 mile and 478 feet gain
highest point: 8,440 feet
map: Nahneke Mountain
time: 3 days
difficulty: strenuous
access: Follow directions in Hike 44 (Queens River Canyon) and Hike 47 (Little Queens River) to hike to the Scenic Lakes Junction.

At High Pass, the orange and black needles of North and South Raker Peaks stick up above a distant ridge like porcupine quills. On the east side of Browns Lake, towers top the crinkled wall of Browns Peak. Across from this wall, tiers of cliffs rising to smooth granite mountains echo the shapes of the benches edging the lake. In late summer, the white island cruising near the lower end resembles a sea monster.

To reach the beginning of this section, follow access directions above to hike to the Scenic Lakes Junction (6,560 feet), which is 6.7 miles and a 1,360-foot climb from the Queens River Transfer Camp. From this junction, the Little Queens River Trail runs in open brush and scattered trees, crosses three side streams and curves east at 1.3 miles. At 1.7 miles, the trail is in a grassy basin with tiny subalpine firs. Where the trail switchbacks left (north) at 1.8 miles in the basin, a path goes south. This is an unofficial .9 mile trail to Diamond Lake, which crosses the river and then climbs 640 feet to the lake. At 2.3 miles, the main trail comes to the Browns Lake Junction (7,800 feet).

The side trail to Browns Lake climbs north of Browns Creek over open slopes and through forest. At .4 mile, it crosses the creek to the right (south) in alders. The path runs along the base of granite benches and then up between them to a meadow with campsites in the trees. It reaches the lake (8,278 feet) at .8 mile. Campsites are on the west shore.

From the Browns Lake Junction, the main trail switchbacks sandy slopes between lodgepoles to 8,440-foot High Pass at 3.3 miles. From here, the canyon of the Little Queens River, the Rakers and gray peaks around Browns Lake are seen.

On the other side, the trail goes left across a sandy slope, switchbacks twice and then continues northwest. Below is the small pond which is shown in a meadow on the map. At 3.6 miles, the trail curves right in woods to an unsigned junction (8,180 feet) at 3.8 miles with a .5 mile side trail to Johnson Lake.

Hiker on Scenic Lake Trail

50 JOHNSON LAKE JUNCTION TO JOHNSON LAKE AND PATS LAKE

Map 17

round trip: 30.2 miles
elevation gain: 4,630 feet
elevation loss (return climb): 1,480 feet
this section one way: 4.6 miles, 1,390 feet gain, 1,220 feet loss
side trip to Johnson Lake: add .5 mile one way and 182 feet
return climb
highest point: 8,350 feet
maps: Nahneke Mountain, Mt. Everly
time: 4 to 5 days
difficulty: strenuous
access: Follow directions in Hike 44 (Queens River Canyon),
Hike 47 (Little Queens River) and Hike 49 (Scenic Lakes Junction
to Browns Lake, High Pass and Johnson Lakes Junction) to hike
to the Johnson Lake Junction.

*A gigantic granite breast swells above the upper end of shallow
Johnson Lake. To the right of it, a second, smaller peak echoes that sil-
houette. Huckleberries and Labrador tea surround the misty emerald
green lake, which contains two granite islands. One is large and plumed
with firs and the other is tiny and rocky. Between Johnson Lake and
Pats Lake, a rugged side trip for experts only reaches Azure Lake. Below
a circle of outcrop-covered peaks, pale granite ledges and talus enclose
the clear water of this lake, which is blue-green rather than azure.*

To reach the Johnson Lake Junction (8,180 feet) which is 10.5
miles and a 3,240-foot climb up the Little Queens River, follow access directions above. Watch for this unsigned junction 200 yards
into the woods below High Pass. To take a side trip to Johnson Lake,
follow the path and blazes east to a crossing of the outlet of a pond.
The path wanders through lodgepoles, then drops to the lower end
of the 7,998-foot lake near a campsite, which is .5 mile from the main
trail. A path continues along the north side of the lake to a marsh.
From here, experts can continue .7 mile cross-country to The Hole
or Glacier Lake.

The main trail to Pats Lake descends through subalpine firs and
lodgepoles, crosses an avalanche area of tiny firs, and at .5 mile

Johnson Lake

makes two switchbacks just above a grassy flat. At .8 mile, the path edges the flat with a glimpse of a small pond hidden in trees. The route runs down the outlet of the pond, then descends through grass, flowers, alders and forest to a ford in alders of Johnson Creek at 2.1 miles (6,960 feet). The first of two sections of the ford has footlogs. At 2.0 miles, the trail joins one down Johnson Creek connecting with the Silver Creek trailhead on the Graham Road. Just above the junction is an old log cabin, pushed down to half height by snow.

The trail to Pats Lake makes switchbacks up to .2 mile long on open slopes of sagebrush and grass with views up Johnson Creek to High Pass and down towards Graham. At 2.8 miles, the trail runs straight along the side of the ridge into forest. The path crosses to the south bank of the creek at 3.9 miles. At 4.0 miles, the way is below talus blocks which pour down from a notch on the skyline to the south. These blocks mark a .5 mile, 400-foot cross-country route for experts to Azure Lake. This point is at the south end of the curve in the trail that is closest to Azure Lake. Just beyond this point, ford back north of the creek in a meadow.

If going to Azure Lake, carry only a day pack and use caution. Do not attempt it in wet weather. The route is along the edge of the trees and ledges just to the right (west) of the talus. From the notch on the skyline, descend a narrow ridge to the lower end of the lake where a granite peninsula shelters a campsite. Note you can't climb directly from Pats Lake to Azure Lake because of cliffs.

Back on the main trail north of the creek, climb between rock ledges, crossing the stream twice before reaching a path to the lower end of Pats Lake (8,350 feet) at 4.6 miles.

Mt. Everly

ATLANTA AREA

51 MIDDLE FORK OF BOISE RIVER: POWERPLANT CAMPGROUND TO ROCK CREEK

Maps 18 and 19

round trip: 17 miles
elevation gain: 960 feet
highest point: 6,400 feet
maps: Atlanta East, Mt. Everly
time: 10 hours or 2 days
difficulty: strenuous
access: From Edna Creek Campground 18 miles northeast of Idaho City on Highway 21, drive to Atlanta, using directions found in Hike 44 (Queens River Canyon). Continue 5 more miles on main road to Atlanta. Go straight ahead where road forks at east end of town and drive 1.5 miles to Powerplant Campground.

The road to the trailhead for this hike wanders through the weathered town of Atlanta. The town nestles in lodgepole pines and aspens in a mountain valley below Greylock Peak, a crumbling giant with a stubble of rock towers. Some of the old buildings have collapsed, some have been torn down to make way for a new lodge, and others are still used as bars, homes, cabins, and small stores. From Powerplant Campground near Atlanta, the trail up the Middle Fork of the Boise River plows through thick forest with a colorful undergrowth of flowers, fluffy grass and bushes. There is a view of the spires and teeth which wall the canyon.

To reach the trailhead, follow access directions listed above. Just before Powerplant Campground (5,440 feet) is a meadow with a trail sign, circular drive and horse loading area. The trail begins to the right (south) of the road. You can drive .5 mile farther to the end of the campground, but do not park there unless you want to pay for camping. From the campground, reach the trail by cutting southeast .1 mile. Trail mileage here is figured from the end of the campground, not from the sign, but Forest Service mileage charts and trail distances on signs are figured from this sign.

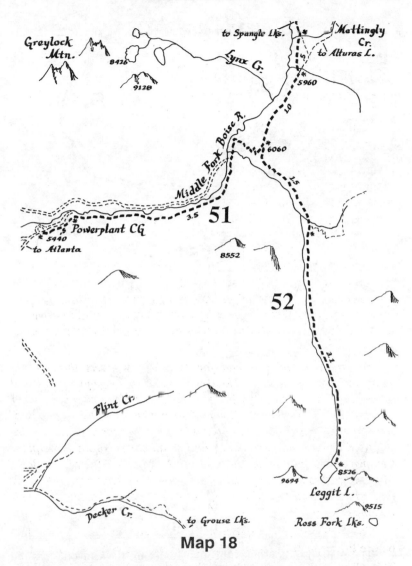

Map 18

The trail parallels the river in forest, across from an old road, passing a meadow and pond at 2.0 miles. At 2.3 miles, the path comes close to the creek above ten-foot cliffs and at 2.6 miles it crosses Leggit Creek. At 2.8 miles, the trail turns 90 degrees east and, at 3.0 miles, switchbacks 200 feet up the canyon wall to the Leggit Lake Junction (6,060 feet) at 3.5 miles. There is a fine view of the canyon from this junction.

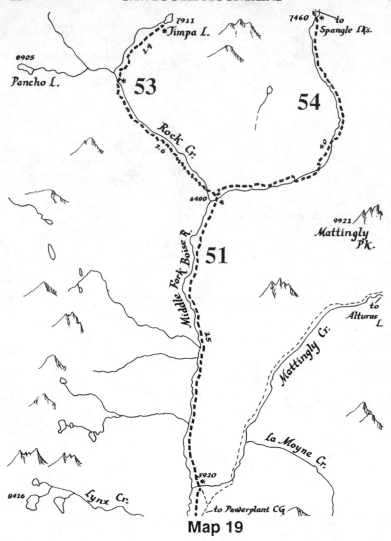

Map 19

The main trail continues through forest up the canyon, crossing an intermittent stream at 4.2 miles. At 4.5 miles is the first of two side trails leading to the Mattingly Creek Trail. The main trail crosses Corral Creek in a grassy flat with a view of a dark rock hill, 100 feet high, standing between the two branches of the Mattingly Creek Trail. At 5.0 miles, in forest just beyond the second of these junctions, the Middle Fork Trail crosses Mattingly Creek on logs at a

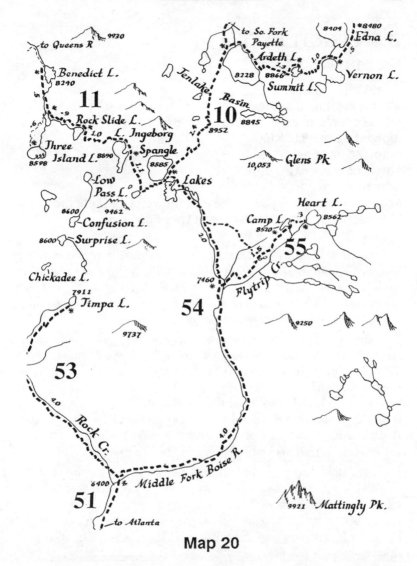

Map 20

spot which can be difficult in early season. Later in the year, it is the only water source along the trail from here to Rock Creek.

The trail continues 3.5 miles through forest to a ford of the river at 8.5 miles (6,400 feet) just beyond its confluence with Rock Creek near campsites. In early season, this ford is deep and rushing. Across it is a junction in a wide grassy area with the trail up Rock Creek to Timpa Lake. The main trail continues up the river to Spangle Lakes.

52 LEGGIT LAKE
Map 18

round trip: 16.2 miles
elevation gain: 3,086 feet
this section one way: 4.6 miles, 2,466 feet gain
highest point: 8,526 feet
map: Atlanta East
time: 12 hours or 2-3 days
difficulty: strenuous
access: Follow directions in Hike 51 (Powerplant Campground to Rock Creek) to hike to the Leggit Lake Junction.

On the way up Leggit Creek, a 1000-foot dark gray cliff reminds hikers of Yosemite. The 500-foot ridges holding Leggit Lake in a rocky cup make it seem like a lake in the sky. These ridges of talus, grass and ledges end in miniature dark gray peaks, one on each side of the lake. The peaked cap of the western one is split by a chimney.

This hike description starts on the Middle Fork of the Boise River Trail at the Leggit Lake Junction (6,060 feet), 3.5 miles and a 620-foot climb from the end of Powerplant Campground. For directions for reaching this junction, see hikes listed above. From this junction on a rock knoll 400 feet above the Middle Fork Canyon, the trail angles steeply up the canyon of Leggit Creek as an old road. Beyond a large campsite at 1.5 miles, the road fords a side stream and leaves the trail to climb the canyon wall to a prospect.

Turn right and go south towards Leggit Creek on the trail. At first there is no path, but it will become obvious in 200 yards. At 1.8 miles, the trail enters a flat, gravelly area opposite the immense black cliff. Beyond the gravel area, it crosses a side stream. At 3.0 miles the forest gives way to rocks, grass, flowers and tiny subalpine firs.

The route becomes steep, rocky and sketchy at 4.1 miles. At 4.4 miles, the trail goes left (east) of the creek to avoid cliffs and disappears. A path climbs the scree past scattered trees east of the cliffs. Look for the path several hundred yards before the cliffs. Follow this path up the ridge ahead to the lake (8,526 feet) at 4.6 miles. A few small campsites are at the lower end. Water is available at two side streams and from the creek now and then in the last 2.5 miles.

53 TIMPA LAKE

Maps 19 and 20

round trip: 25 miles
elevation gain: 2,471 feet
this section one way: 4 miles, 1,511 feet gain
highest point: 7,911 feet
time: 3 days
maps: Atlanta East, Mt. Everly
difficulty: strenuous
access: Using directions in Hike 51 (Powerplant Campground to Rock Creek), hike to Rock Creek.

Turf borders blue-green Timpa Lake and marsh grass waves at the edge of the shallow water. On the west, talus and ledges lead to an elephant-shaped ridge. Beyond the lower end of this small lake, a ridge sweeps up in the center to a wide gable. Up the canyon, several other lakes hide off-trail behind wooded knolls and rock ridges.

To reach the junction of the Middle Fork of the Boise River Trail with the Rock Creek Trail, where this hike description begins, follow directions in Hike 51. At .2 mile, the trail fords Rock Creek to the west and this can be dangerous in high water. The crossing is rocky, so it is difficult or dangerous all summer for saddle or pack stock. The path zigzags up the canyon near the creek, with views of its pools and cascades over granite. At 1.3 miles, the trail passes a huge boulder pile, and becomes more shaded and gradual. The path crosses the creek back to the east at 2.6 miles on a complex of logs.

Above this crossing, Timpa Creek flows into Rock Creek. The trail zigzags up the canyon of Timpa Creek on the right (southeast), then climbs along the side of the canyon to a sudden ending 50 vertical feet above the lake. From here, paths drop to the lake, (7,911 feet) at 4.0 miles. Water is available only at the creek crossings and the lake, and mosquitoes can be a problem.

54 MIDDLE FORK OF BOISE RIVER: ROCK CREEK TO SPANGLE LAKES

Map 20

round trip: 29.0 miles
elevation gain: 3,145 feet
this section one way: 6 miles, 2,185 feet gain
highest point: 8,585 feet
maps: Mt. Everly, Atlanta East
time: 4 days
difficulty: strenuous
access: Hike 9.2 miles from Atlanta up the Middle Fork of the Boise River Trail to Rock Creek. For directions see Hike 51 (Middle Fork Boise River Trail — Powerplant Campground to Rock Creek).

In this section of the canyon, Mattingly Peak forms a dark gray bucket edged by triangular spires. The trail passes under dark, scalloped cliffs and beside wildflowers, from delphinium to grass of Parnassus. From Spangle Lakes, Snowyside Peak resembles a dinosaur with a spine at the neck and a square head with ears. Gullies outline ribs on its side.

To reach Rock Creek at 6,400 feet on the Middle Fork of the Boise River Trail where this description begins, follow directions for Hike 51 (Powerplant Campground to Rock Creek). It is 8.5 miles and a 960-foot climb from the campground to this point. At Rock Creek, ford the river in two sections. This may be difficult in early summer. On the other side is a junction with a trail to Timpa Lake.

Take the right (east) branch of the trail along the river. The route is in the open in snowbrush and ceanothus. At 1.1 miles, cross to the south bank of the river on a log. The trail enters the woods and hops a side creek, then returns to the north at 1.5 miles. Next the path climbs 100 feet away from the river under dark gray cliffs.

At 2.0 miles, the way returns on a log to the right (east) of the river. Then the path enters a grassy field with small trees where a great talus mountain is ahead on the left. The trail jumps two side streams here, passes a pond on the river and returns to the left (west) bank just before a junction with the Flytrip Creek Trail, (7,460 feet) at 4.0 miles. This trail gives access to Camp and Heart Lakes (see Hike 55).

At 4.2 miles, the path crosses back west of the creek. The main trail now zigzags granite benches decorated with lodgepole and subalpine firs. Next, it switchbacks along a small ridge. Across the canyon, granite slabs and cliffs hover above cascades. Parts of the old route are interlaced with the current trail here.

At the top of the switchbacks, experienced hikers descending from Spangle Lakes can turn off on a cross-country shortcut to Camp Lake. At 5.5 miles, the trail crosses the creek and then passes a swamp. Then at 5.9 miles, it reaches an arm of Little Spangle Lake. The shore of Spangle Lake (8,585 feet) is at 6.0 miles at a T-shaped junction with trails to Ardeth Lake and Benedict Creek.

55 CAMP AND HEART LAKES
Map 20

round trip: 28.6 miles
elevation gain: 3,122 feet
this section one way: 1.8 miles, 1,102 feet gain
highest point: 8,562 feet
maps: Mt. Everly, Snowyside Peak
time: 4 days
difficulty: strenuous
access: Using directions in Hikes 51 and 54, (Middle Fork of Boise River Trail—Powerplant Campground to Rock Creek, and Rock Creek to Spangle Lakes), hike 12.5 miles to Flytrip Creek.

At the head of Flytrip Creek, narrow Camp Lake extends from a slim meadow like blue toothpaste from a green tube. Over a wooded ridge lurks the orange dinosaur of Snowyside Peak. On the other side of the ridge, Heart Lake, edged with Labrador tea and granite, faces this monster. A fin-like shoulder connects the dinosaur's head to its pointed back. To the south, low ridges divide Heart Lake from P.S. Lake and a matching dinosaur. Between the two dinosaurs, a conical gray peak stands watch close to the lake.

To reach the Flytrip Creek Trail, hike the Middle Fork of the Boise River from Atlanta 12.5 miles in a 2,020-foot climb or hike 2.0 miles down the river from Spangle Lakes. For directions, see hikes listed above. There is a large campsite at the junction (7,460 feet).

Middle Fork of Boise River

The Flytrip Trail fords the river and ascends the side of the canyon in woods. It crosses three unnamed creeks before two small ponds appear at 1.0 mile. It's another .5 mile to the lake, (8,520) feet. Heart Lake at 8,562 feet is .3 mile beyond, and is reached by a path turning right (southeast) over the low, wooded ridge. Small campsites are at both lakes.

The Flytrip Creek Trail climbs more than 1,000 feet and begins 1,125 feet lower than Spangle Lakes, so from Spangle Lakes it is more fun to go cross-country to Camp and Heart Lakes. To do this, turn east over a low ridge 1.0 mile below Spangle Lakes (just before the steep switchbacks start) and drop to a marsh. From this marsh, go southeast to a larger marsh and cut across at that level, avoiding talus, to the two small ponds .5 mile below Camp Lake on the trail. This route saves 1.5 miles and 600 feet of elevation gain.

trails in the

WHITE CLOUD

MOUNTAINS

Sapphire Lake (Big Boulder Lakes)

GERMANIA CREEK AREA

56 RAINBOW LAKE

Map 21

round trip: 11.0 miles
elevation gain: 2,155 feet
elevation loss (return climb): 905 feet
highest point: 9,200 feet
map: Horton Peak
time: 11 hours or 2 days
difficulty: expert (1.5 miles cross-country, trail indistinct)
access: From Highway 75, turn east 36 miles north of Ketchum on the gravel Pole Creek Road. At 4.5 miles, turn left (north) at a sign "Trail to Champion Creek" and drive 5 miles to an unmarked trailhead where the road makes a 90 degree left turn.

On a peak above Rainbow Lake, a curve of rock, striped rust, white and yellow, forms a rainbow. Along the sketchy trail giving cross-country access to the lake, forget-me-not and pink and yellow mimulus echo the rainbow. On the topo map, a snow pond has been labeled Rainbow Lake, but the map is wrong. The lake is east of this pond, in a spot shown on the map as bog. It is marshy around the edges, but is much deeper than the pond.

The trail provides a fine view of the Boulder Mountains and of a 700-foot high fluted wall east of Horton Peak. The final 1.2 miles are cross-country up a wooded ridge to the small notch leading to the lake.

To reach the trailhead (7,250 feet) follow access directions above. Be sure to stay on the Pole Creek Road. The trail starts up the narrow canyon of Twin Creek in dense forest, and runs left (west) of the creek for the first .3 mile. The path crosses to the east, goes 50 feet above the stream, then returns to the west at .5 mile.

In the next .3 mile, the trail crosses the small creek five more times. Sometimes the trail runs through narrow jaws of rock, where it has been washed out. Hikers must look at their maps to keep on the correct side of the stream. The canyon opens out into a grassy basin where the trail, now on the right side almost disappears. It goes along a grassy shelf above the creek, then drops to the creek and fords it to

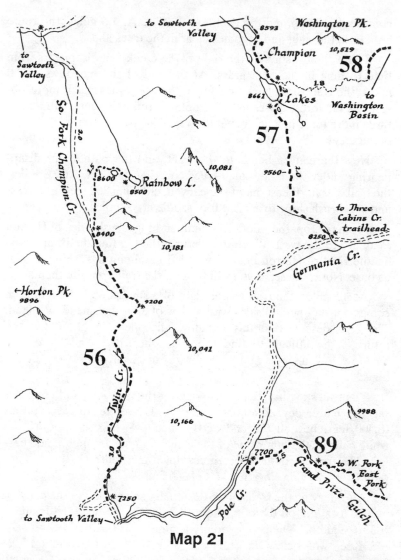

Map 21

the left (south) just beyond where the creek begins a double bend at
1.0 mile.

There is much downed timber here so it is easier to stay on the
right side of the creek in steep sagebrush and pick up the trail again
where it crosses back to the right at 1.2 miles. There are two more
crossings, and these are not shown on the topographic map. The
route returns to the west in a narrow meadow, where the canyon be-

comes more open and the trail less distinct. At 1.6 miles, the route crosses to the right and becomes clear in the trees ahead.

The path now stays on the right of the creek, but disappears from time to time in the high grass. At the end of the meadows at 2.0 miles, the trail fords back and forth, then becomes much more obvious as the forest closes in at 2.1 miles. Around 2.4 miles, there are three more fords in a dell of wildflowers. The trail ends up left (west) of the creek.

Next the canyon bends to the right, and the path keeps disappearing under the many small trees covering the trail. At 2.8 miles, the trail cuts northeast out of the canyon, climbing 300 feet up a grass and sagebrush slope to a 9,200-foot saddle at 3.0 miles.

From the top, the wooded summit and sagebrush sides of Horton Peak are to the west. When descending, the big fluted cliff appears. To the right of Horton Peak, a wooded mountain has white cliffs at its base. Notice these, as you will turn off the trail opposite them.

At 3.5 miles, the trail passes right of a small wooded knoll, then comes out on open hillsides with a view of a big flat meadow ahead. The trail descends to this meadow, disappearing often. On the return, it is difficult to find the spot where the trail leaves the meadow, so you may want to temporarily mark a tree or two with ribbons.

The trail stays in trees on the right of the meadow, and crosses a sagebrush area beyond a horse campsite. Leave the trail at 4.0 miles (8,400 feet) beyond the end of the meadow. This is opposite the white cliffs on the other side of the canyon, which are mentioned earlier. The trail continues three miles down the South Fork of Champion Creek with an elevation loss of 800 feet to Champion Creek.

After leaving the trail, climb diagonally up the side of the canyon. Notice a saddle on the opposite wall between the white cliffs and a rounded hilltop. The notch you are aiming for is due east of this saddle. Keep well below the cliffs and walk north to the wooded hills guarding the 8,600-foot notch at 4.8 miles which leads to Rainbow Lake.

If you are too high on the ridge, find the tea-colored pond below and adjust your route. Descend the other side of the notch through lodgepoles to the pond (8,495 feet) at 5.0 miles. Partly-wooded granite cliffs of the ridge you have just descended shadow the pond. Go around the pond and through forest to the pale green lake (8,500 feet) at 5.5 miles. The lake may appear stagnant in late summer.

This hike is a challenge because the trail disappears often in the grass and because the route from the trail to the notch is heavily wooded. The trip is easier if you camp overnight in the flat meadow at the turnoff for the cross-country route and day hike to the lake.

57 CHAMPION LAKES

Map 21

round trip: 6 miles
elevation gain: 1,310 feet
elevation loss (return climb): 967 feet
highest point: 9,560 feet
maps: Horton Peak, Washington Peak
time: 6 1/2 hours
difficulty: strenuous
access: 36 miles north of Ketchum on Highway 75, just south of Smylie Creek Lodge, turn right (east) on the Pole Creek—Germania Creek Road. Go 2.3 miles on gravel to a junction. Turn right here and go east on a dirt road up to Pole Creek Summit at 9.2 miles. Continue down the other side to a grassy hillside at 10.2 miles. Turn left (north) and drive 100 yards uphill to a register box. The last four miles are rough, rocky and muddy but passable for passenger cars.

From a divide on the trail, to the south shadowed canyons indent the pink and charcoal gray crags of the Boulders. To the north, the blue-green ovals of Champion Lakes sit in a basin of woods, rocks and meadows below the pearl gray sand of Washington Peak. This peak and a pale gray-striped mountain dominate the upper lake, where mats of pink algae float near shore in late summer. At the north end of the lower lake, a gray and white striped ridge ends in a wall of towers.

To reach the trailhead (8,250 feet) follow access directions above. From the register box, the trail goes west across a stream, then fords a creek. The path climbs north along the west side of this creek in grass and sagebrush where blue bells grow in season. At .3 mile the trail crosses back and forth several times over the creek, which is now a tiny stream. At .7 mile, the path turns right (east) uphill and leaves the creek. The route steeply ascends a slope of grass, sand and scattered trees without switchbacks. The 9,560-foot divide is at 1.2 miles.

From here, the trail descends loose rock and crumbled ledges for 30 feet, requiring caution. It then angles down steep scree into a gully of tiny firs. The use of horses and mountain bikes on this trail is discouraged because of the steepness and loose footing. Below the gully, the path crosses a dry flat at 1.5 miles, and climbs an 80-foot wooded ridge. The route drops 300 feet on the other side of the ridge and passes a pond on its way to a meadow at the upper end of the first lake, (8,661 feet) at 2.0 miles.

A path goes around the west side of the lake, but the official trail is on the east. It disappears in the meadow where it crosses the inlet and reappears in the woods on the other side near campsites. Half way around the lake, at 2.3 miles, a trail turns off to go 1.8 miles with a 1,419-foot climb and 700-foot descent over the white shoulder of Washington Peak to Washington Basin.

The main trail goes through boggy meadows below the lower end of the lake to the second lake (8,593 feet) at 3.0 miles. The best camping is at the upper end. Below the second lake, the trail continues 6.7 miles with a 1,493-foot elevation loss to a trailhead on private land in Sawtooth Valley. A third small lake is 200 yards west of the trail half way between the two larger lakes.

58 WASHINGTON BASIN

Map 22

round trip: 9.6 miles
elevation gain: 1,900 feet
elevation loss (return climb): 400 feet
highest point: 9,380 feet
maps: Horton Peak, Galena Peak, Washington Peak, Boulder Chain Lakes
time: 8 1/2 hours
difficulty: strenuous
access: 36 miles north of Ketchum, turn right on the Pole Creek — Germania Creek Road and drive 4.6 miles on dirt road and 7.5 miles on primitive road to trailhead at Three Cabins Creek.

The white rust-striped wall of Croesus Peak hangs above the old cabins, mines and mill ruins of Washington Basin. On a cloudy day, the burnt orange on Croesus Peak looks red, making it peppermint

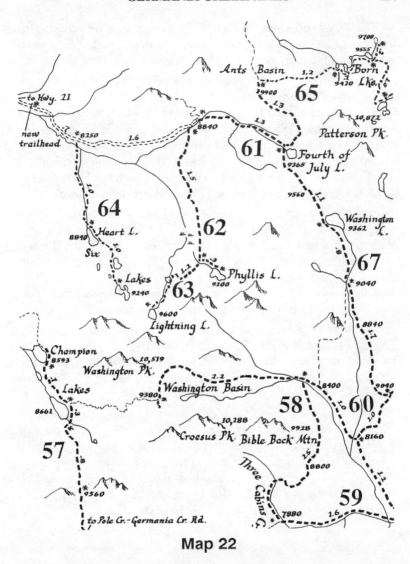

Map 22

striped. *The grooves of chimneys and an "X" of stripes accent the wall. On the east, this wall merges with the two-toned summit of caramel and cream-colored rock called Bible Back Mountain. At the head of the basin bulge the white pillows of Washington Peak and its shoulders. From here, the pleated wall of Castle Peak is a distant backdrop to a narrow green pond in the rocks below.*

This hike is on a steep jeep trail. Passenger cars with four-wheel drive can negotiate it for 2.5 miles, while the upper part of the road is suitable only for four-wheel drive vehicles with a high wheelbase.

To reach the trailhead, follow access directions above. In early season or wet weather, leave ordinary cars .2 mile below the trailhead before the second ford of Germania Creek (not shown on the map). From the trailhead (7,880 feet), the jeep road climbs along Three Cabins Creek in forest and sagebrush. After running over talus for 100 yards at .6 mile, it switchbacks to the right onto a steep section. From here, it wanders back and forth through the lodgepoles to an 8,800-foot summit at 1.5 miles, 920 feet above the trailhead.

Now the track drops to a ford (8,400 feet) of Washington Creek at 2.5 miles and a trailhead for a .5 mile-long spur trail to the Washington Creek Trail. From here, the jeep trail climbs through forest, with bridges at 2.6 and 2.7 miles. At 3.6 miles where the slope lessens, the colorful mountain wall is opposite. Several mines, cabins (private!) and an excellent view are at 3.9 miles. The road then crosses open grassy slopes as it winds to the head of the basin.

At 4.0 miles, a branch road leads right to mines just before the crossing of a small creek. Then the track curves down to a muddy flat. A detour reaches old boilers and mill timbers at the head of this dry pond. The road then climbs past ruins and a log cabin to join a route at 4.5 miles leading left to the Black Rock Mine.

Continue on the main road to a junction with a trail to Champion Lakes at 4.7 miles (9,360 feet). This trail climbs 700 feet over the side of Washington Peak, then descends 1,419 feet to Upper Champion Lake, which is 1.8 miles from here. From the junction, continue on the road to the highest cabin beside a meadow at 4.8 miles. This meadow was once a lake formed by an earthen dam. The narrow green pond and Castle Peak are visible from the cabin.

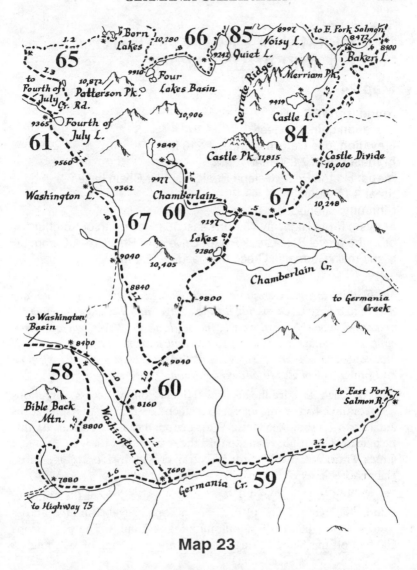

Map 23

59 GERMANIA CREEK TRAIL TO CHAMBERLAIN CREEK

Map 24

round trip: 12.6 miles
elevation gain: 380 feet
elevation loss (return climb): 1,210 feet
highest point: 7,880 feet
maps: Horton Peak, Galena Peak, Boulder Chain Lakes
time: 8 1/2 hours
difficulty: strenuous
access: From Highway 75, turn east 36 miles north of Ketchum onto the gravel Pole Creek Road. Drive over Pole Creek Summit to the main Germania Creek trailhead at 12.4 miles.

In this canyon, Germania Creek changes from a tiny mountain stream to a large creek roaring through gorges and swirling over emerald meadows. Crumbly scalloped cliffs overlook the lower canyon, especially at Chamberlain Creek. As the trail descends, it crosses several meadows and sagebrush slopes and the trees change from lodgepole and spruce to Douglas fir and cottonwood.

To reach the trailhead (7,880 feet) follow access directions above. At 12.4 miles, at a "narrow steep road" sign, the road turns left (north) and becomes the Washington Basin Jeep Trail. At this turn, look to the right (east) to find the register box for the Germania Creek Trail. Within 100 yards, this trail crosses a side stream, Three Cabins Creek.

At .8 mile, Deer Creek joins Germania Creek from the opposite side of the canyon. The trail climbs an open sagebrush area across from a double-humped gray mountain at 1.2 miles. The path drops 100 feet off this slope through trees to a log crossing of Washington Creek at 1.5 miles (7,600 feet).

Beyond a small open area at 1.6 miles, a trail up Washington Creek turns off with no sign. It is 1.0 mile and a 560-foot climb on this trail to a junction (8,160 feet) with the trail to Chamberlain Lakes. Those without four-wheel drive vehicles descend Germania Creek to this point and turn up Washington Creek to go to Chamberlain Lakes. Using the Washington Basin Jeep Trail shortens the distance to Chamberlain Lakes by two miles and the climb by 600 feet.

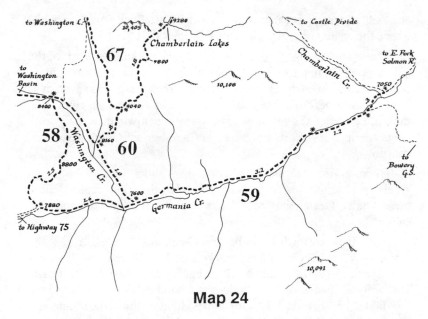

Map 24

Below the junction, the Germania Creek Trail climbs onto a sagebrush hillside, and goes over a volcanic knoll at 2.2 miles. Next the path drops down a wooded ravine to cross Jack Creek at 2.5 miles on rocks onto another sagebrush hillside. At 3.0 miles, the path descends to level woods at the upper end of a mile-long meadow. The way threads clumps of trees, and almost disappears in grass and willows at the edge of the creek at 3.5 miles. At 3.8 miles, the path skirts rock ledges close to the creek, and at 4.0 miles, woods close in again.

The trail runs along a gravel bar and climbs a bank which has slid away. Here the trail has been rerouted. Across from a rock nubbin, the trail drops to ford the creek to the south in gravel at 4.8 miles.

For the next mile, the way is through a thick Douglas fir forest below dark gray cliffs. The route is treacherous where the trail climbs and descends a 30-foot high rocky bluff at 5.5 miles. Level woods beside mossy outcrops and a narrow slot between cliffs and creek are followed by a meadow.

The trail climbs a steep bank at a sign for Bowery Guard Station Cutoff, and disappears in the meadow. This route to Bowery Guard Station turns away from the creek 90 degrees and leads 4.5 miles in a 1,660-foot climb and 2,000-foot descent to that guard station. It is inaccessible by road because a gate on the East Fork Road is locked where the route goes through private property.

Those continuing down Germania Creek to the East Fork of the Salmon or planning to take the Chamberlain Creek route to Chamberlain Lakes need to cross Germania Creek here. However, it is hard to find where the trail crosses the creek. The easiest route is at the upper end of the meadow, where the creek widens over gravel. From the meadow, cliffs tower above Chamberlain Creek across the canyon.

Once across Germania Creek, cow paths join on a steep sagebrush hillside where gray rock knolls edge the creek. Behind these knolls, Germania Creek leaps down in hidden falls and cascades.

Next, the trail fords Chamberlain Creek at 6.2 miles. Across the creek, only a cairn (7,050 feet) marks a trail to the left up Chamberlain Creek. This trail climbs 2,190 feet in 3.7 miles to the Castle Divide Trail .5 mile east of the lowest Chamberlain Lake. Reaching the lakes by this trail is four miles longer than the route via Washington Creek. From this junction, it is 5.0 miles of sagebrush and a 690-foot descent to the East Fork of the Salmon River Road.

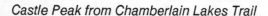

Castle Peak from Chamberlain Lakes Trail

60 CHAMBERLAIN LAKES FROM GERMANIA CREEK

Map 23

round trip: 13.2 miles (8.0 miles with four-wheel drive), additional 1.5 miles one-way to see upper lakes
elevation gain: 2,200 feet (1,640 feet with four-wheel drive), additional 652 feet for upper lakes.
elevation loss (return climb): 800 feet (700 feet with four-wheel drive)
highest point: 9,800 feet
maps: Horton Peak, Washington Peak, Galena Peak, Boulder Chain Lakes
time: 10 hours (7 1/2 with four-wheel drive)
difficulty: strenuous
access: From Highway 75, turn east 36 miles north of Ketchum onto the gravel Pole Creek Road. Drive over Pole Creek Summit to the main Germania Creek trailhead at 12.4 miles. Those with four-wheel drive can continue 2.5 miles farther to a junction of the Washington Basin Jeep Trail with the Washington Creek Pack Trail.

The orange and white 2,500-foot wall of Castle Peak, cut with avalanche chutes, dwarfs the blue-green lakes in Chamberlain Basin, making them look like puddles. From a 9,800-foot divide on the trail, a grassy basin, sprinkled with trees and the lakes, rolls toward this pinnacle-topped wall. The burnt orange of the left side of the wall turns to white on the right, and the white continues in a sharp-pointed shoulder.

Above the lowest lake, three gullies branch to the skyline from the single gully separating the shoulder from the peak. The right (east) gully is the route for scrambling up the peak. Across this green lake from the peak stands a doubled humped white mountain with gray stripes.

A side trail reaches three upper lakes. Hummocks of turf covered with wildflowers surround the turquoise water of the first of these. Above, a maze of orange needles hides the white part of Castle Peak.

To reach the trailhead, follow access directions above. Hike from the register box at Three Cabins Creek (7,880 feet) down the Germania Creek Trail for 1.6 miles. About .2 mile beyond a log crossing of Washington Creek (7,600 feet), turn on an unsigned trail up

The lowest Chamberlain Lake

Washington Creek. This trail climbs 1.0 miles to a junction with a trail to Chamberlain Lakes and one going 1.0 mile to the Washington Basin Jeep Trail. With four-wheel drive, you can drive the jeep trail 2.5 miles and hike 1.0 mile down Washington Creek to this junction.

From the junction at Washington Lake Creek, the trail to Chamberlain Lakes winds straight uphill through the trees. It makes a big switchback in sagebrush and turns back to the left toward ledges. The way then winds among small hills to a junction (9,040 feet) with a trail from Washington Lake at 3.8 miles.

The trail on to Chamberlain Lakes goes straight up a ridge, along the side of a hill and then levels off. The route switchbacks the final pitch to the 9,800-foot saddle with the view of Castle Peak at 5.0 miles. On the other side, the trail cuts northwest through scree and wildflowers, and turns northeast. The path follows a tiny inlet down to the first lake (9,280 feet) at 5.8 miles, which has some campsites in the trees above it.

Below this lake, the route threads two round meadows to the lowest lake (9,197 feet) near its outlet at 6.6 miles. Campsites are off-trail on the south shore. At the outlet is a junction with the trail over Castle Divide to Little Boulder Creek.

The trail to the upper lakes starts from this junction along the north side of the lowest lake and goes through woods into a meadow with a large campsite on the left. Then the path crosses the creek and climbs the right side of a white ravine. Above this is a round green pond in the trees.

The trail follows the stream on the right to the long turquoise lake (9,477 feet). Campsites are east of the lake. The trail ends west of a small round lake just above the large one at 1.5 miles. The highest lake (9,849 feet) can be reached cross-country by a gully to the left of the cliffs above the round lake.

FOURTH OF JULY CREEK AREA

61 FOURTH OF JULY AND WASHINGTON LAKES

Map 22

round trip: 4.8 miles
elevation gain: 720 feet
elevation loss (return climb): 198 feet
highest point: 9,560 feet
maps: Washington Peak, Boulder Chain Lakes
time: 4 1/2 hours
difficulty: easy
access: Drive 46.7 miles north of Ketchum and turn right (east) onto a primitive rough road and go 10.3 miles to the trailhead. The road is gated here just before a private mine road begins. Cars lacking a high wheelbase should be left at the parking area (location of a possible future trailhead) at 8 miles.

Triangular gray cliffs flank the orange sliced-off face of Patterson Peak. Below the peak, wildflowers color the meadows around shallow, green Fourth of July Lake. Over a ridge, an orange wall of crumbled cliffs and scree turns to white at the lower end of blue-green Washington Lake. Meadows on the trail side of this lake thrust two grassy peninsulas into the water.

To reach the trailhead (8,840 feet), follow access directions above. In the future, the lower road will be improved and the upper road may be closed at a parking area 8 miles from the highway.

When this happens, add 2.3 miles one way to all hikes from this trail-head. The section of the road above the future gate requires a high wheelbase vehicle and four-wheel drive is recommended.

From the present trailhead, the trail fords Fourth of July Creek to the right (south) at 100 yards and goes along on the right of a meadow full of willows. The path crosses a side creek, then goes back to the left (north) of the main creek at .8 mile. A side creek not shown on the topo map runs left along the trail here. The trail flattens out in forest near a trail junction at 1.3 miles. Turn right (south) to the outlet just below the lake (9,365 feet) at 1.4 miles and ford it. There are campsites back in the trees.

From this ford, the trail to Washington Lake climbs a ridge of lodgepoles with a view of the Sawtooths. At the flat, sandy top of the divide (9,560 feet) at 2.0 miles is a tiny snow pond. From here, the route descends an open slope to Washington Lake (9,362 feet) at 2.4 miles and crosses an inlet on the way. There are a few campsites in trees at the south end of the lake.

62 PHYLLIS LAKE
Map 22

round trip: 3.6 miles
elevation gain: 700 feet
elevation loss (return climb): 240 feet
highest point: 9,240 feet
map: Washington Peak
time: 6 1/2 hours
difficulty: moderate
access: 45.7 miles north of Ketchum on Highway 75, turn right (east) on the primitive Fourth of July Creek Road and drive 10 miles to a junction in a large meadow.

At Phyllis Lake, a white peak with slanting brown stripes contrasts with water so green it appears to have a light inside it. From this peak, cliffs with ribbon stripes of orange and brown extend to a rounded burnt orange shoulder of Washington Peak. Under this summit, a rocky peninsula guards a lime-green meadow where buttercups and marsh marigolds appear the minute the snow melts.

This hike description begins at a junction in the big meadow below the Highland Surprise Mine on the Fourth of July Creek

Road. The meadow is 2.1 miles and 800 feet above the place where the road may be closed when a future trailhead is created. To reach the meadow (8,780 feet), follow access directions above. Turn right (south) on a jeep trail which fords the creek. Wade the creek and walk up this track avoiding roads downhill to the right and uphill to a prospect. The main road descends gently to a stream (8,980 feet) at 1.0 mile. The slopes are wooded with some open areas.

Across the stream, the road climbs through thick woods and over tiny streams to a junction at 1.5 miles. The right (west) fork which goes to mines at the head of the canyon gives access to Lightning Lake. Take the left (southeast) fork of the road (not shown on the topo map), which ends in 300 yards. From its end, a path climbs left of a creek, then crosses it in a meadow at 1.6 miles and ascends a ravine, where the trail fades. At 1.7 miles, a path turns gradually right (south) over a low saddle to the lake, (9,200 feet) at 1.8 miles.

63 LIGHTNING LAKE
Map 22

round trip: 5 miles (1.8 miles cross-country)
elevation gain: 1,080 feet
elevation loss (return climb): 240 feet
this section one way: 1 mile, 640 feet gain, 40 feet loss
highest point: 9,600 feet
map: Washington Peak
time: 7 hours
difficulty: moderate
access: 45.7 miles north of Ketchum on Highway 75, turn right (east) on the primitive Fourth of July Creek Road and drive 10 miles to a junction in a large meadow. Turn right (south) on the Phyllis Lake Road and walk 1.5 miles to a split in this road.

A furrowed mountain and a scalloped ridge enclose Lightning Lake in a cup of rocks. A few whitebark pines guard the natural rock dam which prevents the blue green water from spilling. Wildflower meadows, the small green rectangle of Thunder Lake and the pale amber saucer of a pond make the route colorful. The lake is also known as Little Triangle.

Lightning Lake

This hike description begins on the old jeep road to Phyllis Lake, where it branches (8,980 feet) 1.5 miles from Fourth of July Creek. To reach this point, see directions listed above. If the road is gated at the new Fourth of July Creek parking area, add 2.1 miles one way to this hike. The left fork of the jeep road goes toward Phyllis Lake.

Walk down the right branch of the road to a campsite at .3 mile. A log cabin and mine diggings are beyond. Where a side road goes up to a tunnel, take the right (northwest) part of the jeep trail down into a meadow.

Turn left (west) off the road at the creek in the meadow and climb the creek to a swamp. Circle the swamp on the right (north) to a sketchy path leading over a small ridge (9,320 feet) to a stream. Ascend this stream to small, green Thunder Lake (9,200 feet) at .7 mile. Walk east of it to the upper end and then up left of the inlet through rocks and grass. The faint path crosses grass and dead logs to reach the amber pond at 1.0 mile. Go right (west) around the pond and up the side of its inlet through rocks to Lightning Lake (9,600 feet) at 1.2 miles.

64 HEART AND SIX LAKES
Map 22

round trip: 4 miles
elevation gain: 1,030 feet
elevation loss (return climb): 40 feet
highest point: 9,240 feet
map: Washington Peak
time: 4 hours
difficulty: cross-country
access: 45.7 miles north of Ketchum on Highway 75, turn right (east) on the primitive Fourth of July Creek Road and drive 8.7 miles to a parking spot. The spot, .7 mile above a large parking area, has blazed trees, two small turnouts, and a view of a chocolate brown mountain ahead.

At the upper end of Heart Lake, the reflections of a charcoal gray lava knoll color the green water inky blue. In the distance behind it, a sweeping pearl gray peak spreads a tidy point. East of Heart Lake the second of the six lakes huddles under a corrugated wall which bristles with gray, brown and orange needles. Below the wall, blobs of chocolate brown rock melt into the talus edging the lake. The turquoise water of the highest lake mirrors gentler, gray peaks at the head of the canyon. The sprawled arms of this lake reach out for clumps of whitebark pines on the shore.

To reach the beginning of this hike at 8,250 feet, follow access directions above. (If the gate is closed at the new trailhead, add .7 mile one way to this hike.) A well-defined path leads south from the road down to Fourth of July Creek. Ford the creek, and follow the path south up the west (right) side of the outlet of the Six Lakes. At an open area, the path climbs a bank to avoid a slide.

At .5 mile in a flat meadow, the path crosses left (east) of the creek for 150 yards. At the lower end of a second meadow, the path goes to the east again briefly. For the last .2 mile, the path climbs along right (west) of the creek through forest to Heart Lake (8,840 feet) at 1.0 mile. The path is not an official trail, and there is downed timber on it.

To reach the higher lakes, go left (east) around Heart Lake to a campsite and creek east of the charcoal cliffs. Climb cross-country right (south) of the inlet meadow on a 15-foot high ridge. Where the meadow turns into talus, cut straight south to the lake at 1.5 miles.

Circle this lake on the right (west) along a wooded slope. At the southwest corner of the lake, climb a gully leading up the wooded knoll separating the lakes. From it, descend to a peninsula on the north edge of the highest lake (9,020 feet) at 2.0 miles. The other three lakes are small ponds. The best campsite at the upper lakes is between them, but you must carry water up to it.

65 BORN LAKES
Maps 22, 23

round trip: 9.4 miles to highest lake
elevation gain: 1,360 feet
elevation loss (return climb) 500 feet
this section one way: 3.4 miles, 825 feet gain, 500 feet loss
highest point: 9,900 feet
maps: Washington Peak, Boulder Chain Lakes
time: 8 hours
difficulty: partly cross-country
access: Using directions for Hike 61 (Fourth of July Lake), hike to that lake.

Talus, wildflower meadows, subalpine firs and whitebark pines enclose the seven tiny ponds of the Born Lakes below orange and gray splintered crags. The largest pond is only 200 yards across, so these lakes seem newborn, but they are actually named for a prospector named Boren. Above the highest lake, a large gray pinnacle on a fractured ridge guards a notch called the Devils Staircase. At sunset, the alpenglow paints the ridge salmon pink.

From a pass on the trail across the green velvet bench of Ants Basin and the abyss of Warm Springs Canyon, some of the White Cloud Peaks gleam like white chalk. This entire range of mountains is called the White Clouds, but among them is a single chain known as the "White Cloud Peaks" for lack of individual names. This chain is mostly white, composed of a metamorphosed limestone similar to marble but containing silica.

To reach the beginning of this hike description, follow directions listed above. Hike to the trail junction just below Fourth of July Lake, 1.3 miles and a 525-foot climb above the present trailhead. Take the left branch of the trail northeast. The right one goes to Washington Lake.

At .2 mile, the trail crosses a meadow where a side trail comes up from the lake. The route climbs northeast with fine views of Fourth of July Lake and the Sawtooths, then cuts back to the northwest. At .5 mile, it passes a small green pond in talus. The trail climbs west along the side of the ridge and zigzags to a saddle (9,900 feet) with the view of the white peaks at 1.1 miles.

The path parallels the saddle for 100 yards and switchbacks down to the edge of Ants Basin (9,560 feet) at 1.3 miles, where it disappears. The trail from Ants Basin down into the Warm Springs Canyon is seldom used and there is no path for it across the basin. This trail descends 1,100 feet in 1.5 miles to the Warm Springs Canyon Trail, which it joins at 4.8 miles above the upper end of The Meadows.

Most hikers are heading to Born Lakes, so there is more of a path on the route to those lakes. To find that route, go east to the edge of the basin at 1.7 miles. Descend a gully to a path on its far side leading across the lower edge of a talus slope, above the trees. Look down on a meadow with a pond in it. If you don't find the path, stay just above the trees and head east.

The first Born Lake (9,420 feet) is at 2.5 miles.. Go along the south edge of the lake and over a small ridge to the second lake at 4.0 miles. To reach the third lake, climb the inlet past a small pond or cut over a wooded hillside directly to it. Above the north side of the third lake (9,555 feet) look for traces of the trail from Warm Springs Canyon as it goes up left of the creek. The route is mostly through open country past clumps of whitebark pines to the highest lake in the rocks (9,700 feet), 3.4 miles from Fourth of July Lake. There are one or more campsites at each of the four main lakes.

66 BORN LAKES TO QUIET LAKE THROUGH FOUR LAKES BASIN

Maps 23, 29

round trip: 13.0 miles
elevation gain: 2,085 feet
elevation loss (return climb): 1,538 feet
this section one-way: 1.8 miles, 725 feet gain, 1,038 feet loss
highest point: 10,280 feet
maps: Washington Peak, Boulder Chain Lakes
time: 3 to 4 days
difficulty: expert (all cross-country)
access: Hike to the third Born Lake at 9,555 feet. For directions see Hike 65 (Fourth of July Lake to Born Lakes) and Hike 61 (Fourth of July Lake to Washington Lakes).

This off-trail pass allows an easier, safer loop trip in the White Clouds than the route from Born Lakes over the Devils Staircase to the Boulder Chain Lakes. Also from the pass, the great gabled wall of Castle Peak, the crinkled ridges of Patterson Peak, and the snow-patched, dark blue crags of the Sawtooths are seen. At the four turquoise lakes in Four Lakes Basin, the few stunted whitebark pines grow only above lake level on talus mounds where it is a little warmer than it is at the lakes.

To reach the beginning of this cross-country route, hike to the third Born Lake at 9,555 feet. From the east end of the lake, go south up a ravine to a big grassy basin on the side of the upper canyon. From the basin, find a faint path zigzagging up the greener parts of the scree. Take this path toward the low point on the skyline, (10,280 feet.)

On the other side, descend a few feet to the large flat area shown on the map at .5 mile. To reach the lakes, you must first get around a big snowbank with a cornice. It is easiest to go to the right (south-west) about .2 mile along a ledge above cliffs until the slope lessens

Pass between Born Lakes and Four Lakes Basin

enough to walk down to Emerald Lake (9,910 feet) 1.0 mile from the third Born Lake. Late in the season, descend left (east) of the cornice to the creek between Emerald and Cornice Lakes. You can't drop directly to Cornice Lake from the saddle because of cliffs. The other two lakes, Rock and Glacier, are south of Emerald Lake.

To get to Quiet Lake, stay north of the lakes and their outlet, avoiding as much talus as possible. Trees and earth between the rocks begin at about 1.4 miles. At 1.6 miles, leave the outlet and descend a ravine to campsites at the upper end of the lake (9,242 feet) at 1.8 miles.

67 WASHINGTON LAKE TO CASTLE DIVIDE AND BAKER LAKE JUNCTION

Map 23

round trip: 23.2 miles
elevation gain: 2,555 feet
elevation loss (return climb): 1,926 feet
this section one way: 9.2 miles, 1,835 feet gain, 1,725 feet loss
highest point: 10,000 feet
map: Boulder Chain Lakes
time: 3 to 4 days
difficulty: strenuous
access: Follow directions for Hike 61 (Fourth of July and Washington Lakes) to hike to Washington Lake.

From Castle Divide, jagged towers on Serrate Ridge, the orange wall behind the Boulder Chain Lakes, and the swirled stripes of Granite Peak near Frog Lake merge with the red rocks of Red Ridge. Closer to the divide, the scree ridge above the Castle Lake route joins the white section of Castle Peak. Between Castle Peak and the divide gleam two white, pointed shoulders, etched with gray stripes.

To reach the beginning of this hike description, follow directions listed above to hike to Washington Lake (9,362 feet). From the lower end of the lake, the trail descends to a flat meadow at .5 mile, and at .8 mile in a larger meadow, it crosses Washington Lake Creek to the left (east). There are campsites on a knoll above the crossing. In the meadow is a junction with a section of the Washington Creek Trail not shown on the topo map. This section descends Washington Lake Creek and climbs over a ridge to Washington Creek, .2 mile downstream from the Washington Basin Jeep Trail.

Just before the crossing of Washington Creek at .8 mile (9,040 feet), a dry gorge to the right (west) divides a pink hump of rock from a white hump. Paths well to the left of the gorge reach an unnamed lake at 9,480 feet.

Beyond the ford, the trail descends through lodgepoles, sagebrush and meadows to 8,840 feet, and then begins to climb the side of the canyon. It turns east to join the route from Germania Creek at 2.5 miles (9,040 feet).

From here the route is identical for 2.8 miles to the one described under Chamberlain Lakes. It climbs over a 9,800-foot divide and passes two of the lakes. For detailed directions, see Hike 60. This description resumes at the lowest of the Chamberlain Lakes (9,197 feet) directly under Castle Peak, at a point 5.3 miles from Washington Lake.

From this lake, the Castle Divide Trail climbs through rolling meadows to a junction (9,240 feet) at 5.8 miles with a trail down Chamberlain Creek. This little-used trail drops 2,180 feet in 3.5 miles to Germania Creek, meeting it 6.2 miles from Three Cabins Creek.

The main trail climbs over a ridge spur in the trees and crosses meadows with a view of the Boulder Mountains. The path ascends scree and talus under red-orange rock walls. Near the top, the trail goes straight up. This section may be reconstructed in the future. At 6.8 miles is the summit of the divide (10,000 feet) between pink outcrops and the white shoulders of Castle Peak.

On the other side, the trail switchbacks through grassy scree to the trees. Then it winds down through forest to a junction (8,400 feet) at 9.2 miles with a .6-mile path to Baker Lake. The section from the summit to the Baker Lake junction was reconstructed in 1986 to an even grade. The trail continues to a junction with the Little Boulder Creek Trail at 9.9 miles. There is no water on the trail between Chamberlain Lakes and a stream one mile north of the divide.

Quiet Lake and Merriam Peak

OBSIDIAN AREA

68 THE MEADOWS ON WARM SPRINGS CREEK

Map 25

round trip: 7.4 miles to meadows, 11.4 miles to view up canyon
elevation gain: 267 feet
elevation loss (return climb): 717 feet
highest point: 8,000 feet
map: Washington Peak
time: 5 1/2 to 7 1/2 hours
difficulty: moderate to strenuous
access: 47.4 miles north of Ketchum on Highway 75, turn right (east) on the primitive Fisher Creek Road and drive 6.8 miles to the Aztec Mine.

More than three miles of wide green meadows stretch along Warm Springs Creek half way between Robinson Bar and Born Lakes. The green meadows carpeting the bottom of the canyon and the green wooded ridges hedging it in form an all-green world. From the upper end of The Meadows, an open hillside above a marshy pond gives a view of the gray and white crumbly peaks of the upper canyon. A shady downhill access trail begins at the old brown Aztec Mine buildings, which are roofed in warped rusty tin.

To reach the trailhead, follow access directions above. The road can be very muddy in early season. The Aztec Mine buildings are picturesque, but are on private property, so respect them. From 8,000 feet, the trail winds down through woods as an old road, passing granite outcrops. At 1.0 mile is a junction (7,600 feet) with the Pigtail Creek Trail from the west. This two-mile trail connects with the Williams Creek Trail which reaches Highway 75 near Obsidian.

The main trail continues through open grass and sagebrush, and then enters woods and a meadow. At 2.4 miles, the way circles the base of a granite knoll, and fords the creek to the east. At 2.8 miles, it crosses back over the creek in a sandy place. The trail continues in woods, flattening out near a junction at 3.5 miles with another old road from the north. This road is the trail down Warm Springs Creek

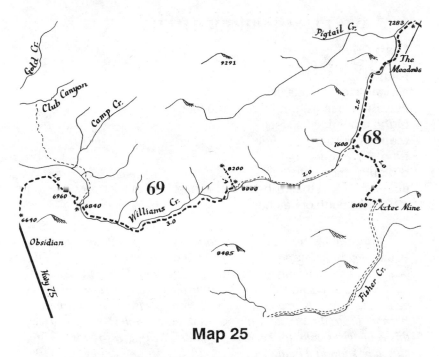

Map 25

going 11.2 miles with a 1,360-foot elevation loss to a CLOSED trail-head at Robinson Bar.

Take the right branch southeast .2 mile to the edge of The Meadows (7,300 feet). This makes a good day hike destination. Those eager to glimpse the upper canyon can continue south along the track at the edge of The Meadows.

Now, the road turns to a trail and then comes close to the creek at 4.0 miles. At a pole fence with a gate, remove and replace the gate poles or climb over them. Follow the trail along the west edge of The Meadows, looking for blazed posts which mark a route across it. Find your way to the creek and ford it to the east. This will be difficult in early summer. A trail soon appears, wandering in the woods and turning east with the canyon. At 5.7 miles, the path climbs the side of the canyon to an open area at 7,550 feet with a view of the upper canyon and of a pond below surrounded by cattle. There is a campsite by the creek.

69 WILLIAMS CREEK TRAIL

Map 25

round trip: 10 miles
elevation gain: 1,480 feet
elevation loss (return climb): 120 feet
highest point: 8,200 feet
map: Obsidian
time: 7 1/2 hours
difficulty: moderate
access: Park at the trailhead on the east side of Highway 75, 49.7 miles north of Ketchum.

A ridge above this trail gives a close view of the white section of the White Clouds. In late afternoon, when the sun shines on this side of the peaks, they resemble mounds of vanilla ice cream. Here you also see a panorama of the Sawtooths emphasizing the glacially-sculptured slopes below the teeth. The gradual, shady climb is pleasant on a warm day. Because the trail starts at the highway and the summit is only 8,000 feet, this route gives entry to the White Clouds when access roads are still closed by snow and mud.

To reach the trailhead, follow the directions above. Park before the house and walk past it to the register box. The trail angles along the side of a sagebrush hill and curves at .4 mile to the right (east) into lodgepoles. At .8 mile, the path turns southeast at a small meadow. It switchbacks over a ridge and 120 feet down sagebrush slopes into a teardrop-shaped meadow at 1.5 miles. The trail crosses Williams Creek on a bridge at the lower end of the meadow at 1.6 miles (6,840 feet) at a junction with a trail from the Idaho Rocky Mountain Ranch.

The main trail goes along east of the meadow. At 2.5 miles, it crosses to the right (south) of the creek on a culvert. The trail curves in and out of ravines across from sagebrush slopes dotted with splintered granite outcrops. At 4.4 miles, it goes back north of the creek. As it begins to climb a sagebrush slope, an old trail joins from the left. From this slope, Mt. Heyburn is visible.

Next, the way edges a basin of lodgepoles to the 8,000-foot summit at 4.6 miles. The trail drops 400 feet on the other side in 2.0 miles to reach the trail from the Aztec Mine to The Meadows.

For the viewpoint, turn left (north) at the divide on a path up a gentle ridge. The Sawtooths appear at 4.8 miles and the White Clouds at 5.0 miles (8,200 feet).

70 BOUNDARY CREEK TRAIL, CASINO LAKES AND BIG CASINO CREEK

Map 26

through trip: 11.4 miles
elevation gain: 2,760 feet
elevation loss: 3,300 feet
highest point: 9,560 feet
maps: Casino Lakes, East Basin Creek
time: 10 hours
difficulty: strenuous
access: From Highway 75, turn right (east) 54.7 miles north of Ketchum at a sign for the Boundary Creek Trail. Drive .8 mile to the end of the dirt road. Avoid side roads to cabins.

Wooded hills, talus ridges and white granite knolls shadow the marsh grass which wreaths the shores of the three Casino Lakes. At the lower lake, asters, gentians, elephant's head, and polemonium decorate a marshy garden. From the highest point on the trail, the long blue rib-bon of Redfish Lake glistens below the overlapping zigzags of the Saw-tooths. From here, the White Clouds Peaks appear to the south and the pink and tan summits of the Salmon River Mountains to the north. From the lakes, the Big Casino Trail descends to the Salmon River be-side the forest flowers and moss-covered rocks of a shady canyon.

A through trip from Boundary Creek to the Salmon River avoids a 960-foot return climb on the Boundary Creek Trail. To reach the Boundary Creek trailhead, follow the access directions above. From the parking area (6,800 feet), the trail winds through sagebrush into aspen, lodgepole and Douglas fir. At .5 mile, a trail joins from cabins across the creek. The main route turns north, zigzagging up a ridge. From the side of this ridge in sagebrush at 1.3 miles, there are views of Redfish Lake and the Sawtooths.

At a saddle at 2.8 miles at the top of the main ridge, the trail returns to forest. On this saddle (8,760 feet), the unsigned Sunny Gulch Trail joins from the left. This trail goes 5.2 miles with a 160-foot gain and 2,400-foot loss to the edge of the Salmon River opposite the Sunny Gulch Campground. At 3.5 miles, it connects with the Little Casino Creek Trail. The route down Sunny Gulch is not shown on the topo map.

From the saddle, take the Boundary Creek Trail to the right (southeast). It winds in trees right of the ridge through a narrow meadow, a dry grass flat, and a lush green meadow with springs. At 3.3 miles, the trail climbs onto and follows the crest of the ridge to an elevation of 9,560 feet at 3.5 miles. From here, the view includes the Sawtooths, the Salmon River and White Cloud Mountains and the highest Casino Lake.

The path descends to a saddle and drops to the east along a spur ridge. This ridge is sprinkled with subalpine fir, lupine, and red mountain heath. At 4.2 miles, the route passes left of a large wet meadow with campsites and crosses a stream (not shown on the map) to the right (south). At 4.5 miles is a junction just east of a 9,120-foot saddle with the Garland Creek and South Martin–Big Casino trails.

From here, the Garland Creek Trail joins the Rough Creek Trail in a mile at one of the Garland Lakes, and then drops 2,240 feet in 5.0 miles down Garland Creek to Warm Springs Creek. The trail to the south passes near two of the Garland Lakes on the way to Martin Creek at 4.3 miles, 1,320 feet below.

Take the Big Casino Trail north. It crosses a stream to the west and then back to the east as it descends to the first of the marshy Casino Lakes (8,800 feet) at 4.8 miles. The trail to the lowest lake (8,600 feet) goes down through forest on the right (east) of the creek, then crosses it to the west just before the lake at 5.3 miles.

The route circles south of the lake in woods, and goes downhill in a lodgepole forest to cross a small side stream. The path fords the main creek to the east at 5.9 miles. There are four more crossings in the next mile before the route finally stays on the east (right). A talus slope at 7.0 miles is followed by Douglas firs and rocks. The path hops a side stream well above the main creek at 7.8 miles. At 8.5 miles, the route follows a stream bed for .5 mile in a level lodgepole forest between Big Casino and Midwinter Creeks, and crosses tiny Midwinter Creek at 9.2 miles.

Two rock outcrops resemble crocodiles when the forest becomes open and the valley widens. At 10.8 miles the trail fords the creek to the west and reaches an old road. The track goes back over the creek at 11 miles, and comes to a posted, locked gate in 200 yards.

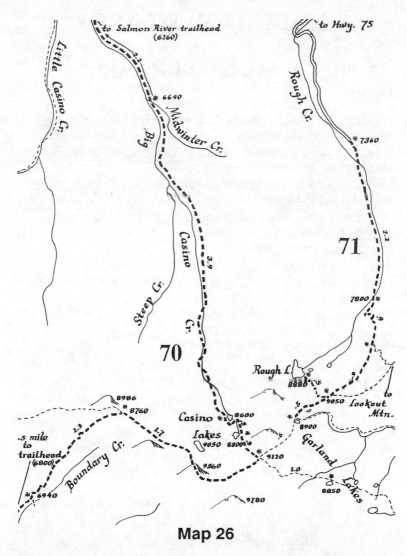

Map 26

Ford the creek back to the left (west) at a crossing not shown on the topo map. At 11.4 miles, the trail reaches the trailhead (6,260 feet). The bridge over the Salmon River to Highway 75 at Casino Creek is .2 mile away and Stanley is 3.0 miles west of the bridge.

ROUGH CREEK AREA

71 ROUGH AND GARLAND LAKES
Map 26

round trip: 9 miles to Rough Lake with 1 mile cross-country, 9 miles for first Garland Lake
elevation gain: 1,790 feet for Rough Lake, or 1,690 feet for first Garland Lake
elevation loss (return climb): 240 feet for Rough Lake, 150 feet for first Garland Lake
side trip to other Garland Lakes: 2.4 miles one way, 320 feet gain, 240 feet loss
highest point: 9,160 feet
map: Casino Lakes
time: 7 1/2 hours for Rough Lake, 10 hours for all Garland Lakes
difficulty: strenuous; expert ability for Rough Lake
access: Drive 10 miles northeast of Stanley on Highway 75. Just beyond Basin Creek, turn south and drive 4.2 miles on the dirt Rough Creek Road to a signed trailhead.

Near the moss and wildflowers of the inlet, a round-topped 100-foot cliff falls into the blue-green water of Rough Lake. Along the shores grow whitebark pine, subalpine fir, Labrador tea and red mountain heath. The first amber-colored Garland Lake sits in a basin of grasses, Kalmia, alpine buttercup, tiny firs, and red and white mountain heaths. Water pipits sometimes fly along the shore and nest among the heaths. From a saddle on the trail, there is a distant view of the high peaks of the White Clouds.

To reach the trailhead (7,360 feet), follow access directions above. A logging road heads to the right at the trailhead, but the trail goes left through shady woods. The trail crosses the creek on a log to the west at .3 mile. The way climbs above the creek, but then returns to it and crosses back to the east at 2.2 miles. The path makes a big switchback to the east at 2.5 miles and then ascends steeply to a turnoff for Lookout Mountain at 3.1 miles. This side trail climbs 400 feet in 2.0 miles to the 9,984-foot summit.

Continue on the main trail, which goes around the head of the canyon. Cross several creeks to a saddle (9,050 feet) at 4.0 miles. A branch of the Lookout Mountain Trail comes in at a junction.

To reach Rough Lake, take a path west up the ridge from the saddle until the slope lessens at about 9,160 feet. Turn right (north) on a branch toward the lake. This path drops steeply to the lake (8,880 feet) at 4.5 miles.

To reach the Garland Lakes, stay on the trail at the saddle and descend the other side. The Garland Creek Trail turns off part way down, not at a lake as shown on the map. Continue on the main trail to a pond. The first tiny Garland Lake (8,900 feet) is at 4.5 miles. To reach the other lakes, go southwest on the same trail for .6 mile. At a four-way junction, turn left (south) onto the Martin Creek Trail. Two additional Garland Lakes are along this trail. The first (8,850 feet) is 1.0 mile from the junction. To reach the second (8,800 feet), turn south off the trail 1.6 miles from the junction and walk .2 mile.

SLATE CREEK AREA

72 HOODOO LAKE

Map 27

round trip: 4.2 miles
elevation gain: 1,727 feet
highest point: 8,677 feet
map: Robinson Bar
time: 4 to 5 hours
difficulty: moderate
access: Highway 75 crosses the Salmon River to the south side 23.7 miles northeast of Stanley. Just across the bridge, turn right (west) on a dirt road along the river. At .8 mile, turn left (south) on a dirt road up Slate Creek and drive to a gate at 7.1 miles.

At the head of emerald-green Hoodoo Lake, a C-shaped groove, often filled with snow, indents the face of a gray mountain. An orange ridge bristling with trees extends from it along the east side of the lake. Behind this, a wide triangular summit with one scalloped side stands across the canyon of Slate Creek. Marsh grass and shrubby cinquefoil

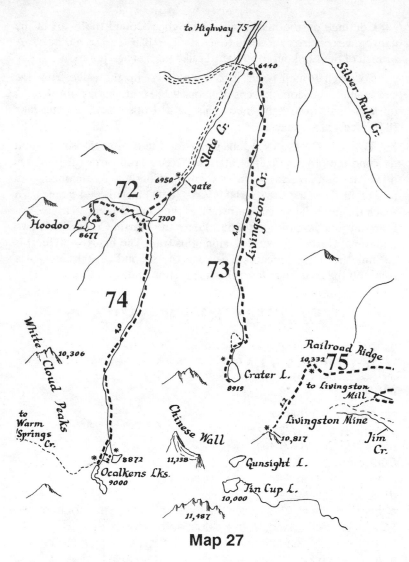

Map 27

line the shores of this lake, whose level was raised years ago by an earthen dam.

   To reach the trailhead, follow access directions above. Before
reaching the gate, park at about 6,950 feet. Walk through this gate
and another, passing a hot spring and inactive mine. Do not enter
any of the buildings. They are private property and contain mine
shafts. Follow the dirt road around the tailings pond and cross the

outlet of the lake on a bridge to a split in the road at .5 mile. (The left branch gives access to an abandoned trail to Ocalkens Lakes.)

Take the right fork of the road, which is now a jeep trail. It begins switchbacks in 150 yards. Keep on the best road, avoiding branch roads leading towards the creek and a dirt road leading southwest from the south end of the first switchback. At .8 mile, the track hops a side creek on a bridge and divides. The track for Hoodoo Lake continues up the canyon of its outlet across an orange talus slope at 1.3 miles. It goes into the woods where the road narrows and deteriorates.

The route turns left to a T-intersection. Take the right branch. This track switchbacks left over the bright green moss of a spring and comes to another T. The intersection at a mine prospect is the only one shown on the map. Stay right again, and go up the middle of the outlet for 50 yards and then into woods right (west) of the creek. When the route returns to the creek, it climbs up the middle of the creek again for 150 yards. This could be difficult in early summer.

The route ascends to the right (west) of the creek and parallels it. At 1.8 miles, the track fords the creek to the left (east) and climbs away from it up a ridge with a view of Slate Creek Canyon. At 2.0 miles, the track turns west along a low ridge above the north side of the lake to the dam (8,677 feet) at 2.1 miles. A campsite near the inlet can be reached by a .1-mile long path.

73 CRATER LAKE
Map 27

round trip: 8 miles
elevation gain: 2,479 feet
highest point: 8,919 feet
map: Livingston Creek
time: 7 1/2 hours
difficulty: strenuous
access: Drive northeast of Stanley on Highway 75 for 23.7 miles to the south side of a bridge over the Salmon River. Turn right (west) on a dirt road along the river. At .8 mile, turn right (west) on dirt Slate Creek Road and drive to a four-way intersection at 5.9 miles. Turn left (east) and drive 200 yards to Slate Creek.

Above the gray talus and cloudy blue water of Crater Lake, three small teeth, joined at the base, block passage across a saddle. On the Chinese Wall to the right of this tower, layers of white rock striped with dark gray tip up at each end, resembling a warped pile of weathered plywood. To the left of the tower, mining roads slash the round gravelly end of Railroad Ridge. On the south, peaks topped with crumbling triangular towers enclose the lake.

To reach the trailhead (6,440 feet), follow access directions above. There is room for only two cars to park. The trail is an old mining road no longer open to motor vehicles and not shown on the topo map. First it crosses Slate Creek on a wooden footbridge, and goes past a cabin to a gate. Beyond the gate, the road crosses Livingston Creek to the east and climbs gently under Douglas firs.

At .5 mile, the track fords two sections of the creek to the right (west), and then returns to the east in 200 yards. Ignore old mining roads which join this track from time to time. Keep on the road nearest the creek. At about 1.0 mile, the route fords to the west again, and returns to the left (east) at 1.2 miles. There are logs or rocks at some of the crossings.

The track passes an old log cabin and side stream, and levels out at 2.7 miles across from talus. The route reaches a basin of talus and grass at 3.5 miles. At an old mine tunnel at the head of this basin, the road crosses the creek again to make a .3 mile-long switchback. To save distance, turn left on a path which climbs talus and ledges on the right (north) of the creek. At 4.0 miles, both routes come out on a grassy area above the gray gravel edging the lake (8,919 feet).

The Chinese Wall and upper Ocalkens Lake

74 OCALKENS LAKES
Map 27

round trip: 9.4 miles
elevation gain: 2,050 feet·
elevation loss (return climb): 40 feet
highest point: 9,000 feet
maps: Livingston Creek, Robinson Bar
time: 8 hours
difficulty: strenuous
access: 23.7 miles northeast of Stanley on Highway 75, cross
the bridge to the south side of the Salmon River and turn right
(west) on a dirt road along the river. At .8 mile, turn left (south) up
Slate Creek and drive to a gate at 7.1 miles.

*Different slopes of three pearl gray summits above Ocalkens Lakes
turn creamy white in the early morning or late afternoon sunlight. On
the nearest peak, two wide bands of charcoal gray cliffs at the summit*

*contrast with the white base. North of the lakes, multicolored layers of
the Chinese Wall curve so the rock layers run vertically on one end and
horizontally on the other. To the south, a scalloped mountain divides
the lakes from the canyon of Warm Springs Creek. Red and white
mountain heaths carpet the shore of the narrow green larger lake. This
lake becomes murky in late summer from lack of an all-year outlet. The
clear blue lower lake nestles against the Chinese Wall.*

The route has been abandoned by the Forest Service to create a
trailless area, and the beginning is difficult to find. However, it is
shown on the Forest Service and topographic maps. To find it, follow
access directions above to reach the gate on the Slate Creek Road at
6,950 feet. Walk through the gate and up the road, keeping away
from the buildings, which contain mine shafts. The road divides after
it bridges the outlet of Hoodoo Lake at .5 mile. Take the left branch
into a logged area. The hillside on the right steepens at .6 mile before
the logging road goes onto a narrow ledge beside the creek and ends.
Before it steepens, climb uphill to the trail.

The trail climbs along talus on the side of the canyon below a
ridge of crumbled cliffs. At 1.7 miles, the path returns to the creek
and levels out. At 3.0 miles in an open basin, the trail fords the creek
to the left (east). Earlier crossings of the creek shown on the topo
map do not exist.

The trail climbs rock benches and, at 4.0 miles, crosses to the
west of the outlet of the smaller, lower lake. A campsite is 100 yards
above the crossing. The way continues along the usually dry outlet of
the larger lake (9,000 feet) and reaches it at 4.5 miles. There are
several campsites. A trail to Warm Springs Canyon has also been
abandoned. The lower lake (8,872 feet) is cross-country .2 mile east
of the ford of its outlet.

EAST FORK OF SALMON RIVER AREA

75 RAILROAD RIDGE
Map 28

round trip: 14 miles
elevation gain: 3,737 feet
elevation loss (return climb): 80 feet
highest point: 10,817 feet
map: Livingston Creek
time: 12 hours or 2 days
difficulty: strenuous; expert ability for last .5 mile
access: 36.5 miles east of Stanley on Highway 75, turn south on the East Fork of Salmon River Road. Drive 14.7 miles on pavement, 2.9 miles on gravel, then turn northwest on the dirt Livingston Mill Road and drive 4.8 miles. At a sign, turn left and go .2 mile to a parking area unless you have four-wheel drive.

From the gables and avalanche chutes of Castle Peak to the fissured white wall of D.O. Lee Peak, the White Clouds seem to reach out toward the summit of Railroad Ridge. From the highest point, talus, ledges and whitebark pines emphasize the bleakness of the timberline site of blue-green Tin Cup and Gunsight Lakes. The ridge also overlooks the blue oval of Crater Lake, which is set in gray talus.

Across a notch, Railroad Ridge faces the Chinese Wall, a textbook example of rock layers warped downward in the center. Down Jim Creek past Livingston Mill stands a layer cake of strawberry and chocolate colored rock. Beyond it are the twin summits of Mt. Borah. Notice the upper and lower timberlines of all of the Lost River Range. To the north stretches a panorama of the Salmon River Mountains from the brown-striped towers of Cabin Creek Peak and the salmon-pink cap of Red Mountain to the two sharp gray points of Twin Peaks. Hard-to-find alpine flowers, such as alpine forget-me-not, grow on this ridge.

To reach the trailhead, follow access directions above. At 22.4 miles, turn left to the transfer camp and leave your car. If you have a four-wheel drive vehicle and plan to travel up the ridge, check with SNRA Headquarters for regulations and road conditions. The road,

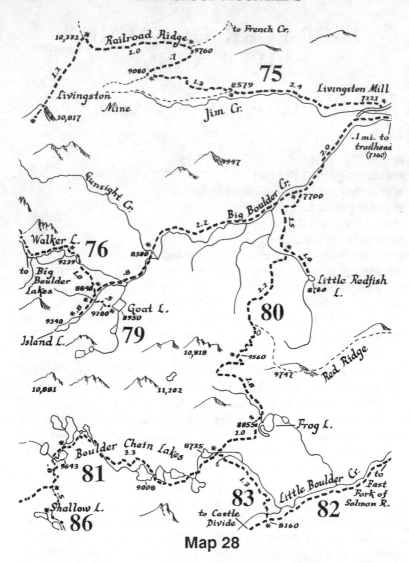

Map 28

which crosses private property and can be impassable in early summer due to snow, is much too steep for two-wheel drive.

From the transfer camp (7,160 feet), walk back to the main road and up it through a gate to Livingston Mill and the junction at .4 mile (7,221 feet) with the road up Railroad Ridge. Leave the gate the way you find it. From the junction to the 2-mile point, the road climbs 1,000 feet up a sagebrush hillside, so this section can be hot.

Tin Cup and Gunsight Lakes from Railroad Ridge

At 2.9 miles, where the road forks (8,579 feet), take the right (north) branch. A large campsite is at 3.5 miles in a grove of trees beside a stream. At 4.1 miles (9,090 feet), the road divides again. This is not shown on the topo map. Take the right branch, which turns sharply to the right (northeast).

The road angles 600 feet up the ridge in .7 mile, crossing a washout half way up. At 4.8 miles, the track bends 180 degrees to the west. At this bend (9,760 feet) the French Creek Jeep Trail, which is no longer open to motor vehicles, turns north.

Keep west on the road along the top of the ridge. The high peaks begin to come into view. Soon the road splits to avoid a washout, and comes together again in 200 yards. At 5.8 miles (10,320 feet), the road divides. Turn left (southwest) on a faint track (not shown on the topo map) along the crest of the ridge. Descend to a notch at 6.1 miles. Crater Lake may be seen by walking downhill a short distance.

To see Tin Cup and Gunsight Lakes, take a faint path from the notch south up a rocky knoll (10,817 feet). Stay near the left (east) edge of the cliffs at first, then move toward the right to the flat summit of the knoll at 7.0 miles. Descend 100 yards toward a notch to see Tin Cup and Gunsight Lakes. Climbing down to these lakes from the knoll is dangerous, but possible for experts carrying only day packs. A sketchy path zigzags from a talus basin .3 mile east of Gunsight

Lake up a trough of scree 500 vertical feet in .1 mile to the knoll, but it is much safer to go up Gunsight Creek from Quicksand Meadows.

76 WALKER LAKE

Map 28

round trip: 12.2 miles
elevation gain: 2,079 feet
highest point: 9,239 feet
maps: Livingston Creek, Boulder Chain Lakes
time: 10 hours
difficulty: strenuous
access: 36.5 miles east of Stanley on Highway 75, turn south on the East Fork of Salmon River Road. Drive 14.7 miles on pavement, 2.9 miles on gravel, then turn northwest on the dirt Livingston Mill Road and drive 4.8 miles. At a sign, turn left and go .2 mile to a parking area.

A village of weathered brown cabins surrounds dilapidated Livingston Mill near the trailhead. From the lower part of the trail, brown and white rock layers on Railroad Ridge resemble melting vanilla ice cream on chocolate cake. Bordering Quicksand Meadows farther up the trail, the pink, brown, rust and white stripes and patches of Granite Peak resemble a patchwork crazy quilt.

North of aqua-green Walker Lake, triangular towers crown the double summit of an orange and white peak. Above the upper end of the lake, the iceberg tips of two of the White Cloud Peaks appear to float over the cliffs early in the morning.

To reach the trailhead (7,160 feet) near Livingston Mill, follow access directions above. From the transfer camp, the trail skirts Big Boulder Creek through sagebrush flats to the register box at .5 mile. The way follows an old road with a view of red rock towers across Big Boulder Creek. At 1.5 miles, the route bridges the creek. The turnoff to Frog Lakes is at 2.1 miles (7,700 feet).

From the junction, the trail to Walker and Island Lakes crosses Big Boulder Creek in two sections, first on a log bridge and then on rocks. The path climbs through sagebrush, lodgepoles, and aspen and at 3.1 miles, it is above a large meadow. The trail climbs a steep grade, and goes through burnt trees above a 100-foot gorge. Next, the

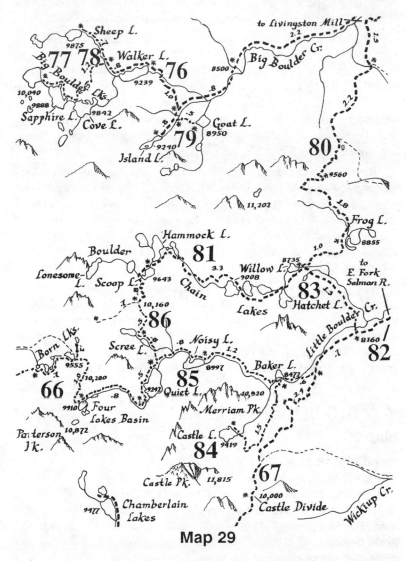

Map 29

path drops into Quicksand Meadows, crosses a creek (8,500 feet), and turns left (south).

Quicksand Meadows is shown as a flat, wooded area on the topo map, with a pond where two creeks join. Out in the meadows, the trail is marked with posts and fords Gunsight Creek on logs at 4.3

miles. It then turns right towards the forest. The lower meadows located off the trail are dangerous to stock because of quicksand.

Quicksand is caused by water upwelling underneath sand with such force that it equals the weight of the sand, and thus separates the sand grains making it possible for an object to sink. A person can float more easily in quicksand than in water because it is denser, so the old tales of people drowning in quicksand are exaggerated. The only way a person's head would sink is in a violent struggle to get free. To get out of quicksand, a person can lie down and swim slowly, but a horse would have to be pulled out.

Beyond the meadows, cross the creek on a log and then return within a few feet to the right (west). The trail switchbacks up a talus slope, then climbs gently through trees, with views of the striped peak on the left. Across cascades in the canyon at 4.8 miles, the outlet of Goat Lake rushes down. The trail makes a switchback beside this cascade, then crosses a side creek. The Walker and Island Lake trails diverge at 5.1 miles.

The trail to Walker Lake is not shown on the topo map and the lake is wrongly labeled Walter Lake. This trail winds up through trees left of a low granite knoll. Beyond the knoll, it descends to a meadow, then skirts a pond on the left (south). The path fords the creek between this pond and another, and then turns away from the creek over granite benches to the 9,239-foot lake at 6.1 miles.

77 BIG BOULDER LAKES
Map 29

round trip: 16.2 miles
elevation gain: 2,880 feet
this section one way: 2 miles, 801 feet gain
highest point: 10,040 feet
map: Boulder Chain Lakes
time: 2 days
difficulty: cross-country
access: Follow directions in Hike 76 (Walker Lake) to hike to Walker Lake, where this hike description begins.

From above, the three Big Boulder Lakes resemble three sapphire blue platters with rims of green pines, turquoise bays and white outcrops. In the distance, the gray, orange and cream-colored stripes of

Cirque Lake, the highest of the three Big Boulder Lakes

Granite Peak paint a backdrop for the lakes. Above them a scalloped, fluted ridge of white rock gleams like vanilla ice cream in the morning, when the sun shines on it. But it turns pearl gray in the afternoon when the sun dips behind it. Recent glacial moraines surround the upper lake, Cirque Lake. The glacier above no longer moves so it is not a true glacier.

The lower end of Walker Lake, where this hike description begins, is 6.1 miles and a 2,079-foot climb from Livingston Mill. To get there, follow directions given above. Take the trail along the north shore of Walker Lake which goes .5 mile to the upper end of the lake.

A path goes right (east) of the right (north) branch of the inlet. Where a stream joins it from a flat area on the left at .7 mile, cross both branches and go west up the left side stream, which is not shown on the map. The path crosses to the right, then back to the left just before the flat meadow. In the meadow, the path turns left (south) and becomes more obvious between rock ledges on the left and the meadow on the right. At 1.0 mile, this path zigzags south 300 feet up rock benches.

Beyond the top of the benches, the path drops to the east end of a narrow pond called Hook Lake, and disappears. To reach Cove Lake, go around this pond and head south between granite benches. From the upper end of Cove Lake (9,842 feet) at 1.5 miles, a faint path ascends right (north) of the inlet to Sapphire Lake (9,888 feet) at 1.6 miles. Climb rock benches cross-country north of its inlet to Cirque Lake (10,040 feet) at 2.0 miles.

It is easier to reach Cove Lake from Island Lake, but the route is less obvious. To do this, go north 300 feet up a gully or ramp from the north corner of that lake to the top of a ridge. Turn left (west) along the ridge to a tiny pond (not shown on the map) under the summit of the ridge. Follow the 9,800-foot contour line west and northwest to Cove Lake, 1.0 mile from Island Lake.

This route is difficult to find on the return from Cove Lake, unless you have reached the lake by it. Don't descend the canyon between Cove and Island Lakes. It is full of boulders and cliffs. Boulders edge the upper end of Island Lake and a big cliff drops into the water on the north side of the lake..

78 SHEEP LAKE
Map 29

round trip: 15.2 miles
elevation gain: 2,715 feet
this section one way: 1.5 miles, 636 feet gain
highest point: 9,875 feet
map: Boulder Chain Lakes
time: 2 to 3 days
difficulty: cross-country
access: Using directions in Hike 76, hike from Livingston Mill to Walker Lake.

Granite benches and ledges softened by bits of meadow sparkling with wildflowers surround Sheep Lake. In the distance below, patchwork designs decorate the wall of Granite Peak. The pinnacles and jumbled cliffs of a peach-colored mountain rise 1,200 feet above the east side of the lake. Across the blue water, a row of dark gray blunt summits faces this peak. Two great rock triangles stand at the head of the canyon above the granite shelves holding Neck and Slide Lakes.

To reach the beginning of this hike description, hike to the lower end of Walker Lake, following directions given above. It is 6.1 miles and a 2,079-foot climb to this point from the trailhead. Go .5 mile to the upper end of Walker Lake on the right (north), and follow a path right (east) of the right (north) branch of the inlet.

Keep straight ahead at .7 mile where a side stream coming in from a flat place on the left marks the route to the Big Boulder Lakes. Beyond, the path is sketchy to Sheep Lake (9,875 feet) at 1.5

miles. There are only one or two small campsites. If you wish, walk .5 mile farther, up granite benches to Neck Lake (a narrow pond) and Slide Lake (10,200 feet), 320 feet above Sheep Lake.

79 ISLAND AND GOAT LAKES
Map 28

round trip: 11.8 miles to Island Lake
elevation gain: 2,080 feet,
this section one way: .8 mile, 400 feet gain; additional .5 mile and 100 feet gain and 200 feet loss for Goat Lake
highest point: 9,240 feet
maps: Boulder Chain Lakes, Livingston Creek
time: 9 1/2 to 11 hours or 2 days
difficulty: strenuous
access: Follow directions in Hike 76 (Walker Lake) to hike to the junction of the Island Lake Trail with the Walker Lake Trail.

The aquamarine water of Island Lake holds two islands, one big enough for whitebark pines and the other just a granite pancake. Granite benches surround the lake except for a narrow boulder-dotted meadow at the upper end and a 200-foot cliff north of it. From the lower end of the lake, a natural ramp gives access to the Big Boulder Lakes. Above Goat Lake, chocolate, gray and buff stripes wander east across Granite Peak to a jumble of pinnacles. Benches, talus and trees surround the green lake below this dramatic wall.

Follow directions above to reach the Walker-Island Lake Junction (8,840 feet), 5.1 miles and a 1,680-foot climb from Livingston Mill. From the junction, the Island Lake Trail climbs the canyon at a distance from the ravine with the creek. The trail crosses and recrosses the creek. At a bog between the two gorges of the creek at .4 mile, the unofficial trail to Goat Lake turns left.

Look east and notice a saddle between a rock knoll and a ridge. An unofficial route is visible across the rocks, heading for this saddle .1 mile from the trail. From the saddle, a sketchy path winds down through the trees to Goat Lake (8,950 feet), .5 mile from the trail.

On the main trail, the route runs along above a second gorge, crosses a side creek and reaches Island Lake (9,240 feet) at a campsite .8 mile from the Walker Lake Junction.

To reach the Big Boulder Lakes from Island Lake, see directions under Hike 77 (Big Boulder Lakes).

80 LIVINGSTON MILL TO FROG LAKE
Map 28

round trip: 15.2 miles
elevation gain: 2,400 feet
elevation loss (return climb): 705 feet
highest point: 9,560 feet
maps: Livingston Creek, Boulder Chain Lakes
time: 2 to 3 days
difficulty: strenuous
access: 36.5 miles east of Stanley on Highway 75, turn south on the East Fork of Salmon River Road. Drive 14.7 miles on pavement, 2.9 miles on gravel, then turn northwest on the dirt Livingston Mill Road and drive 4.8 miles. At a sign, turn left and go .2 mile to the parking area.

This trail has become the standard route to the Boulder Chain Lakes since a landowner put a locked gate across the East Fork of the Salmon River Road below the Little Boulder Creek Trail. From the summit of the Livingston to Frog Lake Trail, two snow-filled ravines gouge the face of Castle Peak, which is charcoal gray on this side. From it the orange needles of Serrate Ridge parade right to the cathedral of Merriam Peak. West of the divide, burnt orange patches and stripes pattern the white face of Granite Peak. Yellow water lilies float near the shores of Frog and Little Frog Lakes. Across the water is a view of Castle Peak. The lakes sit in a wide marshy basin backed by hills of sagebrush and whitebark pines.

To reach the trailhead (7,160 feet), follow directions above. The trail goes along the creek through sagebrush flats to the register box near the old brown cottages of Livingston Mill at .5 mile. Next, the trail is an old road across the creek from red towers. The trail bridges Big Boulder Creek in a small meadow at 1.6 miles.

At 2.1 miles, the Frog Lake Trail turns south. It makes switchbacks not shown on the topo map in a lodgepole forest full of jackstraw-like dead trees. The trail climbs gently because it was constructed for trail bike riders. Even small streams have bridges. At 3.6 miles is a junction with a 1.0 mile side trail to Little Redfish Lake

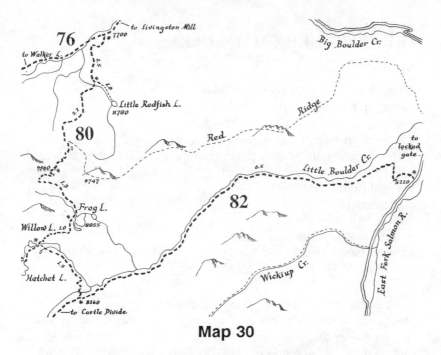

Map 30

(8,780 feet). This route climbs 400 feet to a small lake in marsh grass and water lilies, and is surrounded by wooded ridges.

The main trail continues up in big switchbacks, crossing and recrossing streams. Across Big Boulder Creek from an open grassy area are colorful orange mountains. At a corner at 4.0 miles, white limestone peaks behind the Big Boulder Lakes are visible. The trail climbs through open grassy areas, then flattens out in lodgepoles and passes a pond at 5.1 miles.

Above the pond, long switchbacks in open country culminate at the divide (9,560 feet). The view of Granite Peak is at 5.8 miles. Below the top, the path turns west, then zips back to the east for .2 mile. At 6.5 miles, it turns east again down a small creek through meadows. The trail reaches a tiny pond beside the largest lake (8,855 feet) at 7.6 miles.

81 BOULDER CHAIN LAKES
Map 28 or 29

round trip: 23.8 miles to Scoop Lake
elevation gain: 3,308 feet
elevation loss (return climb): 825 feet
this section one way: 4.3 miles, 908 feet gain, 120 feet loss
(.7 mile additional one way cross-country and 990 feet additional gain to see the highest two lakes)
highest point: 9,643 feet
map: Boulder Chain Lakes
time: 3 to 4 days
difficulty: strenuous
access: Hike to Frog Lake from Livingston Mill (see Hike 80, Livingston Mill to Frog Lake for directions).

A glacier strung these eleven clear blue lakes together like sparkling blue beads on a necklace. A ridge of orange slabs and pinnacles links the first half of the lakes together. On this ridge, a tower with owl-like ears overlooks the second one, Hatchet Lake. Splintered white peaks, rock benches and whitebark pines surround the upper lakes, with bits of meadow brimming with wildflowers touching the shorelines. From the trail to the first lake, the dark snow-slashed face of Castle Peak peers over the orange ridge.

This trail section begins at Frog Lake (8,855 feet), 7.6 miles and 2,400 feet above Livingston Mill. To reach this point, see Hike 80 (Livingston Mill to Frog Lake). Below Frog Lake, the trail drops through trees, then turns west along a sagebrush ridge with a view of Castle Peak.

At 1.0 mile, the route bridges the outlet of Willow Lake (8,735 feet) on a footbridge. The orange ridge overlooks granite knolls to the marsh grass and woods surrounding this lake. The trail goes along the south side of the lake near campsites. Sites are also 200 yards off-trail at a pond called Waterdog Lake.

The trail climbs through trees to Hatchet Lake (8,884 feet) at 1.5 miles. Blue-green water, marsh grass and the pinnacle with ears distinguish this lake. Campsites are off-trail on the northeast side.

The path crosses the outlet. In 200 yards is the inlet from the third lake, Shelf Lake, at 8,939 feet. Woods, bluffs and rock shelves

Hammock Lake, the eighth Boulder Chain Lake

stand on the north side of this lake and the eared mountain lurks behind woods on the south.

The trail climbs next to the cliffs of the orange mountain. It goes through trees under the eared tower to boulders and turf on the south shore of the fourth lake, Sliderock Lake (8,978 feet), at 2.0 miles.

Rock peninsulas clumped with trees elbow this lake. Campsites are located behind the peninsulas. The trail circles the head of the lake, and crosses the inlet on rocks. Next the path goes along the north shore of Lodgepole Lake (9,008 feet). Here the orange ridge sheds talus into the water on the south, and on the north, a clear inlet flows into the lake through marsh grass over golden sand.

Now there is a one-mile gap in the chain of lakes. The route is steep over rock benches and through forest. At 3.4 miles, the trail crosses to the west of the stream, then east and west again just below Hourglass Lake at 3.7 miles.

This upper basin holds three lakes. Hidden (9,517 feet), Hammock (9,514 feet) and Hourglass (9,500 feet) sit below splintered off-white peaks. Campsites are abundant off-trail. The trail continues up onto a shelf to the ninth lake, Scoop Lake (9,643 feet). This lake at 4.3 miles is the last lake on the trail. At the lake in a hollow of solid rock there are only a few stunted whitebark pines and no good campsites.

The trail continues through a pass called Windy Devil (10,000 feet) at 4.9 miles. The two upper lakes, Headwall (9,755 feet) and Lonesome (10,435 feet), are above timberline. They can be reached by going around the west side of Scoop Lake on the trail, and ascending the inlet cross-country for .7 mile. Lonesome Lake is 990 feet above Scoop Lake.

From the pass, the trail climbs out onto a shelf (10,200 feet) and ends at 5.6 miles. The end of the trail is 557 feet and 1.3 miles above Scoop Lake. It is dangerous to try to go over the Devils Staircase from here to Born Lakes.

82 LITTLE BOULDER CREEK TRAIL
Map 30

round trip: 13 miles
elevation gain: 1,940 feet
highest point: 8,160 feet
maps: Bowery Creek, Boulder Chain Lakes
time: 9 1/2 hours
difficulty: strenuous
access: There is no access by road to this trail at the present time, as the East Fork of the Salmon River Road has been closed above the Red Ridge Trail.

The Little Boulder Creek Trail is the shortest route to the Boulder Chain Lakes and Baker Lake. However, access to it has been blocked for several years by a private landowner who closed the East Fork of the Salmon River Road just below the beginning of this trail.

From the Little Boulder Creek Trail, there are two fine views of Castle Peak. One is from a meadow at 3.0 miles and another is from the large meadow at the junction with the Livingston Mill—Castle Divide Trail. Photographs of the view from this meadow of the furrowed dark face of Castle Peak and its burnt orange brother summit, Merriam Peak, have appeared in many books and national magazines, especially during the controversy over mining in the White Clouds in the early 1970s.

From the road at 6,220 feet, the first 1.8 miles of the trail climb 1,000 feet through sagebrush. There is only one grove of trees and no water. At 1.0 mile, the route parallels the red rock formations of Red Ridge. The path enters forest at 1.8 miles and comes close to Little Boulder Creek for the first time at 2.8 miles. A meadow choked with willows at 3.4 miles offers the first view of Castle Peak. The trail then climbs along the creek to the second large meadow at 6.0 miles. At the upper end of this meadow at 6.5 miles (8,160 feet), the trail joins the Livingston Mill – Castle Divide Trail.

83 BOULDER CHAIN LAKES TO BAKER LAKE

Map 29

round trip: 20.4 miles
elevation gain: 2,712 feet
elevation loss (return climb): 1,280 feet
this section one way: 2.6 miles, 312 feet gain, 575 feet loss
highest point: 9,560 feet on Livingston-Frog Lake Divide
map: Boulder Chain Lakes
time: 3 to 4 days
difficulty: strenuous
access: Follow directions in Hike 80 (Livingston Mill to Frog Lake) and Hike 81 (Boulder Chain Lakes) to hike from Livingston Mill to the first Boulder Chain Lake (Willow Lake):

Marsh grass nibbles at shallow, green Baker Lake beneath pearl gray granite ridges. Behind the ridge northwest of the lake, cylindrical orange towers corrugate the wall of Merriam Peak, the highest point on Serrate Ridge. Behind it to the left, the furrowed dark gray face of Castle Peak peers over a wooded ridge. If the Sawtooth National Recreation Area hadn't been formed in 1972, this ridge would now be an open pit molybdenum mine. Dilapidated cabins from the mine exploration still stand beside the lake.

Follow access directions in the hikes listed above to hike to the first Boulder Chain Lake (Willow Lake), 8,735 feet, where this hike description begins. Willow Lake is 8.5 miles with a 2,400-foot climb and 705-foot descent from Livingston Mill.

The trail leads down the wooded canyon of the outlet of Boulder Chain Lakes, and crosses the outlet of Waterdog Lake at .2 mile. At

.8 mile, the path is on an open sagebrush slope decorated with aspens. The way fords Little Boulder Creek at 1.2 miles, and at 1.3 miles, it meets the Little Boulder Creek Trail (8,160 feet). This trail descends 6.5 miles and 1,940 feet to the East Fork of the Salmon River Road in the CLOSED section.

Turn right (southwest) on the Castle Divide Trail and hike up wooded slopes to an unsigned path at 2.0 miles. Turn right (west) on this path and drop down to a prospect. Cross the outlet and climb a few feet to the lake (8,472 feet) at 2.6 miles. Campsites are few and small.

84 CASTLE LAKE

Map 29 or 23

round trip: 23.4 miles via Livingston Mill, 18.2 miles via Castle Divide
elevation gain: 3,699 feet via Livingston
elevation loss (return climb): 1,320 feet
this section one way: 1.5 miles, 947 feet gain, 40 feet loss from Baker Lake
highest point: 9,419 feet
map: Boulder Chain Lakes
time: 3 to 4 days
difficulty: cross-country for experts
access: Using directions in Hike 80 (Livingston to Frog Lake), hike to Baker Lake, or using directions in Hike 61 and Hike 67, hike over Castle Divide to a point .5 mile north of it.

Two snow-filled chimneys form a "V" on the charcoal gray face of Castle Peak above Castle Lake. The lake is so deep and the mountain so dark that the color of the water changes from blue green around the edges to navy blue in the middle. Talus surrounds the lake except for ledges, benches and whitebark pines at the lower end. At the northeast corner of the lake, below the orange sawteeth of Merriam Peak and Serrate Ridge, a rock peninsula sprinkled with bonsai-sized trees encloses a small turquoise bay.

To reach the beginning of this hike description, hike to Baker Lake, following the directions above. It is 10.2 miles and a 2,712-foot climb and 1,280-foot descent from Livingston Mill or 9.1 miles and a 2,105-foot climb and 2,513-foot descent from Germania Creek.

From Baker Lake (8,472 feet), take the right of two mining roads which leave the lake from the west side of a log bridge over the outlet. The road crosses a stream at .1 mile. At .4 mile, just past a clearcut area, the old trail over Castle Divide is close enough to see blazes. The track crosses another stream, switchbacks twice and splits at .5 mile. Go left up the right (west) side of the center of a ridge (9,204 feet). Where the road splits again at 1.0 mile, take the right (west) branch downhill, and then go up across a ravine.

Beyond the ravine, turn left (south) off the road onto a path up a sandy ridge to a spring and old log cabin. Go straight up the ridge above the cabin on a faint path to a .4 mile-long narrow flat area of grass and talus (9,300 feet) at 1.2 miles. There is no water in or near the flat. You can also reach this flat by descending 500 feet in .5 mile from Castle Divide and cutting west along the edge of the timber.

From the flat, the route to the lake is difficult and should only be attempted by experts. To find it, look up on the white scree ridge above you and notice a faint path angling to the right to dead trees and patches of dwarfed pines. Climb this path, using caution where the route has slid away. As it levels, the path curves around the north end of the ridge and plunges to the lake (9,419 feet) at 1.5 miles. There are several campsites among the ledges on the northeast side of the lake.

85 BAKER LAKE TO QUIET AND NOISY LAKES
Map 29

round trip: 24.2 miles
elevation gain: 3,482 feet
elevation loss (return climb): 1,280 feet
this section one way: 2 to 2.5 miles, 770 feet gain
highest point: 9,242 feet
map: Boulder Chain Lakes
time: 3 to 4 days
difficulty: Cross-country for experts
access: Using directions in Hike 80 (Livingston to Frog Lake) and Hike 83 (Boulder Chain to Baker Lake), hike to Baker Lake.

A pointed orange and gray peak guards the upper end of oval Noisy Lake. From the south side of its jade green water, apricot and gray cliffs

Hatchet Lake (second Boulder Chain Lake)

climb the splintery side of Serrate Ridge. A waterfall splashes in a niche in these cliffs most of the summer. Above Quiet Lake, Castle Peak spreads out into an orange and gray face covered with a network of avalanche troughs and outcrops resembling roof gables. From the upper end, the orange pleats and sawteeth of Serrate Ridge zigzag along from Castle Peak to Merriam Peak. The beginning of the route to these lakes climbs granite ledges beside a waterfall.

To reach Baker Lake, hike in from Livingston Mill, following directions given above. It is 10.2 miles and a 2,712-foot climb and 1,280-foot descent from Livingston Mill and 9.1 miles with a 2,105-

foot climb and 2,513-foot descent from Germania Creek to Baker Lake.

At the lake, cross the log bridge over the outlet. Take a path around the south side of the lake and ignore the mine road toward Castle Lake. The path disappears in a marsh. Ford the inlet and walk up its right (west) side to a talus slope with grass below it to the right of a waterfall on Slickenside Creek.. Find a path zigzagging northwest up ledges to the right of it. Descending these ledges with a pack is more difficult than going up. Paths go over to the gorge of the creek and end, but the easiest route stays well to the right of it.

At the top of the ledges 400 feet above Baker Lake, there is a definite path to the right (north) of the creek. The path winds through forest and granite benches to Noisy Lake (8,997 feet) at 1.2 miles.

The trail edges the north side of the lake in woods, crosses the inlet on slippery logs and climbs left (south) of this inlet to the lower end of Quiet Lake (9,242 feet) at 2.0 miles. To continue to the upper end at 2.5 miles, ford the outlet and go along the west shore of the lake on a faint path across grass and talus. One small campsite is at the lower end of the lake. There are several along the trail below the outlet and a few at the upper end.

86 SCREE AND SHALLOW LAKES
Map 29

round trip: 28.0 miles from Livingston
elevation gain: 3,825 feet
elevation loss (return climb): 1,743 feet
this section one way: 2.1 miles, 397 feet gain, 918 feet loss
highest point: 10,160 feet
map: Boulder Chain Lakes
time: 4 to 5 days
difficulty: expert
access: See Hike 81 (Boulder Chain Lakes) and Hike 80 (Livingston to Frog Lake).

The top of Serrate Ridge zigzags across the canyon from the turquoise water of Scree Lake. Whitebark pines cluster along the northeast side of the lake and pale orange granite ledges rim the opposite side. In Shallow Lake, large blocks of granite create pale green rectangles un-

derwater and white islands above it. A ridge containing the gray tower which guards the Devils Staircase stands above the head of the lake.

The trail above the ninth Boulder Chain Lake, Scoop Lake, which is shaped like the scoop of a diesel shovel, climbs through a notch called Windy Devil. It goes out onto a shelf and ends near the Devils Staircase. You can reach Shallow and Scree Lakes cross-country from this trail or from Quiet Lake through a slot in the rocks which is like a secret staircase.

This hike description begins at Scoop Lake (9,643 feet) 11.9 miles from Livingston Mill. For directions for reaching it, see the instructions above. The trail switchbacks across talus above Scoop Lake to a notch in the ridge at .7 mile. From the trail, the tenth lake, Headwall Lake, can be seen on a rocky shelf to the west. Snow may be on the trail here as late as mid-August. Beyond the notch, the trail turns right (west) and climbs an additional 150 feet to a flat, rocky basin where it ends 1.5 miles from Scoop Lake. Taking a cross-country route called the Devils Staircase from here to Born Lakes is not recommended because it is dangerous.

To go to Shallow Lake (9,635 feet), turn south off the trail where it turns west .8 mile from the lower end of Scoop Lake. Descend a ridge and the side of it to the shore. From the lower end of Shallow Lake at 1.3 miles, a trail connects the lakes on the north side of the creek. A few campsites are near this creek.

The path continues around the north side of Scree Lake (9,550 feet) and down its outlet on the left (northeast), then angles away from it to a slot in the cliffs. Descend the slot and follow the canyon of the outlet until it bends east and the pink granite ledges stop. Ford the creek and take a path south .2 mile to the lower end of Quiet Lake (9,242 feet) at 2.1 miles.

trails in the
SMOKY MOUNTAINS

Titus Lake

GALENA AREA

87 HEADWATERS OF THE SALMON RIVER

Map 31

round trip: 5 miles
elevation gain: 700 feet
highest point: 8,300 feet
maps: Frenchman Creek, Galena
time: 4 hours
difficulty: easy
access: From Highway 75 at the bottom of the Galena Summit grade in Sawtooth Valley 33.8 miles north of Ketchum, turn south at a sign for the Salmon River Road. Drive 3.2 miles on dirt road, ford a creek and drive 1.7 miles on primitive road to a ford of river.

This easy hike leads to the place where a branch of the main Salmon River begins in a wildflower meadow just below the divide between Sawtooth Valley and the canyon of Big Smoky Creek. In the meadow, rivulets collect into a three-foot wide stream which rushes down a ravine to begin the river. To the east, two lumpy gray shoulders of 10,225-foot Bromaghin Peak overlook the infant river. Across a divide from the meadow, tiers of cliffs decorate the canyon wall of Big Smoky Creek.

To reach the beginning of the hike, follow the directions above. Two branches join to form the road. At .9 mile, turn right at a sign for Chemeketan Campground. Just before reaching the campground in the woods, the road fords a side creek at 3.2 miles. In the campground, the road becomes primitive. At 3.4 miles, it circles the east edge of a boggy meadow. Park your car (unless you have four-wheel drive) at 4.9 miles, where the topo map shows the road branching at 7,600 feet.

Walk along the road. There are four fords of the river or a branch of it in the next .5 mile. There are no logs for hikers, so it is easiest to cross the river once and walk through sagebrush along the east side to the beginning of the jeep trail shown on the map.

Walk up the jeep trail as it climbs gently up and down in forest. At 1.3 miles, the track fords the river, which is only six feet wide, to

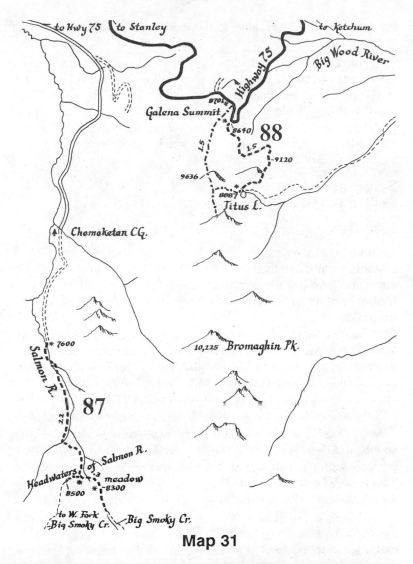

Map 31

the east where there are some campsites in a grassy area. From here, the road switchbacks left up a wooded hillside to a gate at 1.5 miles.

Take a path around the gate and continue up the road, which makes two switchbacks and then winds south along the edge of a 60-foot gorge. Just above the meadow at 2.2 miles, the route leaves the jeep trail. The trail drops into the meadow and fords the three-foot wide river at the lower end at 2.3 miles. The route goes around the northeast side of the meadow to the saddle of the divide (8,300 feet) at 2.5 miles.

From here, hike .5 mile down Big Smoky Creek to see its rugged canyon wall or hike .2 mile up the jeep trail with a 200-foot climb for a view of Bromaghin Peak and a second branch of the river. These two side trips will add 1.4 miles round trip to the hike and 600 feet of elevation gain. The Big Smoky Creek Trail descends 2,920 feet in 18.5 miles to Canyon Campground, which can be reached by road from Fairfield or Featherville.

88 TITUS LAKE
Map 31

round trip: 3 miles
elevation gain: 480 feet
elevation loss (return climb): 233 feet
highest point: 9,120 feet
map: Galena
time: 3 1/2 hours
difficulty: easy, expert for cross-country side trip to peak
access: 28.8 miles north of Ketchum, park .3 mile south of Galena Summit in a large turnout on the east side of road.

Willows and mountain bluebells separate the cloudy emerald green water of Titus Lake from a marshy meadow. A gray and orange ridge of crumbled ledges overlooks the miniature lake. Across Titus Creek, grooves divide the cliffs into lobes which rise to a scalloped skyline. South behind a saddle on the ridge, cliffs and snowbanks slope up to the pointed top of Bromaghin Peak.

From the top of either of the two unnamed peaks north of the lake, the jagged mountains of six ranges (the Sawtooths, Salmon River Mountains, White Clouds, Boulders, Pioneers and Smokies) stretch in every direction. In early July, blueflax, shooting star, phlox and arrowleaf balsamroot color the slopes along the trail.

To reach the trailhead (8,640 feet), follow the access directions. Go west across the highway to a dirt road leading south from the end of the highest big hairpin south of Galena Summit. Walk along the dirt road for 100 yards to a register box.

Take a trail to the left (southeast), crossing a small creek at .1 mile and another at .5 mile. The path runs east in forest along the side of a ridge and gradually climbs over a wrinkle in the ridge at .7 mile. Then it turns southwest at another wrinkle at 9,120 feet and dips into the canyon of the north branch of Titus Creek. At 1.2 miles, the trail turns west and descends 233 feet to the lake (8,887 feet) at 1.5 miles.

Expert hikers can climb .3 mile cross-country above the head of the lake onto a saddle between Peaks 9,921 and 9,636 and walk up either for a view. From here, walking north down the ridge to Galena Summit reaches a path 1.0 mile from the lake and the highway at 1.5 miles. From the outlet of the lake, a faint trail descends Titus Creek 1,598 feet in 3.5 miles to the highway across from Galena Lodge.

Wood River from Gladiator Creek Divide

Castle Lake

trails in the
BOULDER MOUNTAINS

Grand Prize Gulch

POLE CREEK AREA

89 GRAND PRIZE GULCH
Map 32

round trip: 8.4 miles to top of Galena Gulch—Grand Prize Divide, extra 1.0 mile (cross-country) to pond
elevation gain: 1,860 feet to top of divide, additional 100 feet to pond
highest point: 9,560 feet
map: Horton Peak
time: 7 1/2 hours
difficulty: expert
access: Go north on Highway 75 from Ketchum for 36 miles. Turn right (east) onto the Pole Creek Road. Keep right at the Pole Creek—Valley Road Junction at 2.3 miles. At 6.4 miles, turn right at a sign for Grand Prize Gulch and drive on this side road to the creek at 6.6 miles. Because of a 30-inch vertical bank, it is impossible to drive across the creek.

The destination of this hike is the divide between the Grand Prize Gulch and Galena Gulch trails where there is an excellent view. South are the orange and gray peaks of the Boulder Mountains, which are covered with talus, scree and crumbly cliffs. To the north are the creamy summits of the White Clouds. Near the divide, four rounded towers overlook a tiny amber pond. For directions for reaching a viewpoint of Deer Lakes on a ridge above the divide, see Hike 90 (Galena Gulch).

To reach the trailhead (7,700 feet) follow the access directions. Cross the creek on a log and walk up the old road through small lodgepoles. The road angles to the right, then goes back to the left. Avoid side roads.

At 1.5 miles, the road fords the creek to the east and switchbacks above it. Small trees are sprinkled over an old avalanche area across the creek. At a meadow where a road branches to the right, keep straight ahead. At 2.3 miles, the road turns left uphill to a prospect at a "trail" sign pointing right.

Take the trail across a flat meadow. The path climbs gently to the low point on the skyline ahead, reaching it at 3.3 miles. At 3.5 miles, a

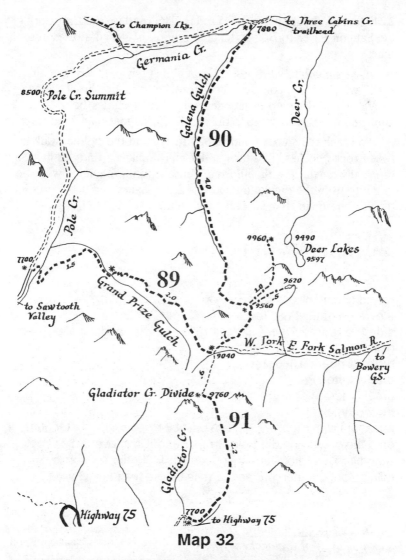

Map 32

rock cairn at 9,040 feet marks the junction with the Gladiator Creek Divide Trail.

Continue 100 yards on the main trail down the West Fork of the East Fork of the Salmon River and turn left off-trail. There isn't a path or sign for this Galena Gulch turnoff even though there is a trail shown on the topo map. (The main trail descends the West Fork of the East Fork, and the East Fork to Bowery Guard Station. It loses

2,240 feet of elevation in this 9.5 miles. The road up the East Fork of the Salmon River to Bowery Guard Station is closed at the present time.)

As you climb towards the Galena Gulch Divide, there are bits of paths which don't connect. The route angles northeast below a spring, which dries up in late season. Then it circles below a rock knoll and heads straight up to the saddle (9,560 feet) at 4.2 miles.

To reach the amber pond (9,620 feet) from the saddle, walk between rock benches. This tarn at 4.7 miles makes a fine destination, especially for those with children. Those with more energy will want to go up from the divide to a view of Deer Lakes at 9,960 feet. (See the description in Hike 90, Galena Gulch.)

90 GALENA GULCH
Map 32

round trip: 8 miles
elevation gain: 1,680 feet
side trip to view Deer Lakes: 1 mile one way, additional 600 feet gain
highest point: 9,560 feet
map: Horton Peak
time: 7 hours
difficulty: expert
access: From Highway 75, turn east 36 miles north of Ketchum onto the gravel and dirt Pole Creek Road. Drive over Pole Creek Summit to a ford of Germania Creek at 12.1 miles, which is .2 mile before another ford and .3 mile before the main Germania Creek trailhead.

In Galena Gulch, lumpy ridges banded with gray and apricot overlook a canyon of avalanche slopes crowded with tiny lodgepoles. The trail offers a view of the white, gold and red peaks around Washington Basin in the White Clouds. From the divide at the head of the canyon, a dark gray tooth on a wall of crumbly cliffs and orange mountains near Bowery Guard Station accents the Boulder Mountains to the south.

This trail allows a loop trip from Three Cabins Creek to Bowery. From a ridge above the divide, Deer Lakes are below hidden cliffs in a basin of gray rock and whitebark pines. Streaks of black sand show

Boulder Mountains from Galena Gulch Trail

through the water of the lower lake, and the upper lake resembles a melted green guitar.

To reach the trailhead (7,860 feet), follow access direction above. Two fords near the end of the road are not shown on the topo map. If you reach a sign for "narrow, steep road", you have driven too far. The unsigned trail begins east of the first ford at the south edge of a campsite at a sign saying "no motorized vehicles."

The trail crosses a tiny stream in moss, and at 150 yards goes left (east) on a footlog over Galena Gulch Creek. Next the path leads uphill away from the creek through Douglas firs, and returns to the ravine of the creek. At 1.0 mile is an avalanche area with small lodgepoles. When the path enters the grassy basin of another avalanche area at 1.3 miles, it disappears.

There are three more avalanche areas with open grassy slopes before the 2.0-mile point. In a few places, downed timber makes walking difficult. There are three additional avalanche areas in the next mile. Use the topo map to help find the trail in the woods beyond each grassy area. Below a meadow at 3.2 miles, the trail fords the creek back to the right (west). The path curves up into forest beneath crumbly outcrops, and goes over a small rock knoll.

Above a little meadow, the trail turns 90 degrees to the right (southwest). Walk along the right (west) side of the meadow to its upper end. Go south across its tiny stream at 3.5 miles and head up into forest. Be sure not to cross the stream at the lower end of the meadow or you'll lose the trail.

Watch for blazes, as some of the paths have been made by animals. The route stays at the edge of the forest below the rocky headwall until it crosses a scree slope just before reaching the saddle (9,560 feet) at 4.0 miles.

To see Deer Lakes, follow animal paths northeast up the sandy ridge. The ridge levels out at 9,960 feet, and the summit of an un-named peak is ahead. Turn left and walk north to a point 1.0 mile from the saddle. The lakes appear below hidden cliffs. North of these cliffs are steep scree slopes, and experts could descend to the lakes, which are at 9,490 and 9,597 feet.

GALENA AREA

91 GLADIATOR CREEK DIVIDE
Map 32

round trip: 4.4 miles
elevation gain: 2,060 feet
highest point: 9,760 feet
maps: Galena, Horton Peak
time: 5 hours
difficulty: strenuous
access: Turn north at Galena Lodge, 23 miles north of Ketchum. Drive 1.7 miles on a dirt road to register box.

This trail climbs steeply and gives a wide view of the Boulder and White Cloud Mountains. It makes you feel as if you are riding in a foot-powered glass elevator. Near the head of the canyon, two grassy basins stairstep up the headwall. On top of this wall, dark green whitebark pines and dark gray and burnt orange towers stand out against a pastel background.

From the divide, knobby gray and orange ridges line nearby canyons in the Boulder Mountains. To the north are the white peaks of the White Clouds, streaked with pink and gold, and the fluted white and orange-gray wall of Castle Peak.

To reach the trailhead, turn north at the Gladiator Creek sign just west of Galena Lodge. Drive 1.7 miles, past Westernhome Gulch and Senate Creek, to a register box at 7,700 feet.

The trail starts southeast as an old road. It gradually turns north, steepens and ends in trees at .5 mile. From here, the trail goes northeast through forest onto a sagebrush slope.

The trail climbs steeply, with only a rare switchback to the grassy basins just below the top. At .8 mile, where a gray peak with a brown top is visible ahead, the path crosses talus. The trail passes a grove of trees, and goes among tiny whitebark pines opposite orange mine tailings at 1.5 miles. It crosses to the right (east) of the creek, which is dry most of the summer.

The lower grassy basin is at 1.7 miles. Orange talus can be seen on the ridge ahead. At the head of the basin, the creek trickles down a rounded gray outcrop. The trail climbs to the right of it to a second, smaller basin at 2.0 miles. Then it goes up through whitebark pines to the divide (9,760 feet) at 2.2 miles.

The trail turns east for 100 feet along the crest of the divide, and drops off across talus. After a 520-foot descent in .6 mile, the trail joins the Grand Prize Gulch Trail at a point 100 yards south of its junction with the West Fork of the East Fork and Galena Gulch trails.

EASLEY AREA

92 SILVER LAKE

Map 33

round trip: 3 miles (2 miles cross-country)
elevation gain: 1,242 feet
highest point: 9,642 feet
map: Easley Hot Springs
time: 5 to 6 hours
difficulty: expert
access: 15.2 miles north of Ketchum on Highway 75, turn right (east) at a sign for Silver Creek. Drive across the bridge and up a steep primitive road on sagebrush and grass-covered hills. Avoid two roads turning left near the bottom. At .3 mile, where the road enters a gully four-wheel drive is needed. Take the right branch at 3 miles and park in an aspen grove at 3.4 miles.

Rocky benches, whitebark pines and subalpine firs ring the clear green water of Silver Lake. Silver-gray mountains sided with talus and broken cliffs enclose the lake basin. Above the lake, ponds and patches of meadow fill dents in gray and orange talus hills. At the mouth of the canyon, white rock between gray layers resembles dripping icing.

To reach the unmarked trailhead (8,400 feet) follow access directions above. Passenger cars will be able to drive only 2 miles up the road. From the aspen grove, walk north up the road to the top of a bluff where the road becomes a path. The route crosses a grassy slope blanketed with blue-violet whorled penstemon in season. At .2 mile, the path goes into the trees. It appears to cross a sandstone bluff at .3 mile, but it drops 50 vertical feet to the left and goes below it. The way continues in trees to a ravine and crosses it.

Beyond the ravine, the path disappears. Stay well above the main creek. At .7 mile, the route crosses talus and then goes through stickseed which covers hidden rocks.

At 1.0 mile, the creek splits into two cascades through wildflowers. At the top of the cascades, turn left (west) across the right stream and climb the right (north) side of the left stream., which splits in 100 yards. Climb the right side of its right branch. This is the middle creek shown on the map. The route goes left of a pale

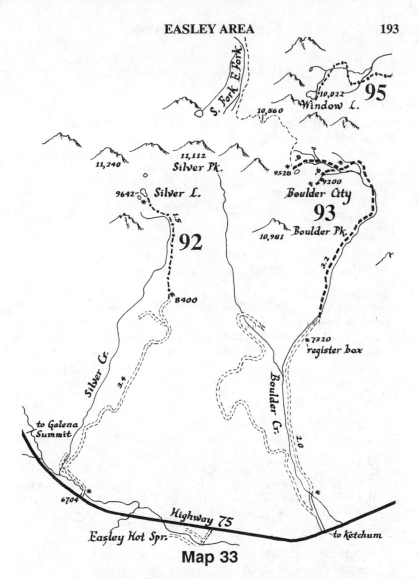

Map 33

orange knoll at 1.3 miles, then comes to a point where the creek splashes over a bluff.

Cross the creek to the left and follow a faint path to the top of this wall. Walk along rock benches left (west) of a bog to the lake (9,642 feet) at 1.5 miles. Two of three nearby ponds are located 200 yards to the southwest.

93 BOULDER BASIN

Map 33

round trip: 7.6 miles from register box to Boulder City, additional .8 mile one way to largest lake
elevation gain: 2,370 feet from ford to Boulder City, 1,880 feet from register box to city, 360 feet additional to lake
highest point: 9,528 feet
maps: Easley Hot Springs, Amber Lakes
time: 9 1/2 hours
difficulty: strenuous
access: 12.2 miles north of Ketchum, turn east on the Boulder Creek Road. For further directions, see description below.

A rusty boiler, tumbled mill building and cabins of silvered logs leaning at odd angles mark the location of Boulder City. Above the mill, a rusted tramway stretches up the mountain to a mine below crinkled peaks. Nearby, meadows sprinkled with gentians in season, fringe a small aquamarine lake below rock buttresses. Behind the buttresses, curving stripes of pink, white and orange swirl across the gray face of Boulder Peak.

A jeep trail leads to Boulder City and the lake, but the upper section is so rough that four-wheel drive vehicles can be damaged. To reach the trailhead, turn right (north) 12.2 miles north of Ketchum on Highway 75 on the Boulder Creek Road. At .2 mile where the Left Fork of Boulder Creek Road turns off, keep right (east) on the Boulder Creek Road to a ford of Boulder Creek at .5 mile. In early season, four-wheel drive may be needed here. If in doubt, park before the ford (6,750 feet), 5.8 miles from Boulder City.

Across the ford, the road goes through sagebrush near the creek to a campsite in forest at 1.8 miles. Leave passenger cars at 2.0 miles at a register box (7,320 feet). Those with pickups can continue to a log cabin at 2.5 miles (7,560 feet). The road crosses the creek to the west at 2.9 miles. The ford and the road beyond it require four-wheel drive, but there is no parking between the log cabin and the ford. Leave four-wheel drive cars at the "mine dump" shown on the map at 3.3 miles (7,920 feet) and start hiking. Park on a branch road beside the creek.

Cabin at Boulder City in Boulder Basin

The main road goes along the base of a talus slope for .4 mile. In the trees beyond this, the road splits. There are several divisions in the next mile. Most of these soon rejoin, so it doesn't matter which you take. Water runs over all of them and some have mudholes. When the track fords the creek to the north at 4.6 miles, the roads have all rejoined.

In a basin of little trees at 4.8 miles, the road makes a sharp left (west) turn. At 5.0 miles, it crosses a branch of the creek to the left (south) in sand in a big meadow. At 5.2 miles (9,100 feet), the road splits. The right fork goes to tiny lakes at the head of the canyon, while the left one goes to Boulder City.

The left branch crosses to the south of the main creek in a ravine at 5.4 miles. The road crosses another part of the creek at 5.7 miles and goes out into a grassy basin below talus and crags. Two leaning cabins are on the left and on the right up the hill are the old mill and tramway at 5.8 miles (9,200 feet).

Back at the junction, the right branch of the road goes through woods north of the creek in a gorge. The gorge ends at 5.7 miles. The road skirts a meadow on the right, and fords the creek to the left (south). The road comes to a T-intersection at the head of the meadow at 5.8 miles. Take the left fork, which makes a hairpin turn, to reach the largest lake (9,528 feet) 6.0 miles from the ford.

The right branch at the "T" goes past tiny ponds and through talus to a pass at 10,560 feet. From here an unmaintained trail descends the South Fork of the East Fork of the Salmon River 3,400 feet in 7.5 miles to a trail along the East Fork 4.5 miles above Bowery Guard Station.

NORTH FORK AREA

94 EAST FORK OF NORTH FORK BIG WOOD RIVER

Map 35

round trip: 7 miles
elevation gain: 1,460 feet
highest point: 8,300 feet at end of official trail
maps: Amber Lakes, Rock Roll Canyon
time: 8 1/2 hours
difficulty: expert
access: From Highway 75 at SNRA Headquarters 7.4 miles north of Ketchum, drive 3.9 miles on the gravel and dirt North Fork Road to a side road .3 mile past Camp Manapu. Drive .3 mile up the north branch of the side road to its end.

This trail is a pleasant walk below crumbly orange, apricot and gray peaks. Half way up, an enormous snowbank covered with the pine needles of many avalanches spans the creek. Beyond this point, downed timber covers much of the trail. There is a good chance no one else will be around, so look for wildlife.

From the end of the trail, you can climb cross-country over a 10,000-foot divide to a trail connecting Trail Creek with the West Fork of Trail Creek. The East Fork of the North Fork Trail is not maintained, and this provides opportunities for volunteers, especially from the nearby church camps, to do some work on it.

To reach the trailhead, follow the access directions. After turning off the North Fork Road, follow the left (north) branches of the side road. Avoid a road uphill to an aspen clump. Use caution when the road drops down the side of a small hill. Park passenger cars before the hill. Others can park on the other side of the hill where the road splits. Walk along the right fork until it becomes a trail.

At first, grassy slopes alternate with groves of Douglas fir. At .7 mile, the path enters forest, but at 1.0 mile it comes out into another open area across from talus cross-hatched with animal paths. Then the trail goes through 200 yards of timber close to the creek. At 1.2 miles, the way climbs above the creek between talus and forest.

The path ascends along an open hillside at 1.3 miles. It reaches the needle-covered snowbank at 1.9 miles, and fords a side creek at 7,650 feet. Then the sketchy trail returns to forest well away from the East Fork. The route threads forest and two narrow open areas with much downed timber. At 2.5 miles, in another open area below a pinkish-gray mountain, willows line the canyon bottom.

After going through a strip of trees, the path reaches a grassy open area where the canyon curves left. The trail is hard to find in thick downed timber in the woods beyond. The path crosses two small side creeks and ends. You may want to continue a few yards to a fork in the canyon at 3.5 miles (8,300 feet) for a better view of a wide peak of apricot talus up the rugged East Fork Canyon.

95 WEST FORK OF NORTH FORK BIG WOOD RIVER AND WINDOW LAKE

Map 34

round trip: 9 miles (3.4 miles cross-country) to Window Lake, 7.6 miles to end of West Fork North Fork of Big Wood River Trail
elevation gain: 3,122 feet to Window Lake, 2,260 feet to end of trail
highest point: 10,022 feet
maps: Amber Lakes, Easley Hot Springs
time: 10 hours
difficulty: expert
access: Turn right (east) 7.4 miles north of Ketchum at the SNRA Headquarters and drive on dirt road to end of the road at 5 miles.

Red and white mountain heath, marsh marigold, alpine buttercup and dwarf lupine create an alpine garden among the pink, orange and gray rocks around blue-green Window Lake. On a knoll above the shore stand the only trees, dwarfed and flattened whitebark pines. From the colorful rocks, talus rises to crumbling gray peaks. A rough cross-country route from the West Fork of the North Fork of the Wood River Trail reaches Window Lake. If you choose instead to go to the end of

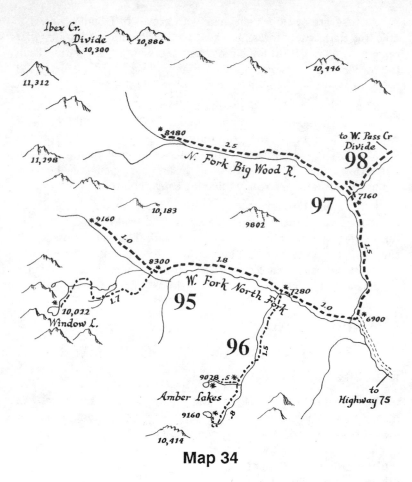

Map 34

that trail, you will find a wide valley of wildflowers below sheer-walled peaks. At the head of this valley, a feathery waterfall glides down a niche in a black cliff. Along the lower parts of this trail, other waterfalls hide in mossy gorges.

To reach the trailhead, follow access directions above. From the end of the road (6,900 feet) ford the North Fork of the Big Wood River to the west bank. The trail starts as an old road in the woods. Beyond a register box at 150 yards, the trail turns left off the road and begins to climb within 200 yards. It returns to the creek in an avalanche area full of little trees. At Amber Gulch at 1.0 mile, the trail turns up to the right, and descends to an open area of stumps and grass.

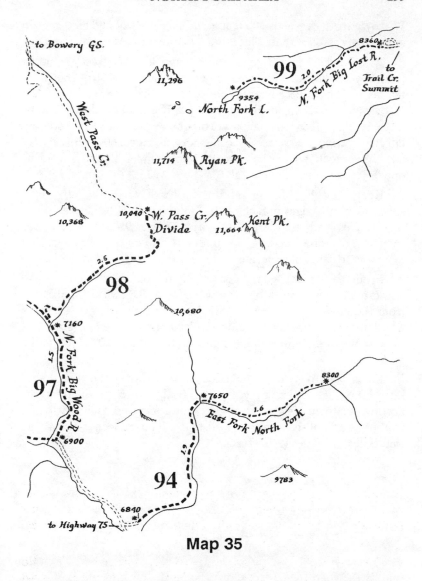

to Bowery GS.

8360

99   2.0   N. Fork Big Lost R.   to Trail Cr. Summit

11,296

9354

North Fork L.

11,714   Ryan Pk.

10,368   10,040   W. Pass Cr. Divide   Kent Pk.   11,664

West Pass Cr.

2.5

98

10,680

7160

57

N. Fork Big Wood R.

97   8300

7650   1.6

6900   East Fork North Fork

1.9

94   9783

6840

to Highway 75

Map 35

At 1.5 miles, the trail disappears in a meadowy area 1.2 miles long. There is a view of peaks above Window Lake. A path close to a waterfall at the head of the open area is not the trail; the correct route is uphill. At 2.3 miles, the trail reappears in the trees 100 feet above the creek and climbs in woods with occasional switchbacks.

When the path descends 100 feet at 2.6 miles, a wooded side canyon appears across the creek. This is not the canyon of Window Lake.

At 2.8 miles, a narrow open area of grass and tiny trees extending vertically up the ridge is across the creek. This open strip shown on the map is the easiest route to Window Lake. Leave the trail at 8,300 feet, cross the creek and climb this slope. The total climb to Window Lake is 3,122 feet, so plan accordingly. At 3.5 miles, where the hillside becomes less steep for a short distance 600 vertical feet above the creek, turn right (west) to two streams. The right (north) one descends from Window Lake.

Keep left of both streams at first. In .1 mile where the left stream splits, climb the right branch of this split, which is usually dry, in a ravine. This leads to a large flat grassy area at 9,400 feet, which is shown on the topo map as a wide interval between contour lines. You may want to camp here because there is no level ground at the lake.

From the flat area, go right (north) to the outlet of Window Lake and cross it to the north below a waterfall at 3.8 miles. Climb away from the creek around a rock bench, and return to it at 4.1 miles where it meets a creek from a pond. Ford back to the left (south) of the creek and walk over rock benches to the lake (10,022 feet) at 4.5 miles.

If you want to go to the end of the trail instead of the lake, do not turn off at 2.8 miles. Stay on the trail, which gradually turns northwest into an open valley of grass and rocks at 3.0 miles, where a feathery waterfall is seen in the distance. The trail ends below the waterfall at 3.8 miles (9,160 feet).

96 AMBER LAKES
Map 34

round trip: 6.6 miles to higher lake, 1.0 mile additional to see lower lake also
elevation gain: 2,260 feet
highest point: 9,160 feet
map: Amber Lakes
time: 9 hours
difficulty: expert
access: Leave Highway 75 at the SNRA Headquarters 7.4 miles north of Ketchum. Drive 5 miles on the gravel and dirt North Fork of Big Wood River Road.

In some lights, the two tiny Amber Lakes reflect amber-colored peaks, but in others, they reflect the blue of the sky. Jumbled pieces of silvered wood from old avalanches line the edges of both shallow lakes and debris from a recent avalanche has flattened the trees at the upper lake. The climb provides excellent views of the colorfully striped Boulder Mountains. This is a rough cross-country hike and scramble for patient experts only, as the trail has almost disappeared under repeated avalanches (if there ever was a constructed trail).

To reach the trailhead, follow access directions above. Hike 1.0 mile along the West Fork of the North Fork of the Wood River Trail. The Amber Lakes turnoff (7,280 feet) is just beyond a split in the trail in an open grassy area with a few dead trees. Turn off before the main trail turns up 90 degrees into woods. You can see the gulch across the canyon. At 1.0 mile, cairns mark a faint path down to a ford of the West Fork of the North Fork.

On the other side, the path crosses to the left (east) of the stream from Amber Gulch. The trail climbs straight up without switchbacks. At 1.3 miles, the path leads below a small boulder field and then down to the creek. Do not follow a path with cairns up the hillside because downed timber above is thick. Instead, take a path in grass and firs at the edge of the willows and along the steep stream bank.

The trail curves into a side gully to avoid downed timber, and turns up the gulch again. It disappears at 1.7 miles in a grassy bowl full of little trees. A cairn beside the creek marks where the trail crosses to the right (west) bank.

Beyond this point, there are only occasional bits of trail. Blazes in the woods are hard to find because of downed timber. The route continues up a wooded ridge to another grassy valley at 2.5 miles, where the outlet of the lower lake cascades into the gulch.

To reach the lower lake, climb .5 mile up the ledges and grass on the right (north) of this creek to the lake (9,028 feet). To reach the upper lake, climb to the right of a small wooded knoll and pass left (east) of the round pond shown on the map 2.8 miles from the trailhead. The way continues up grassy slopes next to the creek with woods above on both sides.

Beyond a wooded hill at 3.0 miles, the canyon opens out into a meadow. The route to Konrad Creek shown going south on the map does not exist. The climb to the lake (9,160 feet) at 3.3 miles is easier on the left side of the creek from this point, but no path or blazes exist. From either lake, hikers can reach the other by climbing over a saddle between them.

97 NORTH FORK OF BIG WOOD RIVER
Map 34

round trip: 8 miles
elevation gain: 1,620 feet
elevation loss (return climb): 40 feet
highest point: 8,480 feet
maps: Amber Lakes, Ryan Peak
time: 6 1/2 to 7 hours
difficulty: moderate
access: 7.4 miles north of Ketchum, turn right (north) at SNRA Headquarters. Drive 5 miles on gravel and dirt to the trailhead.

This hike through wildflower meadows under the orange and gray Boulder Mountains passes a series of waterfalls hiding in chasms. Avalanches have created these meadows by repeatedly felling trees, and avalanche areas stretch up the canyon walls. Some are beginning to be filled with tiny subalpine firs. From the upper trail, the pleated, jagged top of Kent Peak bars the lower canyon. At 4.0 miles, the trail disappears in downed timber, but energetic experts can hike cross-country another 1.5 miles and 1,800 vertical feet to a 10,300-foot divide overlooking Ibex Creek.

Canyon of the North Fork of the Big Wood River

To reach the trailhead (6,900 feet), follow access directions above. The trail first climbs 80 feet up a wooded ridge, then goes down to the edge of the creek. Next, it climbs the side of the canyon to avoid a washout, then returns to the creek at a grassy flat at .4 mile. Where the official trail fords the river to the west bank for .4 mile, it is easier to stay on the east bank and climb a steep path onto an open hillside, and across it to a sagebrush flat at .6 mile. After a stretch of woods at .8 mile, the path rejoins the main trail in another sagebrush flat.

The trail next crosses some talus and two or three side creeks. It makes a 100-foot long hairpin turn to the right in the forest and comes back. The route again goes straight up the canyon in a smaller sagebrush flat. In this flat at 1.5 miles, cairns and a path mark the turnoff for the trail up West Pass Creek Divide.

The main trail returns to the edge of the creek in willows. The first of the wildflower-sagebrush meadows is at 2.0 miles and there is a view of peaks and avalanche chutes. The creek runs in cascades and then in a gorge. To avoid confusion, watch for cairns marking the path through the meadows.

At 2.4 miles, cross a side stream and climb an outcrop. At a gully full of rye grass, the trail ascends a bluff to the left. At 2.6 miles, waterfalls in a gorge are close as the trail goes back into trees. The way levels at a campsite, and at 2.7 miles, it enters another long meadow. At the far end of it at 3.6 miles, the trail climbs another bluff and traverses more woods. A third, much shorter open area with downed trees is at 3.7 miles. The route fords a side creek, but it does not cross the river at 3.6 and 3.7 miles as shown on the map. Beyond the point where the river splits into a "Y" at 3.8 miles, the trail enters the woods. At 4.0 miles (8,480 feet) it disappears in downed timber.

98 WEST PASS CREEK DIVIDE
Map 35

round trip: 8 miles
elevation gain: 3,140 feet
highest point: 10,040 feet
maps: Ryan Peak, Amber Lakes
time: 8 hours
difficulty: strenuous
access: 7.4 miles north of Ketchum on Highway 75, turn north on the North Fork of Wood River Road at SNRA Headquarters. Drive 5 miles on gravel and dirt to the trailhead.

Across West Pass Creek from this divide, Glassford Peak and the peaks around it are tinted red, gold and orange. In the distance east of these peaks float the white peaks of the White Clouds. Above the divide, the orange-streaked cliffs of Ryan Peak merge with the crinkled wall of towers of Kent Peak. This trail climbs almost 3,000 feet in 2.5 miles, so plan for the steep ascent.

To reach the trailhead, follow access directions above. For the first 1.5 miles of the trail along the North Fork of the Wood River, detailed directions are given in Hike 97 (North Fork of the Wood River). On this trail beyond a long sagebrush area in forest at 1.5 miles, the trail turns 90 degrees to the right for 100 yards. It comes back 180 degrees and then goes straight up the canyon into a sagebrush flat. In the flat (7,160 feet), cairns mark an unsigned trail to the right (east).

Take this path to the edge of the forest where blazes begin. The trail angles up the canyon for 200 yards, and makes two switchbacks, each 400 yards long, in the forest. At 2.0 miles, the way comes to the edge of the canyon of a branch of the North Fork of the Big Wood River where a waterfall plunges below. The trail turns up the canyon on an open slope. It hops two small side creeks, which are dry in late season, and goes below a grove of Douglas firs.

At the head of a gorge at 2.8 miles, the trail returns to the creek. After crossing a third side creek, the path climbs scree and talus. At 3.0 miles, the creek splits in a basin full of tiny subalpine firs. Above, rock ledges stairstep a dark gray triangular peak.

The route curves west in whitebark pines near a marginal campsite at 3.2 miles. The trail edges the creek at 3.4 miles, and disappears in moss. It winds northwest up a steep rocky slope onto a talus ridge dotted with whitebark pines. At 3.7 miles, the path runs along left of a gully across from a burnt orange outcrop. It goes into a grass and talus basin at 3.8 miles. After climbing the head of this basin, the trail disappears in turf below the top of the divide at 4.0 miles. On the other side, the trail descends the canyon of West Pass Creek 2,000 feet in 2.5 miles to a road from Bowery Guard Station.

TRAIL CREEK AREA

99 NORTH FORK LAKE

Map 35

round trip: 4 miles
elevation gain: 994 feet
highest point: 9,354 feet
maps: Meridian Peak, Ryan Peak
time: 6 1/2 hours
difficulty: expert (all cross-country)
access: From Main Street in Ketchum, drive on the paved and gravel Trail Creek Road over Trail Creek Summit. At 20.6 miles, turn left (west) on the dirt North Fork of the Big Lost River Road and drive along it to Blind Creek at 30.8 miles. Turn left and cross the North Fork on a bridge. Continue on a primitive road, and take the right branch at 32 miles. At a split in the road at 32.9 miles, go left and park in aspens at 33.3 miles.

The narrow strip of aquamarine North Fork Lake separates a gray mountain wall from an orange one. At the head of the lake, orange rock meets gray in a row of orange cylinders divided by strips of gray. Gray talus on the south side of the lake rises to a sheer gray wall, and orange talus on the north slopes up to a mottled orange mountain. This cross-country hike is the only one in this book which is just over the border from the Sawtooth National Recreation Area. Possibly, it will be included in the proposed White Cloud-Boulder Mountain Wilderness so it is described here.

To reach the beginning of this hike, follow access directions above. Above the parking area, red, orange, gray and cream twisted stripes scribble the high peaks of the Boulder Mountains. Walk southwest up the ridge for 200 yards. You can follow the ridge through downed timber and across steep talus, but it is much more difficult than going up the creek.

Turn right off the ridge and gradually descend to the North Fork at .5 mile, where a side branch joins from the west. Climb south away from the creek a few yards onto a wrinkle to stay out of the creek's ravine. At a meadow at 1.0 mile, ford the creek to the right (north). The route climbs a steep slope with ledges and then goes above a 100-foot gorge. Be careful.

Above this, the slope lessens and the gorge widens opposite a slope of tiny firs and downed timber. At 1.3 miles, go down to the creek and walk along the grass beside it. Keep well away from the creek at 1.5 miles as you climb along a steep grassy hillside. After the ground flattens at 1.7 miles, walk through grass to the lower end of the lake at 2.0 miles.

APPENDIX
TRAILS NOT COVERED IN TEXT

Sawtooths

BENCH CREEK: Access: Highway 21. From Highway 21, .4 mile south of road to Bull Trout Lake, southeast to Swamp Creek Trail .1 mile north of Marten Lake. Only .7 mile of this trail is in the SNRA. 5.5 miles, 1,280 feet gain, 644 feet loss. Map: Banner Summit.

BENEDICT CREEK: Access: Grandjean. From South Fork of Payette River Trail 2.9 miles above Elk Lake, southwest to junction of Queens River Trail and trail to Benedict Lake. Trail from this junction to Spangle Lakes, considered a part of Benedict Creek Trail, is covered in text. 3.5 miles, 960 feet gain. Map: Mt. Everly.

BRAXON LAKE: Access: Grandjean or Redfish Inlet Transfer Camp. Originally from Baron Creek Trail 1.0 mile below Baron Lake to old trail crew camp below Braxon Lake. Now peters out half way to lakes. Not maintained, not shown on maps. Mileage and elevation gain not available. Map: Warbonnet Peak.

BULL MOOSE: Access: Decker Flat. From Decker Flat to Redfish—Decker Lake Trail .2 mile southwest of junction with Redfish Ridge Trail. 4.5 miles, 1,020 feet gain. Map; Mt. Cramer.

DIAMOND LAKE: Access: Atlanta. From Little Queens River Trail .3 mile west of Browns Lake Junction to Diamond Lake. Old trail, no longer maintained and not on any maps. Fords river, steep. .9 mile, 640 feet gain. Map: Nahneke Mountain.

ELK CREEK: Access: Elk Meadows or Stanley Lake. From Elk Meadows-Elizabeth Lake Junction south up to Elk Summit and then east down to Stanley Lake Creek Trail. 9.5 miles, 1,780 feet gain, 1,520 feet loss. Maps: Banner Summit, Grandjean, Stanley Lake.

EUREKA GULCH (jeep trail): Access: Alturas Lake Road. From Alturas Lake Road .3 mile west of ford of Alpine Creek to mines of old mining settlement of Eureka. No buildings. Good view of Alpine Creek Canyon. 3.0 miles, 1,580 feet gain. Maps: Snowyside Peak, Marshall Peak.

FLAT TOP LAKES: Access: Queens River Road. From Scenic Lakes Trail 2.5 miles from Little Queens River to first of two Flat Top Lakes. No path, just a line of blazes. .7 mile, 800 feet gain. Map: Nahneke Mountain.

HUCKLEBERRY CREEK: Access: Decker Flat. From Decker Flat southwest to Redfish-Decker Lake Trail .7 mile north of Hell Roaring Lake. 3.8 miles, 1,430 feet gain. Map: Mt. Cramer.

JOE DALEY: Access: Atlanta. From Queens River Trail south to roads near Atlanta airstrip which lead to bridge and Riverside Campground. Very steep trail. 4.5 miles, 1,320 feet gain. Map: Atlanta West.

JOHNSON CREEK (near Graham): Access: road to Graham Guard Station. From Johnson Creek Campground east and north to Bayhouse Trail. Upper end covered in text. Four fords of creek. 5.0 miles, 700 feet gain. Maps: Swanholm Peak, Nahneke Mountain.

JOHNSON CREEK (North Fork Ross Fork): Access: Alturas Creek Road. From Mattingly Creek Divide Trail south past a junction with the North Fork of Ross Fork Trail at .6 mile, then southeast to Ross Fork of Boise River. Provides cross-country access to Johnson Lake and access to Ross Fork, Perkons and Bass Lakes without the need to drive around by Dollarhide Summit or Fairfield. 7.6 miles, 235 feet gain, 2,055 feet loss. Map: Marshall Peak.

MEADOW CREEK: Access: BLOCKED by posted private land. From pasture 3.0 miles southwest of Stanley to Alpine Way Trail 2.8 miles north of Marshall Lake. 1.2 miles, 450 feet gain. Map: Stanley Lake.

NEINMEYER CREEK: Access: Queens River Road or Graham Road. From Johnson Creek Trail .6 mile south of Bayhouse Trail Junction southeast over Grouse Creek Pass down into Black Warrior Creek, over another divide and down to the Little Queens River 6.2 miles from the trailhead. 7.6 miles, 2,320 feet gain, 2,080 feet loss. Parts of the trail are very narrow on steep side hills and so it is not recommended for stock. Map: Nahneke Mountain.

NORTH FORK OF BOISE RIVER: Access: Grandjean or Silver Creek trailhead on Graham Road. From South Fork Payette River Trail 3.8 miles from Grandjean south to Bayhouse Trail 1.0 mile east of Graham Road. North end begins with 120-foot ford of South Fork of Payette, which can be dangerous or impassable in early summer. South end connects with trail to Graham Road, a rough, primitive road recommended only for four-wheel drive vehicles. 11.8 miles,

2,271 feet gain, 1,656 feet loss. Maps: Edaho Mountain, Nahneke Mountain, Swanholm Peak.

PICKET MOUNTAIN: Access: Grandjean. From North Fork of Boise River Trail over Picket Mountain (within 100 feet of summit) and out of the SNRA to junction with Wapiti Creek Trail. 4.5 miles, 1,404 feet gain, 280 feet loss. Map: Edaho Mountain.

REDFISH RIDGE: Access: Decker Flat Road. From Bull Moose Trail .2 mile from trailhead to Grand Mogul Trail 2.5 miles from Sockeye Campground. 3.0 miles, 740 feet gain. Maps: Mt. Cramer, Stanley.

SMILEY CREEK: Access: Smiley Creek Road. From Vienna south to divide between Smiley Creek and West Fork of Big Smoky Creek. Covered in *"Trails of Western Idaho"* by the author. 3.0 miles, 1,440 feet gain. Map: Frenchman Creek.

SWAMP CREEK: Access: Highway 21. From .7 mile south of Thatcher Creek Campground to Trap Creek Trail at Marten Lake. 6.0 miles, 910 feet gain. Map: Banner Summit.

THREE ISLAND LAKE: Access: From Atlanta or Grandjean or Yellow Belly Lake. From Benedict Creek Trail between Rock Slide and Benedict Lakes south to Three Island Lake. .6 mile, 200 feet gain. Map: Mt. Everly.

White Clouds

BIG LAKE CREEK: Access: East Fork of Salmon River Road. From end of 1.3-mile spur road up Big Lake Creek northwest past Jimmy Smith Lake at .2 mile and then west up Big Lake Creek to French Creek Jeep Trail 1.5 miles north of Railroad Ridge. Most of trail in sagebrush. 10.5 miles, 3,020 feet gain. Maps: Potaman Peak, Livingston Creek.

BLUETT CREEK: Access: East Fork of Salmon River. From East Fork of Salmon River Road west and then north to Big Lake Creek Trail 5.8 miles from trailhead. Not signed, not maintained, not on topo map. About 6 miles, 2,500 feet gain. Map: Potaman Peak.

CHAMBERLAIN CREEK: Access: Pole Creek—Germania Creek Road. From Germania Creek Trail to Livingston—Castle Divide Trail .5 mile east of the lowest Chamberlain Lake. 2.3 miles along trail, Chamberlain Creek Falls lies in chasm .2 mile south of

Galena Peak and Boulder Mountains from Governor's Punchbowl

trail. Provides loop to Chamberlain Lakes and back by way of Washington Creek. 3.7 miles, 2,190 feet gain. Map: Boulder Chain Lakes.

CHAMPION CREEK: Access: Valley Road through private land. From spur road up Champion Creek east to Champion Lakes (and on to Germania Creek, which is covered in text). From trailhead to lower lake 6.7 miles, 1,513 feet gain. Maps: Washington Peak, Horton Peak.

FRENCH CREEK: Access: Highway 75 between Sunbeam and Clayton. From Highway 75, 1 mile east of Yankee Fork Guard Station south to Railroad Ridge. Former jeep trail, now closed to vehicles. 11.5 miles, 4,160 feet gain. Maps: Clayton, Potaman Peak, Livingston Creek.

GARLAND CREEK: Access: Rough Creek or Boundary Creek. From Rough Creek Trail 4.5 miles from trailhead east to Warm Springs Creek 6.8 miles south of Robinson Bar. 5.5 miles, 2,020 feet loss. Maps: Casino Lakes, Robinson Bar.

GOVERNORS PUNCHBOWL: Access: Highway 75, 25.3 miles north of Ketchum. From parking area north of highway to small, greenish-gray pond. Trail is only a strip cleared of timber long ago for a stock driveway. Lower part marked with yellow stock driveway signs. Starts along branch road closest to highway leading west. Unsigned, no path after the first 200 yards, rough ground. Beautiful wildflowers and view of Boulder Mountains. 1.2 miles, 1,672 feet gain. Map: Horton Peak.

HORTON PEAK: Access: Valley Road. From spur road at Taylor Creek to lookout no longer manned. Excellent view of Castle Peak. Poor condition, not signed, no water. 3.5 miles, 2,956 feet gain. Maps: Horton Peak, Alturas Lake.

LITTLE CASINO CREEK: Access: From Highway 75, 3 miles east of Stanley by Big Casino Creek Bridge. From dirt road along river southwest to junction with Boundary Creek Trail. 9.0 miles, 2,800 feet gain. Maps: East Basin Creek, Casino Lakes.

LITTLE REDFISH LAKE: Access: Livingston Mill—Frog Lake Trail. From that trail 1.5 miles south of junction with Big Boulder Creek Trail southeast to Little Redfish Lake. 1.0 mile, 400 feet gain. Map: Boulder Chain Lakes.

LOOKOUT MOUNTAIN: Access: Rough Creek. From Rough Creek Trail 3.1 miles from trailhead northeast to summit of Lookout Mountain. Lookout no longer manned but slated for restoration. 2.5 miles, 420 feet gain. Map: Casino Lakes.

MARTIN CREEK: Access: Rough Creek or Boundary Creek. From Big Casino—Boundary Creek Junction southeast to Martin Creek and east to Warm Springs Creek at north end The Meadows. 6.0 miles, 1,680 feet loss. Maps: Casino Lakes, Robinson Bar.

RED RIDGE: Access: East Fork of Salmon River Road. From that road west along Red Ridge to Livingston—Frog Lake Trail near divide. Not signed, not on topo map, hard to follow in sagebrush. About 9 miles long, about 3,500 feet gain and 700 feet loss. Maps: Bowery Creek, Boulder Chain Lakes.

SULLIVAN LAKE: Access: From Highway 75, 2.5 miles east of Yankee Fork Ranger Station. From dirt road of ranch 200 yards off highway to Sullivan Lake. Covered in *"Trails of Western Idaho."* Unsigned, mostly sagebrush, but colorful canyon. 2.6 miles, 1,170 feet gain. Maps: Clayton, Potaman Peak.

SUNNY GULCH: Access: Highway 75 at Sunny Gulch Campground. From Sunny Gulch Campground to Little Casino Creek Trail 3.5 miles northwest of Boundary Creek Junction. No bridge over Salmon River at beginning of trail. Not on topo map. About 1.5 miles, 1,040 feet gain. Map: Stanley.

WARM SPRINGS CREEK (lower): Access: From Highway 75 BLOCKED by posted private property and gate. Other access from

Aztec Mine and Pigtail Creek Trail (see Hike 68, The Meadows and Hike 69, Williams Creek). Four fords of Warm Springs Creek and five fords of large side creeks. Provides cross-country access to Swimm Lake via Swimm Creek. 11.2 miles from Salmon River to The Meadows, 1,360 feet gain. Map: Robinson Bar.

WASHINGTON BASIN TO CHAMPION LAKES: Access: Washington Basin Jeep Trail. From jeep trail to Champion Lakes Trail at Upper Champion Lake. 1.8 miles, 680 feet gain. Map: Washington Peak.

WICKIUP CREEK: Access: East Fork of Salmon River Road in section CLOSED by gate and posted private land. Other access from Livingston–Castle Divide Trail. From East Fork of Salmon River Road southwest and then northwest to Castle Divide Trail .6 mile north of divide. Not maintained. 7.0 miles, 3,140 feet gain. Maps: Bowery Creek, Boulder Chain Lakes.

Boulders

BOWERY CUTOFF: Access: Access to Bowery Guard Station is CLOSED by gate and posted private property on East Fork of Salmon River Road north of Little Boulder Creek Trail. Hot spring 1.0 mile from guard station. From Germania Creek Trail 6.7 miles east of Three Cabins Creek trailhead to Bowery Guard Station. 4.5 miles, 1,660 feet gain, 2,000 feet loss. Maps: Boulder Chain Lakes, Galena Peak, Ryan Peak.

KONRAD CREEK: Access: Highway 75 at Wood River Campground near SNRA Headquarters. From Wood River Campground to head of canyon. Unsigned. Does not continue to Amber Lakes. Not on topo map. About 2.5 miles and 2,200 feet gain. Map: Amber Lakes.

SOUTH FORK EAST FORK SALMON RIVER: Access: Bowery Guard Station, but access CLOSED by gate and posted private property on East Fork of Salmon River Road north of Little Boulder Creek. Other access from West Fork East Fork Trail or Highway 75 via Boulder Basin. From Bowery Guard Station south to divide above Boulder Basin. Section from station to West Fork East Fork shown as road is not open to four-wheeled vehicles. Section from West Fork East Fork Trail to Boulder Basin not maintained, hard to find. 12.0 miles, 3,790 feet gain. Maps: Easley Hot Springs, Galena Peak.

WEST FORK OF EAST FORK SALMON RIVER: Access: Grand Prize Gulch. From Grand Prize Gulch Trail at Gladiator Creek Junction to South Fork East Fork Trail. 5.0 miles, 1,840 feet loss. Maps: Horton Peak, Galena Peak.

Smokies

BAKER LAKE: Access: Baker Creek Road. From that road west to Baker Lake. Not in SNRA; in and administered by Ketchum Ranger District, Sawtooth National Forest. Covered in *"Trails of Western Idaho."* 1.0 mile, 870 feet gain. Map: Baker Peak.

MILL LAKE: Access: Prairie Creek Road. From Prairie Creek Road to Mill Lake. The road (not the trail and lake) is in the SNRA; administered by Ketchum Ranger District. Covered in *"Trails of Western Idaho."* 2.0 miles, 1,020 feet gain. Map: Galena.

MINER LAKE: Access: Prairie Creek Road. From Prairie Creek Trail 2.5 miles south of trailhead to Miner Lake. The road (not the trail and lake) is in the SNRA, but area is administered by the Ketchum Ranger District. Covered in *"Trails of Western Idaho."* 1.5 miles, 1,100 feet gain. Map: Galena.

NORTON LAKE: Access: Baker Creek Road. From 1-mile spur road up Norton Creek to Norton Lakes. Not in SNRA; in Ketchum Ranger District. Covered in *"Trails of Western Idaho."* 2.2 miles, 1,460 feet gain. Map: Baker Peak

PRAIRIE LAKES: Access: Prairie Creek Road. From that road to Prairie Lakes. Road (not the trail and lakes) is in the SNRA; area is administered by Ketchum Ranger District. Covered in *"Trails of Western Idaho."* 5.0 miles, 1,500 feet gain. Map: Galena.

WEST FORK OF PRAIRIE CREEK: Access: Prairie Creek Road. From that road northwest up canyon to dead end. Originally it continued to the head of the canyon, over a divide and back down to Prairie Creek. In Ketchum Ranger District. Existing trail about 1.8 miles, 600 feet gain. Map: Galena.

Suggestions for Loop Trips

Trailhead	Points on the trail	Miles	Days
Grandjean	Baron, Alpine, Hidden, Elk Lakes	43	4 - 6
Hell Roaring Creek	Imogene, Edith, Edna ,Hidden, Cramer, Alpine, Baron, Trail Creek, Stanley Lake Creek, Alpine Way, Marshall, Redfish, Bench Lakes, Decker Lakes, Hell Roaring Lake	92	11 - 14
Silver Creek at Graham	North Fork Boise, Big Meadows, Elk Lake, Edna, Ardeth, Spangle, Ingeborg, Benedict, Pats; Johnson Creek, Bayhouse Trail	46	5 - 7
Queens River	Queens River, Pats, Johnson, Browns, Little Queens	33	4 - 6
Powerplant CG at Atlanta	Rock Creek, Spangle, Ardeth, Edna, Cramer, Baron, North Fork Boise, Silver Creek, Johnson Creek, Pats, Benedict, Ingeborg, Spangle, Rock Creek	74	7 - 10
Livingston Mill	Walker, Frog, Boulder Chain, Quiet, Baker, Livingston Mill	35	5 - 7
Germania Creek	Germania Creek, Bowery Guard Station, East Fork Salmon, West Fork of East Fork Trail, Galena Gulch	26	3 - 4
Fourth of July	Fourth of July Lake, Born Lakes, Four Lakes Basin, Quiet Lake, Noisy Lake, Baker Lake, Castle Lake, Castle Divide, Chamberlain Lakes, Washington Lake, Fourth of July Lake (partly cross-country; for experts only)	21	3 - 5

Guide to Trips

EASY TRIPS (not more than 7 miles; less than 1,000-foot elevation gain; no cross-country travel)

Elk Meadows (must ford creek)	Headwaters of Salmon
Farley Lake	Hell Roaring Lake
Fishhook Creek	Phyllis Lake
Fourth of July Lake	Redfish to Flatrock

MODERATE TRIPS (5 to 10 miles and 1,000 to 1,800-foot elevation gain, no cross-country travel)

Bench Lakes	Marten and Kelly Lakes
Sawtooth Lake	Warm Springs Meadows
Alpine Way (north)	Mays Creek to McDonald Lake

PARTLY CROSS COUNTRY or on unofficial trails (for exerienced hikers only)

Alpine Creek Lakes	Heart and Six Lakes (White Clouds)
Amber Lakes	Leggit Lake (trail disappears)
Bench Lakes 3, 4, and 5	Lightning Lake
Big Boulder Lakes	Lucille and Profile Lakes
Born Lakes	North Fork Lake
Cabin Creek Lakes	Quiet and Noisy Lakes
Castle Lake	Rainbow Lake
Decker Lakes	Rough Lake
Elizabeth Lake (trail disappears)	Saddleback Lakes
Four Lakes Basin	Shallow and Scree Lakes
Goat Lake (Sawtooths)	Sheep Lake
Goat Lake (White Clouds)	Silver Lake
Hanson Lakes	Upper Redfish
Heart Lake (Sawtooths)	

HIKES FOR EXPERTS (poor footing and/or route difficult to find)

Alpine Creek Lakes

Amber Lakes

Big Boulder Lakes

Castle Lake

East Fork North Fork

Elizabeth Lake

Elk Lake to Hidden Lake
  Junction (at high water)

Four Lakes Basin

Galena Gulch

Goat Lake

Leggit Lake

Lucille and Profile Lakes

North Fork Lake

Quiet and Noisy Lakes

Rainbow Lake

Rough Lake

Saddleback Lakes

Scenic Lakes

Shallow and Scree Lakes

Silver Lake

Upper Redfish Lakes

West Fork North Fork Wood River

LIKELY TO BE OVERCROWDED

Alice Lake

Alpine Lake (Redfish)

Alpine Lake (Iron Creek)

Baron Lakes

Bench Lakes

Boulder Chain Lakes

Cramer Lakes

Farley Lake

Fishhook Creek

Frog Lake

Hell Roaring Lake

Imogene Lake

Mattingly Creek Divide (lower, by
  trail bikes)

Sawtooth Lake

Toxaway Lake

Twin Lakes

Walker Lake

Williams Creek

SELDOM VISITED

Bayhouse and Johnson Creek

Benedict, Rock Slide, and
  Ingeborg Lakes

Boulder Basin

Bridalveil Falls and Hanson
  Lakes

Camp and Heart Lakes

Casino and Garland Lakes

Castle Lake

Elizabeth Lake

Elk Lake to Hidden Lake Jctn.

Everly and Plummer Lakes

Lake Ingeborg

(SELDOM VISITED)

Johnson Lake

Leggit Lake

Marten and Kelly Lakes

North Fork Wood River

Pats and Arrowhead Lakes

Quiet and Noisy Lakes

Rock Creek to Spangle

Rough Lake

Scenic Lake

Shallow and Scree Lakes

Washington Basin

West Pass Creek Divide

RARELY VISITED

Amber Lakes

Decker Lakes to Redfish Inlet

East Fork North Fork Wood
   River

Four Lakes Basin

Galena Gulch

Gladiator Creek Divide

Mays Creek

North Fork Baron Creek

North Fork Lake

Ocalkens Lakes

Rainbow Lake

Silver Lake

Timpa Lake

West Fork North Fork Wood
   River

OVERNIGHT TRIPS

TWO OR THREE DAYS REQUIRED ON FOOT

Baker Lake

Baron Lakes

Big Boulder Lakes

Boulder Chain Lakes

Browns Lake

Castle Lake

Chamberlain Lakes

Edna Lake

Four Lakes Basin

Leggit Lake

Livingston Mill to Frog Lake

Lucille and Profile Lakes

North Fork Baron Creek

Observation Peak

Quiet and Noisy Lakes

Rainbow Lake

Sand Mountain, Imogene Divide

Scenic Lakes

Shallow and Scree Lakes

Sheep Lake

THREE TO FIVE DAYS ON FOOT

Ardeth and Spangle Lakes

Arrowhead and Pats Lakes

Camp and Heart Lakes

Everly and Plummer Lakes

Hidden Lake

Ingeborg, Rock Slide, and
   Benedict Lakes

Johnson Lake

Timpa Lake

OPEN ABOUT JULY 1 IN AN AVERAGE YEAR

Alpine Way Trail

Alpine Lake (near Sawtooth)

Bench Lakes

Bridalveil Falls

Elk Lake

Farley Lake (from Pettit)

Fishhook Creek

Grand Prize Gulch

Little Queens River to
   Scenic Lakes Junction

Marshall Lake

Mays Creek

Middle Fork Boise to Rock
   Creek

Williams Creek

OPEN EARLY OR MID-AUGUST

Alpine-Baron Divide

Ardeth-Spangle Divide

Big Boulder Lakes

Castle Divide

Cramer Divide

Divide at Ingeborg Lake

Elizabeth Lake from
   Stanley Lake

Four Lakes Basin

High Pass

Imogene Divide

Pass above Scoop Lake

Pats Lake Divide (latest pass in the
   SNRA to open)

Sand Mountain Pass

Snowyside Pass

ACCESS ROAD FOR TOUGH VEHICLES AND EXPERIENCED DRIVERS

Fourth of July Creek (but future reconstruction of lower road and closure of upper two miles is being considered)

Graham Guard Station (four-wheel drive recommended)

Hell Roaring Creek (slated for closure and trailhead change in 1989)

Yellow Belly Lake (planned future reconstruction so it will be suitable for passenger cars)

Bibliography

Fuller, Margaret, *Mountains: A Natural History and Hiking Guide,* John Wiley & Sons., Inc., New York, (tentatively Spring 1989)

Bradley, Jim, *Environmental Outfitting,* Moose Creek Ranger District, Nez Perce National Forest, 1975

Craighead, John J. and Frank C., *Field Guide to Rocky Mountain Wildflowers,* Houghton Mifflin Co., Boston, 1963

D'Easum, Dick, *Sawtooth Tales,* Caxton Printers, Caldwell, Idaho, 1977

Miller, Robert W., *Guide for Using Horses In Mountain Country,* Montana Wilderness Association, 1974

Off Belay, Renton, Washington, February 1975

— Bachman, Ben, "Sawtooth Prolog", page 4

— Stur, Louis, "Sawtooth Pioneering", page 10

— Bachman, Ben, and Smutek, Ray, "Sawtooth Mountaineering", page 18

Reynolds, Gray; Fournier, Edwin; and Hamre, Vern, *General Management Plan: Sawtooth National Recreation Area* and *Final Environmental Statement,* United States Forest Service, Department of Agriculture, 1975

SUGGESTED READING

Brower, David, *Sierra Club Wilderness Handbook,* Sierra Club, Ballentine Books, New York, 1971

Hart, John, *Walking Softly In the Wilderness,* Sierra Club, San Francisco, 1977

Little, Elbert L., *The Audubon Society Field Guide to North American Trees, Western Region,* Alfred A. Knopf, New York, 1980.

Maley, Terry, *Exploring Idaho Geology,* Mineral Land Publications, Boise, 1979

Manning, Harvey, *Backpacking, One Step at a Time,* Vintage Books, New York, 1980

Mountaineering; The Freedom of the Hills, The Mountaineers, Seattle, 1974

Petzoldt, Paul, *The Wilderness Handbook*, W.W. Norton Co. New York, 1974

Preston, Richard Jr. *Rocky Mountain Trees*, Dover Publications, New York, 1968

Rethmel, R.C., *Backpacking*, Burgess Publishing Co., Minneapolis 1974

Simer, Peter, *The National Outdoor Leadership School's Wilderness Guide*, Simon & Schuster, 1985

Sparling, Wayne, *Southern Idaho Ghost Towns*, Caxton Printers, Caldwell, Idaho, 1976

Spellenberg, Richard, *The Audubon Society Field Guide to North American Wildflowers, Western Region*, Alfred A. Knopf, New York, 1979

Udvardy, Miklos, *The Audubon Society Field Guide to North American Birds, Western Region*, Alfred A. Knopf, New York 1977

Whitaker, John O. Jr., *The Audubon Society Field Guide to North American Mammals*, Alfred A. Knopf, New York, 1980

Wilkerson, James A., *Hypothermia, Frostbite, and Other Cold Injuries*, The Mountaineers, Seattle, Washington, 1986

Yarber, Esther and McGown, Edna, *Stanley - Sawtooth Country*, Publishers Press, Salt Lake City, 1976

Basic Backpacking Equipment

CLOTHING

broken-in hiking boots	wool boot socks
*long pants	*long-sleeved shirt
sweater	*warm jacket
*wool hat	sun hat
*rain poncho or jacket	rain pants or chaps
*sunglasses	complete change of clothes
mosquito headnet	

GENERAL

comfortable backpack	*topographic map

(General equipment)

*flashlight	plastic trowel
extra batteries and bulbs	toilet paper
*compass	20 feet of 1/8" nylon rope
plastic bags	mirror and whistle for signalling

COOKING

aluminum cooking pots	cup and spoon per person
utensils	backpacking stove
folding plastic washbasin	extra fuel
biodegradeable soap	work gloves or pot grippers
pot scrubber, nylon filament	*pocket knife
pot scrubber, metal mesh	*firestarter
*waterproof matches	*extra food
water filter	

SLEEPING

tent (breathable fabric with waterproof rainfly; single wall tents aren't warm enough)

down or synthetic fill three-season sleeping bag inside plastic bag and waterproof stuff sack

open or closed cell foam pad or foam-filled air mattress

FIRST AID

mosquito repellant	sunburn cream
*minimum first aid kit	lip salve

    pain pills, moleskin, Bandaids, salt tablets, gauze, adhesive tape, antibiotic ointment, electrolyte balance restoring powder (such as Infalyte) to treat shock, and other items recommended by your doctor

* ESSENTIAL ITEMS FOR EVERY HIKER

Margaret Fuller

About the Author

Margaret Fuller was born and raised in Palo Alto, California. While growing up, she hiked extensively in the Tahoe, Muir Trail and Mt. Lassen areas in California. She received her B.A. in biology from Stanford University in 1956 and has lived in Idaho since 1957.

The idea for a trail guide to the Sawtooths came when she, her husband, Wayne, and their five children found it difficult to find information about good short hikes suitable for families. She has hiked every trail discussed in detail in this guide. For this revision, she repeated 66 of the original 73 hikes and did 24 new ones. In writing her guidebooks, she has hiked over 3,500 miles on Idaho's trails.

"Trails of the Sawtooth and White Cloud Mountains" was first published in 1979 by Signpost Books, Edmonds, Washington. She is the author of three other books: *"Trails of Western Idaho"* (Signpost Books, 1982), *"Trails of the Frank Church—River of No Return Wilderness"* (Signpost Books, 1987) and *"Mountains: A Natural History and Hiking Guide"* (John Wiley & Sons, Inc., New York, Spring 1989).

Mrs. Fuller has taught backpacking in community education courses, led backpacking treks for the Idaho Lung Association and given over 150 slide shows about Idaho mountains. In 1982 she received the Writer of the Year Award from the Idaho Writer's League. Her hobbies are hiking, writing, photography, nature study, playing the flute, skiing and sewing. Her husband, Wayne, is a district judge for the third District in Idaho, with chambers in Weiser.

Index